The Great Global Transformation

The Great Global Transformation

National Market Liberalism in a Multipolar World

BRANKO MILANOVIC

ALLEN LANE
an imprint of
PENGUIN BOOKS

ALLEN LANE

UK | USA | Canada | Ireland | Australia
India | New Zealand | South Africa

Allen Lane is part of the Penguin Random House group of companies whose addresses can be found at global.penguinrandomhouse.com.

Penguin Random House UK
One Embassy Gardens, 8 Viaduct Gardens, London SW11 7BW

penguin.co.uk

First published in Great Britain by Allen Lane 2025
001

Copyright © Branko Milanovic, 2025

Penguin Random House values and supports copyright.
Copyright fuels creativity, encourages diverse voices, promotes freedom
of expression and supports a vibrant culture. Thank you for purchasing
an authorized edition of this book and for respecting intellectual property
laws by not reproducing, scanning or distributing any part of it by any
means without permission. You are supporting authors and enabling
Penguin Random House to continue to publish books for everyone.
No part of this book may be used or reproduced in any manner for the
purpose of training artificial intelligence technologies or systems. In accordance
with Article 4(3) of the DSM Directive 2019/790, Penguin Random House
expressly reserves this work from the text and data mining exception.

The moral right of the author has been asserted

Set in 12/14.75pt Dante MT Std
Typeset by Six Red Marbles UK, Thetford, Norfolk
Printed and bound in Great Britain by Clays Ltd, Elcograf S.p.A.

The authorized representative in the EEA is Penguin Random House Ireland,
Morrison Chambers, 32 Nassau Street, Dublin D02 YH68

A CIP catalogue record for this book is available from the British Library

ISBN: 978–0–241–67893–0

Penguin Random House is committed to a sustainable future
for our business, our readers and our planet. This book is made from
Forest Stewardship Council® certified paper.

Contents

Preface	ix
Introduction	1
1. The Rise of Asia	5
Countries	5
People	30
2. Convergence and Conflict	46
Does international trade lead to peace or war?	52
Why are we afraid of convergence?	79
Complexity of the world	88
3. The Elites	104
America's new ruling class: homoploutia with credentials	105
China's new ruling class: capital ownership with CPC membership	123
4. National Market Liberalism	141
National market liberalism	146
Statism	162
Multipolarity: in an uncertain struggle	177
5. Nationalism, Greed and Property	193
Bibliography	199
Acknowledgements	209
Notes	211
Index	245

The Great Global Transformation deals with three global developments that have taken place over the past half-century and are likely to influence the world in the decades to come. They all stem from the economic and technological rise of Asia compared to the rest of the world, and in particular compared to the West. Economically, the rise of Asia has shifted the centre of global production and trade to the Pacific. At the level of nations, and thus politically, the rise of China has sharpened geopolitical competition with the United States in both Asia and perhaps globally. At the level of individuals, the rise of Asian middle classes has displaced parts of Western middle classes from the high global income positions they have enjoyed for the past two centuries. It has thus led to the greatest reshuffling of incomes since the Industrial Revolution. The dissatisfaction of the Western middle classes was translated into a political reaction that has shaken the post-Cold War domestic political order in Western democracies.

Preface

One day, in the spring or summer of 1989, at lunchtime, I went to a Bookstore on I Street in Washington DC. There I ran into Jeffrey Sachs and David Lipton, two American economists whom I had known from their involvement in the Polish economic reforms, long before the change of government in June 1989. They were carrying a pile of books on Eastern Europe and the history of communism that they had just bought, and I mentioned to Jeff that my book *Liberalization and Entrepreneurship* had been published only a couple of months ago. He asked me whether a copy was available in the bookstore. I checked and found one. Jeff bought it. It was then up to me to write a dedication. I wrote, 'To Jeff who is trying to save socialism (despite itself)'. The part between the brackets was supposed to be cute, and to refer to the Communist blockheads who were undermining all efforts at reform in the region. But the part before the brackets was very genuine. Jeff looked up at me in some bewilderment: 'But I am trying to bury socialism, not to save it,' he exclaimed. I gave him some lame explanation, probably mentioning socialist market economy or something similar – there was no time to say more: Jeff was juggling with difficulty a dozen books in his hands.

But my thinking then went as follows. The mid- to late 1980s was a period of rising Reaganism and Thatcherism in the West (only later known under the umbrella framework of 'neoliberalism') and sharp crisis of growth in socialist economies. Their decline began in most cases with an inability to repay foreign loans, incurred in hard currencies after the twin oil shocks of the 1970s. This is the often-forgotten background to the rise of the Solidarity movement in Poland, centrifugal forces in Yugoslavia, brutal austerity in Romania, the slowdown of goulash socialism in Hungary, and East Germany's begging for Soviet and West German money.

Preface

I saw the socialist crisis as a perfect analogue to the 1929–32 Great Depression in capitalist countries. The Depression was overcome thanks to Keynesian policies. What Keynesianism did was introduce a dose of statism in an otherwise free-market economy that simply could not, on its own, get out of the Depression. Thus, capitalism was saved thanks to what many regarded as proto-socialist policies of government spending, unemployment benefits, public works and the nationalization of private companies. By analogy, I reasoned in 1989, the grave crisis of socialist economies had to be solved through the introduction of doses of capitalism: a greater role of the market, a more incentivized wage structure, liberalization of the small and medium sector for private companies, greater independence in decision-making for state-owned enterprises and paring down of central planning. It seemed to me perfectly clear that the way out of the socialist crisis was more capitalism – yet, as in the analogous case of the Great Depression – without the abandonment of the main socialist model. Just as capitalist economies did not cease to be capitalist when a greater role of the state was introduced, socialist economies, I thought then, would not cease to be socialist if the private sector played a much greater role than before.

Indeed, in the book that Jeff bought, I developed this argument, even before the socialist crisis became obvious, by among other things showing the data on the size of the private and state sectors in various economies. Capitalist economies ranged from having less than 5 per cent of Gross Domestic Product (GDP) produced in the public sector to having more than 20 per cent; socialist economies ranged from almost 100 per cent of GDP produced by the state sector to only 70 per cent. I argued: why could not the percentage of the state sector in socialist economies be reduced to a range from (say) 50 to 70 per cent without changing the fundamental nature of socialism? Eventually, the two systems may still be recognizably 'socialist' and 'capitalist' in ideology, but in reality they would both be 'mixed' systems with relatively small differences between them. Instead of studying varieties of capitalism as branches of only one system, we would then be studying a much richer set of economies that combined, in various proportions, the market and the state. System convergence would 'solve' the ideological dispute between them and make world peace more tenable. It seemed to me a win-win proposition. This was my thinking underlying the book and its dedication.

But reality went the other way. 1989 was an important year on the road to total domination of neoliberal economics across the world. Reagan's economic policies were continued by his Republican successor, George H. W. Bush, and a few years later consolidated by the Democrat Bill Clinton. Margaret Thatcher was on her way to becoming the longest-serving UK Prime Minister in modern history. Reagan's and Thatcher's anti-union stance, deregulation, privatization of infrastructure and housing, and lower tax rates for capital owners and the rich, all hallmarks of policies that aimed to refashion the New Deal order and reduce the welfare state, continued unabated. Moreover, such policies expanded geographically to include no longer only the West and Japan. Between 1989 and 1992, all formerly communist economies folded and flipped to the other side: some went from 100 per cent public to 100 per cent private ownership. They did not go 'mixed' as I imagined. Most moved towards a Thatcherite system where the public sector (or the government) had no business in the production of anything, not even in infrastructure, and hopefully, it was thought, not much role in spending either. Of course, such extreme precepts were impossible to implement for any length of time and 'transition' economies still ended up keeping an important role for the state, especially so in Central Europe. Nevertheless, all of them were unmistakably capitalist and neoliberal.

Elsewhere, things changed in the same direction. In 1991, India entered neoliberalism with the dismantlement of numerous regulations that had stymied the growth of the private sector. The famous Indian 'Licence Raj' ended with the government of Manmohan Singh and the International Monetary Fund (IMF) bailout. After the Tiananmen Square crackdown in 1989, China, following the historic Southern Tour by Deng Xiaoping, accelerated its pro-capitalist development. It turned out that lots of youthful energy that had been directed towards political reform in the late 1980s could be easily rechannelled into economics and self-enrichment. The youthful proponents of Mr Democracy became millionaire entrepreneurs. The Soviet Union not only disappeared from the map but all new states espoused extreme versions of the neoliberal creed. It helped that the new elites interpreted neoliberal capitalism as an ideological licence to steal. They were thus very happy to be neoliberal.

The peak of global neoliberalism came around the turn of the millennium when China entered the World Trade Organization (WTO); the Glass-Steagall Act was repealed in the United States; the euro became a common European currency; and globalization was accepted as the new normal. Intellectual prophets of political liberalism and unfettered market economy believed that this particular combination of democracy and market commanded universal support, and would soon be accepted even by those small recalcitrant islets that, like the Gaulish village in *Asterix*, stubbornly clung to the old ways.

In the developing world, the triumph involved an ideologically coherent trinity of the Washington Consensus, basic needs (reduction of absolute poverty globally) and protection of human rights. The role of the nation-state, especially of the weaker nation-states, became nil: they received their policy prescription straight from the Washington-based international organizations, whether about the budget deficits or the best ways to organize social assistance, and then from the equally Washington-based, and often State Department-affiliated, human rights non-governmental organizations (NGOs).

Two events put paid to the neoliberal domination. Both were brought about by its success. The success of globalization made China increasingly rich and powerful. That triggered the geopolitical response among the politicians, geo-strategists and militaristic circles in the West that saw China as a competitor and even as a foe, at least in the East Asian region, and in the future possibly globally as well. China, too, emboldened by its success and seeing clearly the advantages that its vast size, long history of concentrated state power, high literacy and hard-working ethic of its population gave it, developed, at times even if jejunely, a hubristic mentality. For the first time in two centuries, China was challenging Western supremacy. Its century of humiliations was over.

China's success, which owed so much to neoliberal globalization, brought on another issue: the loss of jobs, income and self-esteem among the workers of the Western countries who were either replaced indirectly by Chinese imports or directly through Western, and especially American, offshoring of production to cheaper locales. The counterpart of China's geopolitical rise was the increase in incomes for large swathes of its population who, for the first time in two centuries, moved into the secluded ranks of the top one or two richest global income deciles, displacing from their global income positions parts of the Western middle class. The latter did not like it.

The rise of China that was made possible thanks to global neoliberalism made the end of global neoliberalism inevitable.

The second success of neoliberalism – the enrichment of the elites in the West – became, after the Global Financial Crisis in 2008, unsupportable for the left-behind and other, to use Hillary Clinton's term, 'deplorables'. The costs of the crisis were not borne by those who caused it but by those who lost because of it. The crisis undermined the ideological basis of neoliberalism, not only by showing that not all are likely to benefit equally from globalization, but by clearly displaying the irresponsibility of the rich and their ability to manipulate governments. Inchoate coalitions of malcontents formed in practically all Western countries. Their amalgam of complaints ranged from economic (low income growth) and cultural (cosmopolitanism and deracination of the elites) to social (elite contempt for those who were not educated and smart enough to profit from opportunities in the globalized world).

Thus, the end of neoliberal ideological and 'factual' hegemony came as a by-product of its two biggest successes: the rise of Asia and the new wealth of the highly educated Western elites. The so-called populist revolt was led by a great variety of forces, reflecting in turn the variety of complaints. Its success is not only dubious in the sense that its leaders are not likely to come to positions of authority; but even when they do, the policies the 'rebel' movements apply once in office are not so different from the policies they reviled when fighting for power. This is due to their ideological confusion and inability to think through, and prosecute, alternative policies. But it is wrong to judge the success or failure of these movements by simply looking at whether they are in power, or noting that they offer much less in terms of actually different policies than they claim. The importance of the movements of malcontents is in their being 'anti', that is, in bringing to an end the hegemony of global neoliberalism and questioning the power and the ideological and cultural bases of the newly created elites. Most importantly, they have forced the elites to change many ideas that defined neoliberalism in the past several decades. Tariff wars and reversal of parts of globalization through 'friend-shoring' and similar discriminatory practices have entered the lexicon of mainstream parties; so has concern with immigration and a desire to curb it; as well as the use of economic coercion through innumerable sanctions to achieve international political or economic goals. All of these things put together represent a departure from the ideology of global neoliberalism. The global or international part no longer applies. Instead, the new ruling model can be appropriately called 'national market liberalism'. It retains key features of neoliberalism in the domestic market sphere, but abandons its internationalism, and often even the application of liberalism to domestic social issues. The epithets or qualifiers 'national' and 'market' are needed to show where the new order still uses classical liberal or neoliberal principles: they are restricted to the domestic market, revised as to the social sphere, and almost entirely abandoned in the international space.

This book is about these two developments that have marked the apogee and the decline of global neoliberalism: the rise of Asia, and China in particular, and the emergence of new plutocratic ruling elites in the United States and China. These new elites were brought into existence, and power, thanks to global neoliberalism, and their success created the conditions for its decline. The actions of a Trump or a Xi Jinping, and many other leaders since, are, despite what they and even their supporters might think, reactions against the winners of neoliberal globalization and their excesses. These reactions have ended one historical period and opened another whose contours are only dimly apprehended today.

Introduction

This book deals with two important topics that have attracted a huge amount of interest and a groundswell of literature and debate. They are the rise of China and more generally of Asia, and the increasing questioning of the power and position of domestic elites who have benefited from global neoliberalism. The contention of this book is that the two topics are interrelated. The rise of China has created geopolitical tensions because the global neoliberal order is hierarchically structured and cannot easily accept a country as big and potentially powerful as China. This has led to the reversal of globalization. But the rise of Asia has also displaced many people in the 'political West' from their global income positions, reinforced the gap between the educated well-to-do and the rest of the population within Western countries, and created a state of incipient political unrest.

The rise of Asia represents a return to the distribution of economic power that existed before the Industrial Revolution. It is therefore as momentous an event as the Industrial Revolution of the nineteenth century that enabled European countries, benefiting from economic and military superiority, to conquer different parts of the world. With the rise of China and Asia this period has come to a close.

This change in economic power has impacted two areas. First, it has transformed the relative economic standing of states and thereby the geopolitical balance of power. In terms of international relations this can lead to tensions, conflicts and even wars; or differently, greater trade and interdependence may be associated with incentives for peace. Second, it has had an impact on individuals in the sense that it has altered their positions in the global income distribution. For the past two hundred years, citizens of Western countries and Japan have been practically the only ones in the top quintile (20 per cent) of the global income distribution. Citizens of other countries, of the three continents of Asia, Latin America and Africa, were there only sporadically and never in large numbers. That too is changing with the rise of Asia. It is not only the Chinese who are entering the top 20, the top 10, or the top 5 per cent of the global income distribution; they are being followed by people from India, Vietnam, Indonesia, Thailand and other Asian countries. As they enter these top groups, some people who were there previously are pushed down. The change is dramatic given the numbers of people involved in the reshuffling.

These global changes (at the country level: geopolitical; at the individual level: economic) are accompanied by political conflicts at the national level. What has happened during the past forty years of neoliberalism is the formation of new moneyed elites in all large countries of the world. Their ways to the top might have been different but they were all beneficiaries of neoliberal policies. These policies have, however, also created opponents among people in the West: those who have been left out of the benefits of globalization, lost their jobs, or feel socially slighted by the new elite. They have become increasingly critical of the status quo. In the case of China, there is growing discontent among those who believe that the Communist Party should retain its leading role in the running of the country, and who are afraid that the rich, with their greater numbers and economic power, might come to dominate the Party, and thereby determine the direction of the nation.

The excesses of wealth and the power accumulated by the new elites have created what might be called the 'counter-revolutionary' feelings among the people who, for various reasons, feel left out – ideologically, economically, or socially.

It is the contention of this book that it is only within this context that we can grasp and understand the rear-guard or counter-revolutionary action, in the most powerful nations, spearheaded by Donald Trump and the so-called populists in the United States, by Xi Jinping and those in favour of reinforcement of the Party role in China, and by Vladimir Putin and the national security complex in Russia. In all three cases the policies are the reaction to the dominant political and economic position of the neoliberal ruling class and the narrative that accompanied it. In the case of Trump, the counter-narrative is directed against the liberal and cosmopolitan establishment; in the case of Xi Jinping, it is directed against the nouveaux riches who have infiltrated the Party; and in the case of Putin, it is directed against the oligarchs who have tried to control the state. But we see this pattern spread all over the world. Nationalism is blended into domestic politics and narratives as a way to make policies look 'tougher', harden them and present them as a defence of a nation, not just of a group.

This book revolves around these great themes: the realignment in economic power between countries around the world (Chapter 1, 'Countries'; and Chapter 2); the reshuffling of global income positions (Chapter 1, 'Peoples'); the creation of new elites (Chapter 3); and the 'counter-revolutionary' reaction to the accumulated power and wealth of the elites (Chapter 4). A brief Chapter 5 speculates on the main ideological forces that shape the current era.

I.
The Rise of Asia

The most important economic fact of the past fifty or even one hundred years is the economic rise of Asia. It has displaced the centre of gravity of the global economy and trade towards the Pacific and the Indian oceans, brought the most populous part of the world to play a role that is broadly equivalent to its importance in the world population, and reshuffled the global upper class in such a way that, for the first time since the Industrial Revolution, it contains a sizeable share of non-Western citizens. This chapter is dedicated to documenting this dramatic change and asking the question: how has it impacted the world and its people?

Countries

The New International Economic Order: the first challenge to the West[1]

Exactly fifty years ago to the time of this writing, the Group of 77 (G77), the non-aligned countries – or as they were colloquially called, the 'Third World' – came up with a proposal for the New International Economic Order (NIEO).[2] The aim of the NIEO was to give greater voting power to the Third World countries in international organizations, most notably the IMF and the World Bank, to pressurize rich countries into providing more aid to the poorest countries, improve the terms of trade for developing countries' exports, establish the rules of non-interference in political and economic matters of the countries of the Third World, and, in a nutshell, to have developing countries treated as equal members of the international community, neither subject to the externally organized coups, nor treated with hauteur by the IMF.

At that time, as Figure 1.1 shows, countries of the Third World produced just under a quarter of the global GDP even if they accounted for almost one-half of the world population. In other words, their GDP per capita was about half of the world average. There were of course two other worlds: the 'First World' composed of rich capitalist (or core) countries that included North America, Western Europe, Oceania, and Japan and South Korea, and the 'Second World' of the socialist countries aligned with the Soviet Union. The First World produced 62 per cent of global GDP with 21 per cent of the world population; the Second World produced 13 per cent of global GDP with 9 per cent share of the world population. The three worlds

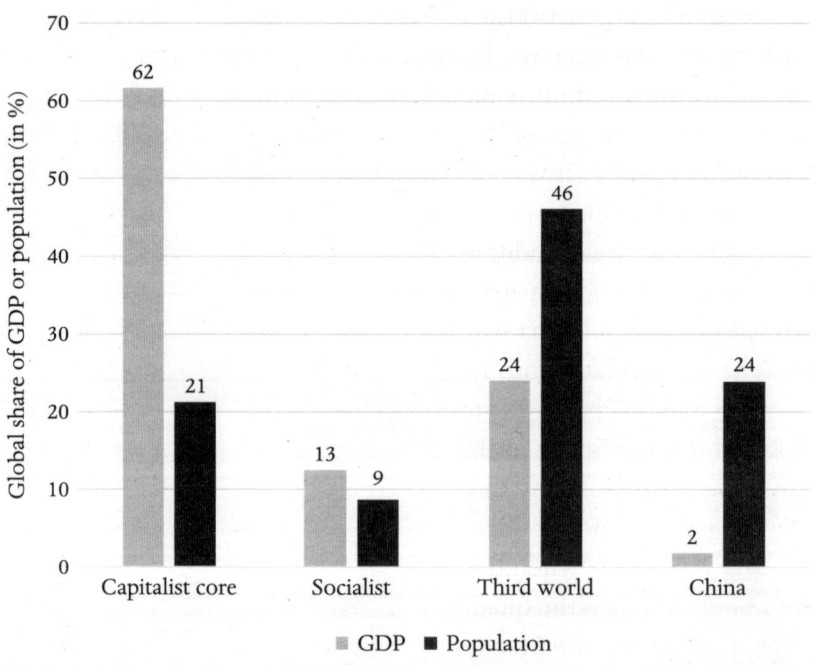

Figure 1.1. Geoeconomics of the world in 1974. Percentage shares of world GDP and world population[3]

between them accounted for 98 per cent of global output but 'only' three-quarters of the world population.

One large country stood outside this simplified order: China. While a communist state, China was in conflict with the Soviet Union since the mid-1950s, and even had a brief military conflict in 1969 along its border with the Soviet Union. Although it was a poor country, only liberated from all forms of foreign control after the 1949 Revolution, and thus had a lot in common with the Third World countries of Africa, Asia and Latin America, it stood apart from that group. Thanks to the support of the Third World, it had, just two years earlier, joined the United Nations, expelling the island of Taiwan, which pretended to represent the mainland of China. Yet the People's Republic failed to officially join the non-aligned movement or the Group of 77. China already by then stood apart. This apartness, and even aloofness, will, as we shall argue throughout, continue to be one of its main features.

Despite its population size, the aloofness of China did not matter that much. The three worlds produced, as we have seen, 98 per cent of the world's output. China's contribution was minuscule: 2 per cent, even if one person out of each four in the world lived in the People's Republic. It was obviously a very poor country, and many thought it was likely to stay so.[4] But there were others, fewer in number, who thought differently. Alain Peyrefitte wrote an influential book in French in 1973, *Quand la Chine s'éveillera . . . le monde tremblera* ('When China wakes up the world will shake'). The book was never translated into English, but its French edition alone sold some 2 million copies. Peyrefitte saw the rising power of China but located it much more in the size of the population, its work ethic and ancient philosophy than in economic prowess. Nobody could imagine the economic success that China would become.

1974 was a year when the First World was on the defensive. The doubling and then the quadrupling of oil prices, following upon the Egyptian–Israeli war the year before and the oil embargo, shook the rich capitalist world. The scourge of stagflation appeared: prices went up while output stagnated. In fact, many years later, that period, and even that very year (1974), would be taken as the endmark of an era that became known as *Les Trente Glorieuses* ('the glorious thirty years'), popularized by the French economist Jean Fourastié.[5] It represented the end of the extraordinary post-war boom of the United States, Western European economies and Japan. It included at least two 'economic miracles' of Japan and West Germany, although one should not forget the almost equally dramatic transformations of France and Italy. Not only did Western countries in that period become richer, but their GDP per capita grew compared to the global GDP per capita, as we shall see in the 'People' section below. Thus the countries of the First World became better off in real (inflation-adjusted) and relative (with respect to the rest of the world) terms. For example, Italian GDP per capita was less than twice as high as the world average in 1952; by 1974, it was almost three times as high. Meanwhile, inequalities in most rich capitalist countries went down. This facet of development became known as the Great Compression (the term was probably introduced by Goldin and Margo in 1991, originally in reference to wage, not income, compression).[6] Finally, rich capitalist countries' incomes converged among themselves. This means that the poorer Western countries grew on average faster than the richer Western countries, and the gap among them diminished. This, in turn, led to the first studies of economic convergence within the rich countries, members of the Organization for Economic Cooperation and Development (OECD). Since it was established early on that this convergence did not spread to other parts of the world, it became fashionable to speak of 'club convergence', with the 'club' in this case including the OECD, or what the World System Theorists called the 'capitalist core'.

All these fine developments of the First World were called into question by the crisis of 1973–74. The oil weapon was in the hands of less developed countries, and not surprisingly, they felt emboldened. The non-aligned movement that existed officially from 1961, and de facto since the Bandung Conference in 1955 that brought together twenty-nine newly liberated Asian and African nations, was the natural vehicle through which the newly found self-confidence would be expressed.

The Second World, in the meantime, was languishing with gradually decreasing growth rates, widening economic distance from the rich world, and unsuccessful economic reforms that, from the mid-1960s, tried to lift the anaemic growth rates. But more than slow growth, the problem of the Second World was slow technological progress and inefficiency of investment that left it increasingly lagging behind the capitalist core. In order to solve the latter, East European countries turned to borrowing from the West, to buy the newest technological equipment and relaunch growth. It was, as we shall see, an expensive mistake that would, to a large extent, lead to the fall of communist regimes some fifteen years later.[7]

It could be thought that the natural allies of the Third World countries would be the socialist bloc. And indeed, the Soviet Union insisted on that, most strongly at the Havana 1979 conference of the non-aligned movement. Yet it was not obvious how this 'natural alliance' would work, except perhaps in a few matters of international politics like the vote, on certain issues, at the General Assembly of the UN. The Second World was, by its own decision, excluded from the most important international economic organizations. Only a few communist countries were members of the World Bank and the IMF, or participated in the General Agreement on Tariffs and Trade (GATT), and in none of these institutions did they play any important role. After 1945, the USSR stayed, demonstratively, out of all worldwide economic 'entanglements'. The socialist bloc experienced a constant shortage of 'hard currencies', a feature it shared with the Third World. It could not help the Third World in that area. It could not help much with direct investments either, or when it tried, it did it very inefficiently. Overall, compared to the activism, money and intellectual ferment regarding development provided by the West, the Soviet Union and its allied states looked more like observers. The British economist Peter Wiles, in his summary of fifty years of Soviet economic influence on Third World countries, lists only two instances of that influence: Mexican agrarian reforms under Lázaro Cárdenas, and India's First Five-Year Plan.[8] For sure, the USSR provided enormous credits, mostly in goods and military matériel, to a select group of countries (Syria, Vietnam, Angola, first Eritrea then Ethiopia, Afghanistan), but their economic, as opposed to possible military effects, were small.[9] Many of these debts, after the USSR dissolved and both the Soviet debts and credits were taken by Russia, ended up not being repaid.

Thus, the Third World, in challenging the core capitalist countries in the international economic arena in 1974, was alone. Worse than that, the Third World, despite the single appellation that it shared, was hopelessly divided among itself. It included countries that were staunch US allies like Suharto's Indonesia, those with the elites in the pay of the US (most of Central America and the Caribbean), countries militarily dependent on the US (Iran and South Vietnam), and, at the other end of the spectrum, communist countries like Cuba that were suffering from the US trade embargo (at that time, for more than a decade). The ruling classes in most Third World countries depended, in order to remain in power, on US benevolence. Some leaders, like the Shah of Iran, encouraged by the sudden inflow of dollars, could afford to hector the West while skiing in St Moritz, but most knew well enough that their personal fortunes, in the literal as well as the figurative sense, were linked with the capitalist core. Moreover, the weapon of oil had an ambiguous role. Indeed, it was a tremendous help to countries that had oil (some of them only tenuously part of the Third World: Saudi Arabia, United Arab Emirates and Qatar), but it made life much more expensive and difficult for the Third World countries that were importers of oil. They never got much, if any, subsidized oil from their Third World fellow-members.

The NIEO challenge fizzled out within a period equal to one five-year plan. By the late 1970s or early 1980s, the world had changed dramatically. Ideologically, the West abandoned the development of an ever more progressive welfare state, and turned towards neoliberalism, the movement that would continue until the Global Financial Crisis in 2008 and the rising challenge of China. The West was willing to risk a deep recession in 1981 to break the stranglehold of trade unions (in Great Britain), to weaken organized labour (as in the United States), to slash inflation through inordinately increased interest rates (the Volcker effect) and thus to change the domestic political set-up. That domestic change produced dramatic effects on the rest of the world. Countries that borrowed the plentiful dollars in the mid-1970s (as the petrol-states could not use them profitably and had to lend them through the intermediary of Western banks) ran into the crisis of repayment. They borrowed with the expectation that the real interest rates would be low or even negative. After the US jacked up its own rates of interest to control double-digit inflation, the effects of higher rates propagated throughout the rest of the world and brought to the edge of bankruptcy Mexico, Brazil, Argentina, Venezuela and several other Latin American countries. In Eastern Europe, in a development that I have already mentioned, high costs of repayment, combined with the failed strategy to ramp up the efficiency of domestic investment through Western technology, led to popular unrest, most notably in Poland, and to either default or all-but-default to Western creditors in Poland, Hungary, Yugoslavia and Romania.[10] The Soviet Union, as we now know from officials' notes and transcripts of Politburo meetings, was unable to cover the income shortfall of its allies, or to provide more subsidized gas and oil, or to lend the foreign exchange of which it was itself short.[11]

The promises made to the working classes by the political parties in power had to be broken in both West and East. In an excellent book, American historian Fritz Bartel describes the process of promise-breaking in the First and Second Worlds in the 1980s, from coal miners in Britain to shipyard workers in Gdansk. 'The international financial system attacked the communist world for the same reason it attacked debtor countries in the Global South at the same time: the high interest rates and budget deficits in the United States began to monopolize the world's capital, and there was little left for everyone else.'[12] Only the strongest survived. The strongest was the West. It was able, after a deep but relatively short recession, to return to growth – even if by now growth began to assume all the usual features of unequal income gains across classes that were to continue for the next forty years and that were so different from what had happened before 1974. Figure 1.2 shows the real (inflation-adjusted) income gains by decile in the United States between 1964 and 1979, and then between 1979 and 2019. The first line is downward sloping throughout, implying that proportionately higher real income gains were made by the lower deciles. The second-period line is entirely different. Not only is it upward sloping, implying the reverse, namely, that income gains are greater the higher one is in income distribution, but towards the very top the line becomes almost vertical, highly exponential, showing us what by now we all know: the top 1 per cent

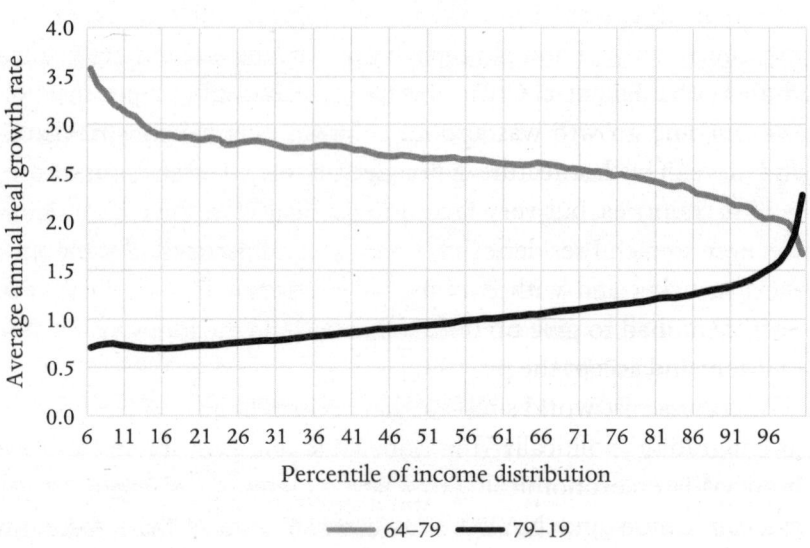

Figure 1.2. United States: Growth incidence curves for 1964–79 and 1979–2019 (average annual real per capita growth)[13]

Note: The growth incidence curves show the real (inflation-adjusted) average per capita growth rate for the periods 1964–79 and 1979–2019. The second period ends before the Covid-19 pandemic. The upward sloping curve implies that the relative (percentage) gains were greater for the rich than the poor. The downward sloping curve implies the opposite.

benefited enormously from neoliberal policies. It is also noticeable that all income groups except the top percentile had higher real growth in the first period than in the second. Further, everybody below the median had, in the second period, real average growth that was less than 1 per cent per year. The equivalently positioned people in the period 1964–79 experienced an average annual growth of above 2.5 per cent per capita. Therefore, the two periods were very different both in terms of real growth and its distribution.

The epilogue of the NIEO challenge came ten years after it was launched. The West fought off the challenge, by not yielding on any key point to the Third World: the Third World was not less subject to Western political meddling and diktat than before, nor was its role in international financial organizations greater. The capitalist core returned to growth, even if that growth was much slower than before. OECD countries grew at an average rate of 3.3 per cent per person between 1952 and 1974 and then at 2 per cent between 1974 and the Global Financial Crisis in 2008, and in many countries such slower income growth was also much more unequally distributed than before. This last feature will indeed come to bedevil the core capitalist countries, but very few thought of that in the early 1980s when even French President François Mitterrand, newly elected on a socialist ticket and with communist ministers brought into the government, had to give up on the idea of nationalizing the banking system and accept the privatize, deregulate, stabilize mantra.

The communist world simply collapsed, with most of the countries 'migrating' politically (many people migrated literally), and somewhat later economically, to the First World, by joining the European Union and NATO. The heterogeneous Third World returned to where it was before 1974. As socialism collapsed, many countries adopted or pretended to adopt the 'end of history' view that capitalism and liberal governance were the way of the future. The non-aligned movement almost entirely disintegrated; some countries moved to become de facto US protectorates (Morocco, Jordan, Thailand, the Philippines), others even asked to be accepted into NATO however geographically remote they were from the original North Atlantic-based alliance (Colombia, Argentina under Javier Milei), while others became subimperial powers.[14] A part of the Third World went in another direction: it turned to religion, like Iran, where the Shah, only a few years after what seemed like the peak of his power, was unceremoniously kicked out and had to beg for asylum in the United States and end his days as a lowly and undesired exile in Egypt. Algeria, one of the founding members of the non-aligned movement, descended into a brutal civil war with Islamic insurgents; the same fate, plus secessionism, befell Ethiopia. Yugoslavia, straddling the Second and the Third Worlds, disappeared from the map.

In this, the first story of the Third World's challenge against the capitalist core, we hardly mentioned one country: China. We hardly mentioned it because it hardly mattered. Despite some attempts to present Maoism as a global ideology (Julia Lovell, 2019) it was neither: Maoism was not a coherent ideology, but was instead programmatically, and sometimes bemusedly, an arranged jigsaw of different ideologies. Nor was its reach ever global, despite its influence over the fringe movements in Peru and Cambodia, or perhaps among the Parisian intellectuals when they were in search of a new girlfriend.

But the sleeper-country in 1974 would 'explode' in the next half-century and transform the world.

China: the second challenge to the West

The world in the early twenties of the twenty-first century is very different from the world that we have just described. Most of the 'merit' for this profound change goes to one country: China, and more broadly to one continent: Asia.

Figure 1.3 is equivalent to Figure 1.1 except that the 'picture is taken' just short of half a century later. The core capitalist countries have expanded in geographical terms as the Second World imploded and many of the erstwhile Soviet-aligned countries changed camp. However, despite the geographical and thus population and income extension, the share of the First World has shrunk from 62 per cent

The Rise of Asia

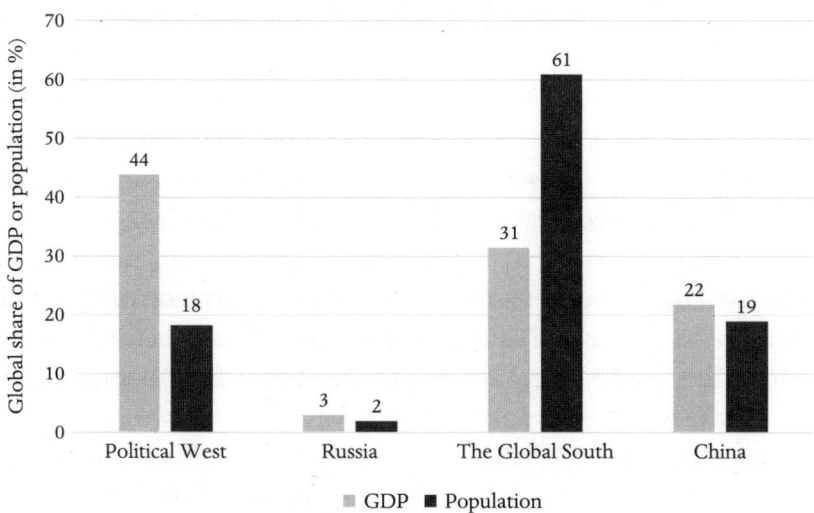

Figure 1.3. Geoeconomics of the world in 2022. Percentage shares of world GDP and world population[16]

to 44 per cent of global output. This is a remarkable decline that, as we shall see below, is reflected not only at an aggregate level, but in income positions of individuals from the capitalist core throughout global income distribution. Even the appellation of the First World is no longer meaningful. If there is no Second World, and if the Third World has, as we shall see, become even more economically and politically diverse than it was, there is no sense in speaking of the First World. A much more appropriate term is, I believe, the *political West*. It is no longer the West limited to what traditionally was called the West; the capitalist core now includes Eastern Europe, the Caucasus, even Central Asian republics, and certainly (as before) Japan and South Korea.[15] This is the new classification that I shall use.

The Second World has disappeared; but given the geopolitical stance of Russia that is in opposition to the 'collective' West, we can replace the Second World with Russia alone. The importance of Russia, economically and population-wise, however, is rather small: representing 3 per cent of global output and 2 per cent of the world population. An inspection of Figures 1.1 and 1.3 easily reveals that, in purely numeric output terms, Russia has taken the place occupied by China in 1974.

China has 'exploded': from producing 2 per cent of global output in 1974, its share has risen to 22 per cent in 2022. This was achieved by a prowess unrecorded in world economic history. Between 1978 and 2022, China has grown at an average (compounded) annual rate of 8.1 per cent per capita. Never in history have so many people improved their incomes so much over such a long uninterrupted period. To illustrate that, we can compare China's rise to the case of Japan. In the Chinese case, we have more than a billion people (the average number of Chinese citizens during the period 1978–2022 was 1.23 billion), growing at 8.1 per cent per annum over forty-four years. A simple calculation (1.081) on the 44th degree multiplied by 1.23 billion gives a total gain of 38 billion (people/income) units. Japan, during its most successful period, 1952–91, produced income growth of approximately 105 million people over thirty-nine years at an average rate of 7.1 per cent per capita per annum. The same calculation gives in turn 1.9 billion people/income units, i.e. *one-twentieth* of what we obtain for China. Finally, a calculation for the United States over the period of its economic take-off between 1865 and 1914 yields an average annual growth rate of 1.3 per cent per capita for an average population of 63 million, and thus an overall gain of 0.13 billion units. In other words, the gains created during China's extraordinary rise were of an altogether different order of magnitude compared to those of Japan and the United States during their economic take-offs.

What used to be called the Third World can now be more appropriately called the Global South. Its share, in both population and total output, has risen: currently it accounts for 61 per cent of the world population (vs 46 per cent in 1974) and 31 per cent of global output (vs 24 per cent in 1974). However, these two numbers, while indicating the increasing importance of the Global South, also illustrate its weakness. In effect, the average per capita GDP of the Global South has slightly decreased from 52 per cent of the global average (easily obtained as 24/46 = 0.52) to 51 per cent of the global average (31/61). In other words, the growth in importance of the Global South is driven by its population expansion, and not by it becoming (compared to the world as a whole) richer. As we shall see next, this overall performance conceals large differences between various parts of the Global South, with India and other Asian countries growing at above world-average growth rates, and Latin America and especially Africa growing at below global average rates. Thus to speak of global 'convergence' requires a very careful use of the term: for in reality, in the past fifty years, the world has in some sense become more uniform (in terms of geographical distribution of economic activity and, as we shall see in the 'People' section below, in terms of individuals' standard of living). But there were also significant parts of the world where this convergence did not take place – moreover, where divergence was 'the order of the day', most notably regarding Africa.

In a political sense, we now have a unified (or collective) political West that produces 44 per cent of global output, a politically (obviously) unified China producing half of that amount, and a politically heterogeneous periphery creating almost a third of global GDP (with much less political power, because of that heterogeneity). Finally, Russia is trying to punch politically above its weight. It is tempting to compare this Russia, circa 2022, with China in 1974, both because they cut a solitary figure politically – not belonging to, or heading, a political or economic bloc – and because, in terms of global output, they have the same weights of about 2 to 3 per cent. The difference, however, was that China in 1974 accounted for almost a quarter of the world population while Russia has only one-tenth of that number. The element, however, that we do not take into account here is Russia's greater military potential than China's in 1974; but measuring that potential is of course much trickier than measuring economic output or population.[17]

How significant is China's challenge to the West? We shall deal with this in the second half of this chapter. But for now, it is useful to compare it to the previous challenge of the New International Economic Order. That challenge was fairly limited as it bore only on international economics, and only in passing on international political relations, trying, in the case of the former, to 'extract' more aid and more favourable policies from the developed capitalist countries, and in the latter, to reaffirm political independence of the Third World.[18] The Soviet challenge with which we did not deal here was, at its peak in the 1950s and early 1960s, much more comprehensive. It included a challenge to the internal organization of the capitalist countries, as well as to their international power. But the economic weight of the socialist bloc was never too great, and even its population share (if we exclude China) was limited. As the economic performance of socialist countries deteriorated, in comparison to capitalist ones, the challenge fizzled out. I think that we can date the end of the attractiveness of the socialist model to the early 1970s, and perhaps even more specifically to the Portuguese Revolution in 1974. Portugal was one of the poorest Western European countries, with the experience of half a century of a conservative or even quasi-fascist regime, with a banned communist party that played an important role in the overthrow of the dictatorship, including among the military. It thus seemed to share many prerequisites for a successful pro-communist revolution. But although the Party and its sympathizers were, at the outset of the Revolution, quite influential, it soon became clear that Portugal would join the West politically and economically, discarding the possibility of nationalization of private companies and a single-party regime. This dating is somewhat ironic because it coincides with the end of the Thirty Glorious years of Western growth, and thus the Portuguese Revolution could have been seen to come at a particularly propitious time to challenge the West. But the Soviet model was by then even more threadbare than the Western one – and it clearly, and easily, lost.

In light of these two examples, how can we then treat the Chinese challenge? Is it similar to, or different from, the geopolitical shifts that we have seen before? Is it more serious or less? China's political system has not been much copied in the rest of the world, and it is not even obvious that China is particularly interested in 'exporting' it. (This could change, however.) In international relations and especially economically, China's challenge is much more important than the previous Soviet and Third World challenges. This is obvious even from the cursory inspection of the numbers: China produces more than one-fifth of the world's GDP while the socialist countries' share was less than one-tenth. Yet it lacks a clear ideological model that the Soviet Union had (despite what I just mentioned about its lack of attractiveness in 1970s Europe) and which exerted a significant pull among many liberation movements in the Third World for at least thirty years after the end of World War II. China does not have a similar ideological appeal precisely because its model, or rather its contrast with the Western model, is not clear and well defined. We could thus say that China scores well in 'weight' (meaning economic importance) but rather poorly in 'softness', implying not only the lack of soft power of culture but of an alternative way of organizing society.

Not by China alone: the rise of Asia overall

The role of Asia appears very clearly when we go beyond an essentially political classification of countries, as we have seen in the chapter so far, to one based on geography. Figure 1.4 highlights again the extraordinary position of China, but also showcases the rise of India, which experienced a rate of per capita growth that was two and a half times greater than that of the political West, as well as the significant, if somewhat less impressive growth record of 'Other Asia'.[19] It is notable that the top three growth 'regions' are all Asian (Figure 1.4). At the very end of this growth ranking are the two other continents belonging to the erstwhile Third World: Latin America and Africa. It is the performance of Africa that is of most concern since it is the poorest continent and also the one with the lowest rate of growth, under 1 per cent per capita annually. The share of Africa in global output has, however, remained constant during the past half-century because its low per capita growth was 'compensated' by high population growth. (Of course, it could be argued that the two developments are not independent: high population growth, the denominator in a per capita measure, reduces GDP per capita and thus its growth.)

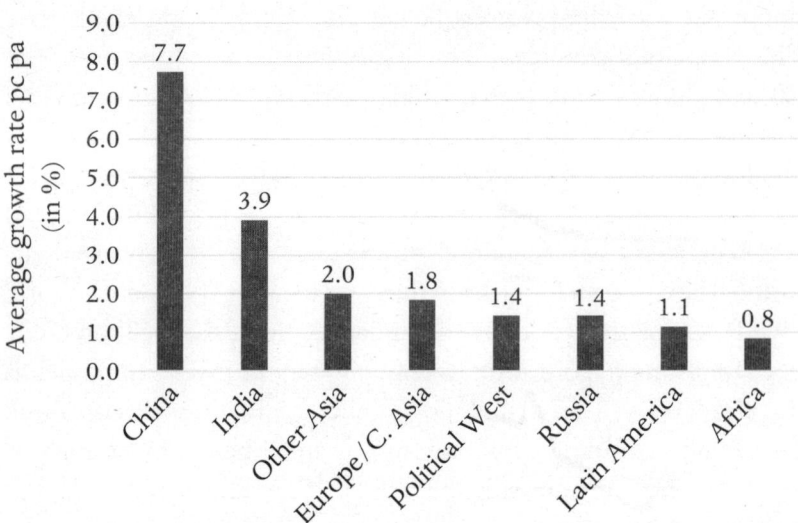

Figure 1.4. The rise of Asia I: Average growth rate of GDP per capita by region 1974–2022 (in per cent, per capita, per year)[20]

Note: 'Other Asia' includes all Asian countries except China, India, and South Korea and Japan. The latter two are considered the 'political West'.

The global economic importance of Asian countries has dramatically increased over the same period. Figure 1.5 gives the share in total world output for four Asian countries (China, India, Indonesia and Vietnam), each paired with a relevant Western country, respectively: the United States, UK, the Netherlands and France. The data reveal the uniformly increasing global importance of Asian countries, and diminishing importance of Western countries. China has overtaken the United States as the largest economy in the world (in purchasing power parity terms, or PPP) in 2015. Its current share is 22 per cent of global output; America's share is 15.5 per cent. Less noticed, but in many ways even more extraordinary, is the change in the shares of Great Britain and India. While in the mid-1970s, the two economies were of about equal size, India's is now four times larger, and accounts for about 8 per cent of global GDP. Similar developments are observable in the two other cases shown in Figure 1.5.

The Rise of Asia

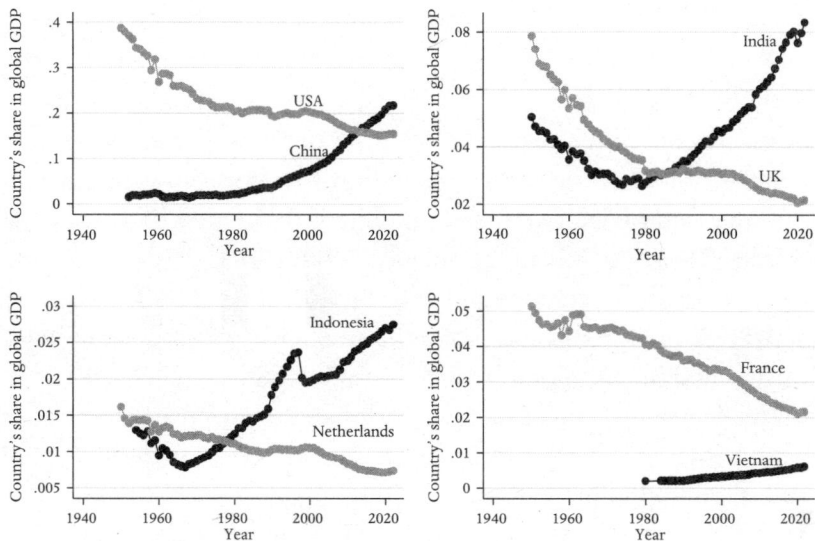

Figure 1.5. The rise of Asia II. The share in global GDP of several Asian countries and the political West, 1952–2022[21]

Note: The share is expressed in ratios; 0.1 means 10 per cent.

In the previous paragraphs we have looked at the size of entire economies. Some of these changes between the regions can be driven in part by the relatively fast population growth (e.g., India's rate of population growth over the period was 1.8 per cent per year, while Great Britain's population grew by only 0.3 per cent per year). The change in economic importance is, however, also driven by the increasing relative wealth of Asian countries, where 'relative wealth' is measured by contrasting GDP per capita of a given country with the world average. We ask the following question: in what year was a country's GDP per capita, expressed as the ratio with respect to the world average GDP per capita, at its maximum? We call it the year of the 'relative income peak'. Clearly, for the countries that are currently growing faster than the world average, the relative income may be at its historical peak at the present; for those that are growing less than the world average, the peak is likely to lie in the past.[22]

The results are shown in Table 1.1: we focus only on selected Asian and Western countries. All large Asian countries, comprising more than 3.5 billion people, are at their relative income peak presently, that is after 2017. Several (China, Vietnam and Bangladesh) are at their peak 'now', that is at the time of the latest available data (2022). For most countries of the political West, the best year was at the very end of the twentieth century or in the first decade of the twenty-first century, and for only four countries is the peak income reached in the recent period (South Korea, Turkey, Ireland and Malta). For Germany and Japan the peak year was 1992, Italy 1995, Austria and Belgium 1999, France 2001, Australia 2002, UK 2003. The United States and Canada are a special case: their relative income peak was in 1952 (at the beginning of our data series) – when the United States' per capita income was 4.7 times greater than the world average. This was due to the very special conditions prevailing after World War II with most of the rest of the developed world in ruins, and Africa and Asia still colonized and poor. The United States is unlikely ever to achieve that relative income level again.

Asia	Year of the peak	Political West	Year of the peak
Thailand	2018	United States	1952
Bhutan	2019	Germany	1992
Cambodia	2019	Japan	1992
India	2019	Italy	1995
Malaysia	2019	Austria	1999
Myanmar	2019	Belgium	1999
Indonesia	2020	France	2001
Laos	2020	Netherlands	2001
Singapore	2021	Australia	2002
Bangladesh	2022	Spain	2002
China	2022	Sweden	2002
Vietnam	2022	UK	2003

Table 1.1. The year of the relative peak income in selected countries in Asia and the political West[23]

Note: For Asia, the data are shown only for the countries whose relative peak income was achieved after 2017.

Emblematic of the developments in the West is Italy. Its income relative to the world average peaked, as we have seen, in 1995, after a period of some forty years when it steadily increased from 1.8 times the world average to the maximum of 3.5 times. It has since equally steadily declined, and it stands today at about 2.2 times the world average, the level at which it was in 1959. Italy's development is paralleled by other Western countries. Generally speaking, their relative 'wealth' increased during the 'Glorious Thirty' years, continued on that trajectory, albeit with some slowdown, for another ten to fifteen years, and has been in decline ever since. The decline is due to the fast growth of populous Asian countries that raised the bar for the global average income by more than the Western countries' income went up. Thus, we see very clearly that the relative position of Asia has improved not only when we consider total output, wherein population growth plays a part, but also when we consider more narrowly economic 'wealth' as represented by per capita GDP compared to the world average.

Within-Asia convergence. It is worth looking at developments within Asia more carefully. To fix ideas, we need to highlight that Asia is an extraordinarily heterogeneous continent in terms of income levels, both of the countries that compose it, as well as of people within countries. In 2022, the range of GDP per capita went from Nepal with less than $PPP 3,000, to Singapore which was close to $PPP 100,000, and Qatar far exceeding it. This gives a top to bottom ratio of 33 to 1. One can compare this with the range for Latin America, which goes from $PPP 1,500 for Haiti to $PPP 25,000 for Chile, a ratio of 17 to 1; and of course with a much more compact political West where the range is even narrower. We find the same levels of between-country heterogeneity in Asia if, instead of computing the ratio of the extremes, we calculate the Gini coefficient of inequality by taking each country's per capita GDP as a single observation, not accounting for population size.[24] This is what I call Concept 1 inequality. In Figure 1.6, in which we observe Concept 1 inequality globally, we see high heterogeneity (or inequality) of incomes in Asia compared to the world, but also that the

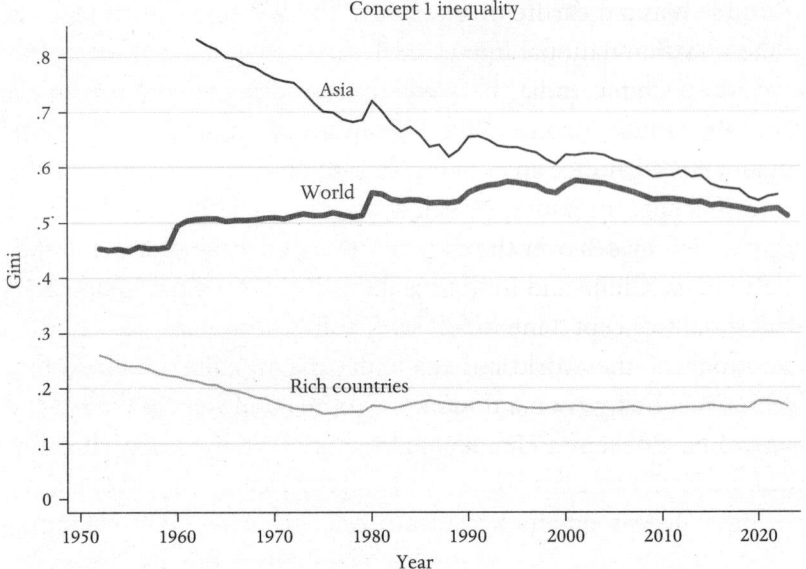

Figure 1.6. Unweighted inequality of GDPs per capita (Concept 1 Gini for the world, Asia and rich Western countries)[26]

Note: Concept 1 measures inequality of unweighted GDPs per capita. The vertical axis shows the Gini coefficient.

Asian between-country inequality has been in decline since the mid-1960s (when our data begin). This contrasts with the rest of the world, where inequality has been broadly constant, albeit with an increase in the 1990s and an equivalent decline in the first decade of the twenty-first century; and also the West, where convergence has stalled since the mid-1970s.[25]

While Concept 1 inequality does not consider a country's population size, it is included when we use Concept 2 inequality, which calculates inequality over population-weighted GDPs per capita. In this measure, each individual technically enters the calculation with the GDP per capita of the country where he or she lives. To put things very clearly: while Concept 1 treats China's importance to be the same as that of Brunei, in the Concept 2 measure, China matters much more. Yet another way to think of Concept 2 is to see it as a measure of inequality across individuals that would exist if within-national inequalities were zero, that is if every individual in China, India, etc. had the same income (equal to the country's mean income). If we now look at Asia, using Concept 2 inequality, we notice an even faster decrease of inequality than with the Concept 1 measure, explained of course by the extraordinary high growth rates over the past fifty years of the two Asian population giants, China and India (see Figure 1.7). They have also driven the *global* Concept 2 inequality down. This last point means that if we think of the world by discarding inequalities within nations, global inequality is on a downward trend. The decrease from 1990, when the Concept 2 Gini shown in Figure 1.7 was around 60 Gini points, to the present value of 45 is quite dramatic. For Asia, that decrease is even greater and amounts to almost 30 Gini points.

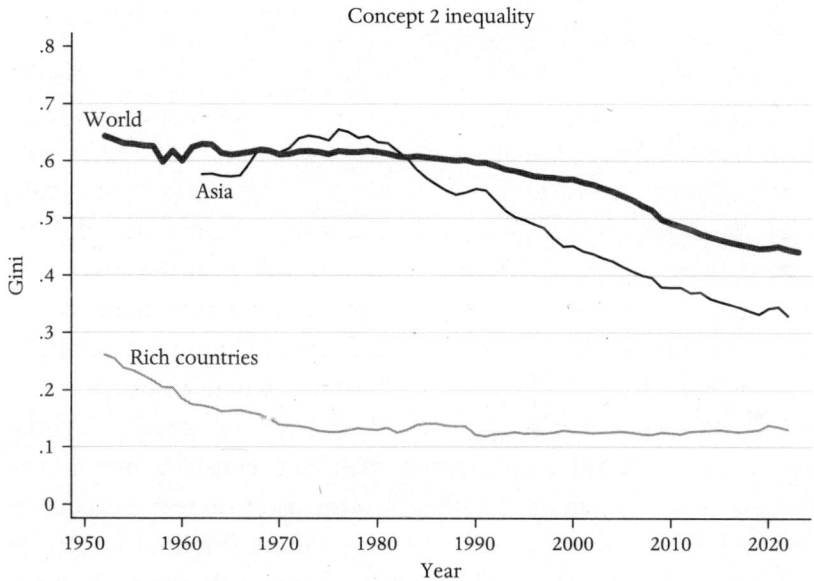

Figure 1.7. Population-weighted inequality of GDPs per capita (Concept 2 Gini for the world, Asia and rich Western countries)[27]

Note: Concept 2 measures inequality of population-weighted GDPs per capita. The vertical axis shows the Gini coefficient.

We thus see, even before we move to account for personal incomes in the calculation (which we shall do in the 'People' section below), that not only has the importance of Asia in the global economy increased in the past half-century, but Asia has become much less unequal (or less heterogeneous), both when measured with and without population-weighting. It is therefore important to highlight more explicitly these two developments: first, in absolute and relative terms, the increased economic weight of Asia, which moves the centre of gravity of the world economy towards the Pacific and the Indian oceans; and second, the convergence of income among Asian countries. In other words, we are highlighting two *changes*: change towards greater Asian economic importance in the world, and change towards less income heterogeneity within Asia.

Is the United States on the decline?

Whether the United States is on the decline is a question that is often asked, and in the broader Western context the query goes back at least to the end of World War I and Oswald Spengler's *The Decline of the West*, the first volume of which was published in 1918. There is an unmistakable thrill among Western audiences when such an idea is posited, because it is pleasant to speak of a decline that is being permanently announced and then equally permanently postponed and that in reality most expect never to happen, or not to happen in their lifetimes. In fact, not only has the talk of the decline been long in existence and repetitive (with various countries, periodically, being supposed to take over), but the facts do not support it. It is not even clear what 'the decline' means. Is 'the decline' a decrease in the amount of things that are being produced in the United States, or is 'the decline' when the increase in the amount of things that are being produced in the United States is slower than such an increase elsewhere (or in the world)? Does 'the decline' mean that the US has to have lower absolute GDP than another big country, or that its growth rate should be less over the long run even if the absolute amount of GDP remains greater?

How do we correlate economic to military or political decline? On each of these complex issues, the answer is not clear. Can the United States be on a military decline when it holds 750 bases in eighty countries against three Chinese foreign bases and three Russian? Can the US be on the decline when it hierarchically controls the only effective military alliance in the world that currently has thirty-two formal member-countries, twice as many as during the Cold War, that produce a third of global output? Can the US be on a political decline when NATO is now expanding globally, adding de facto members in Oceania (Australia, Japan, South Korea, the Philippines, and possibly New Zealand) and even in Latin America (Colombia and Argentina)? China, on the other hand, has not a single official ally. Russia's only ally is Belarus. Finally, can one speak of a decline when the US population is increasing at the rate of 0.6 per cent per year and it attracts millions of immigrants with some 15 million allegedly living in the country without documentation?

When we look at some other, economic, criteria the situation is not as clear cut. Figure 1.8 shows the shares of the United States and China in global GDP; the left panel, when GDPs are calculated in international (PPP) dollars (as also seen in Figure 1.5), and the right panel, when they are calculated at market exchange rates. The former gives a better indication of actual production capacity, the latter of the power of that productive capacity to purchase things in the world. In the early 1950s, the United States was producing almost 40 per cent of global output (with 5 per cent of global population). One needs to put that number in context, though. It was the time when most of continental Europe, Japan and the USSR were devastated, India and most of Africa were colonies, and China was in the midst of a civil war. If most of the world is at war and in turmoil, whereas the United States was not only unaffected by the war directly, but used the war to expand spectacularly its industrial capacity, it is not surprising that it then produced 40 per cent of world output.[28] People who use these 1950s numbers as a yardstick against which the current situation should be judged are employing the wrong measurement. It was a unique situation, unlikely to be repeated in peacetime, and even if another big war were to take place, it is unlikely that it would leave the United States unscathed as the first two global wars did. Secondly, the elementary economics tell us that despite the destruction wrought over continental Europe, Japan and the Soviet Union, the technological level of development and skills of labourers in these countries were much less affected (despite large losses in lives and also, in the case of Germany and the USSR, large outflows of scientists and technicians). So, these countries had to recover, and while doing so, they obviously reduced the global share of US output. In other words, the post-war situation cannot be used, as some supporters of *Make America Great Again* do, as the 'normal' point where the United States should be at any one time, nor can the decline from that point be taken as an indication of the secular decline of the United States.

The US 'decline' is seen, however, if the country is compared with China over the long term. As Figure 1.8 shows, China overtook the United States in total GDP, measured in PPP terms, by 2015, but is still significantly below the US when GDP is measured at market exchange rates. Periods of dollar strengthening, in the 1980s and after 1995, are quite well displayed in the right panel. They obviously do not have anything to do with greater production of goods and services in the US, but indicate that the international economic power of the GDP produced in the United States is greater. Thus

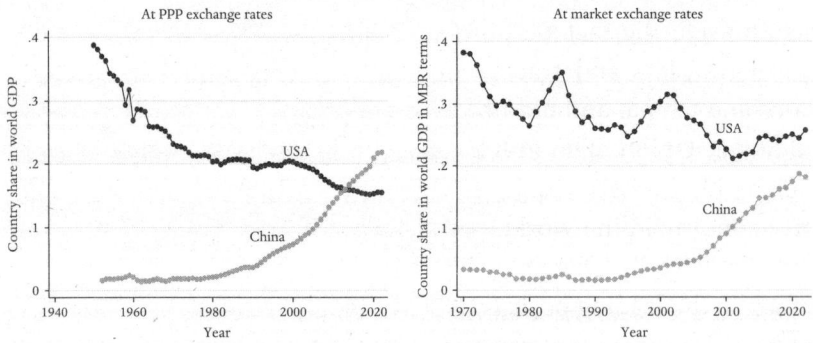

Figure 1.8. Shares of the United States and China in world GDP[29]

Note: Shares expressed as ratios: 0.1 means 10 per cent.

whether the Chinese catch-up of the United States will occur also when GDP is measured at market exchange rates will depend not solely on how fast the two economies are churning out goods and services, but whether the dollar remains the dominant global reserve currency. This shows how the issues of the decline, catch-up and overtake, even when defined in purely economic terms, are difficult to resolve conclusively. I shall discuss below, when we look at how the great transformation of economic power affects not only the position of countries, but people, the way in which we may redefine the point where China may be said to have caught up with the United States. But that point is still one to two generations away – under the assumption that Chinese per capita growth rates remain several percentage points higher than America's.

The current or likely forthcoming cold war with China is sometimes compared with the Cold War between the United States and the Soviet Union. There are indeed many similarities, but when it comes to the economics, that war was much less challenging for the US than the current conflict with China. Figure 1.9 shows the shares of the two largest economies in the world from 1965 until 2022 (in PPP terms). It is notable that while the Soviet Union, all the way to its dissolution in 1992, was the second largest economy in the world, its share never exceeded 10 per cent of the global GDP, which is less than one-half of China's world share now. So, the Soviet Union was economically much less of a strong competitor than China, even leaving aside the fact of much greater interdependence, technological transfers and trade that exist today between the United States and China, and did not exist between the United States and the Soviet Union. The graph also shows that economically, for a brief period in the 1990s, Japan took the position of the second largest economy in the world, only to be overtaken by China in 1999, with China finally overtaking the US in 2015. How long China might remain in the leading position is anyone's guess: but the period may not be short, given that possibly the most likely contender for the top slot, India, has the current global GDP share of a little over 8 per cent (compared to the Chinese 22 per cent). India, of course,

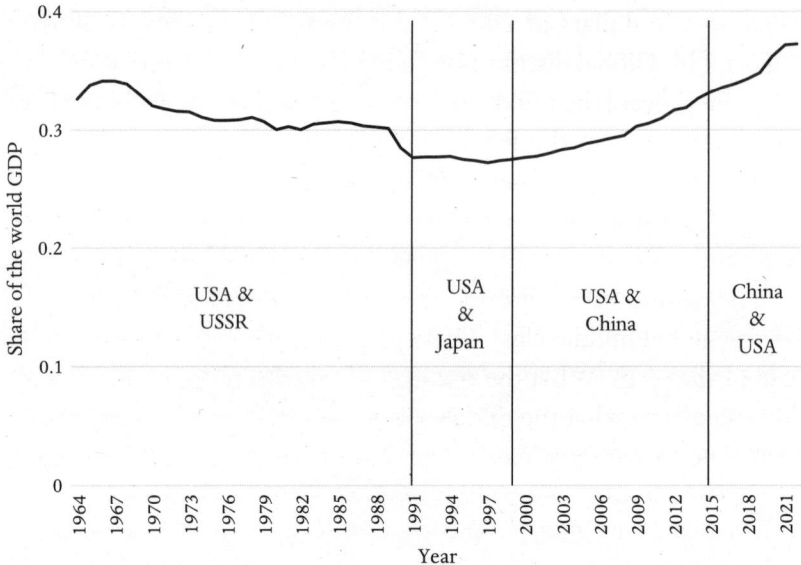

Figure 1.9. The share of two largest economies in world GDP, 1964–2022 (in PPP terms)[30]

Note: The share on the vertical axis is expressed in ratios; 0.1 means 10 per cent.

has the advantage of a rising population that China no longer does, and high growth rates; yet the distance is still too big.

People[31]

The emergence of the global 'middle class'

The growth of Asia has created a global middle class, or more exactly the global median class. When the country-level data that we have considered so far are 'translated' into household or personal incomes, we find that a much greater percentage of people (and of course, much greater absolute *number* of people) are located around the middle of the global income distribution in 2018 than thirty years earlier.[32] (Global income distribution is defined as the distribution of after-tax income among world citizens, with incomes measured in dollars of equal purchasing power). This is shown in Figure 1.10. Global distribution in 2018 is, as can be observed, much 'thicker' around the middle than in 1988 when the bulk of the world population was in the left part of the graph, at very low income levels. The change happened in an 'evolutionary' way, that is, gradually: the distribution in 2008 stands somewhere between those in 1988 and 2018.

The concentration around the global median allows us to speak of the global middle class. However, one has to be careful with the use of the term. What the middle class means in a global context is different from what the middle class means in a richer Western context. The global middle class is much poorer than what is normally considered in the West to be a 'middle-class' income. The reason is obvious. The (political) West is a very rich part of the world: a person with the Western median after-tax income, which is around

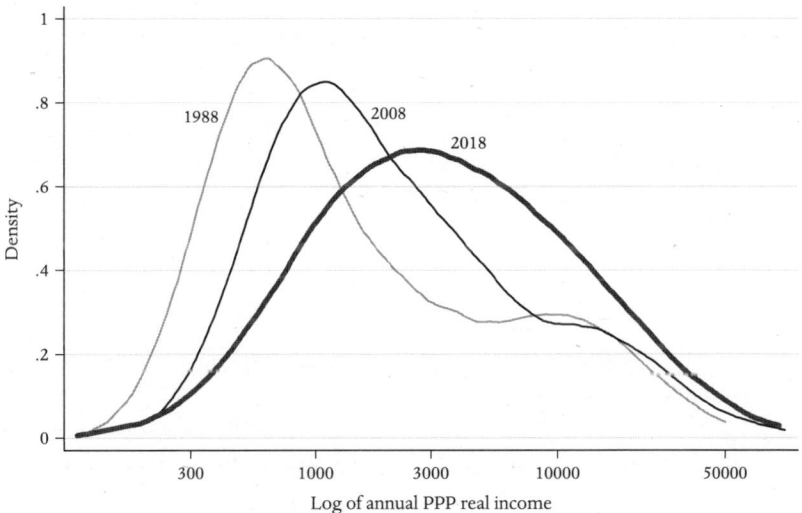

Figure 1.10. Global income distribution in 1988, 2008 and 2018[33]

Note: The graph shows global income distributions as obtained from nationally representative household surveys that cover approximately 120 countries and about 95 per cent of the world income and population. Individuals are ranked by their household per capita real (PPP) income.

$PPP 18,000 per person annually, is at the 90th global percentile. It is only such a relatively high income that, from the Western point of view, tends to be associated with a 'middle-class' life.[34] The global middle class is much poorer. Its per capita incomes range between $PPP 2,600 and $PPP 3,900.[35] Some 770 million people, or 11 per cent of the world population, are in that range.

Despite the fact that such global middle-class incomes are seen as low from the Western perspective, the extent of change, or improvement, in the global income distribution is remarkable. For the first time in two hundred years, global income distribution looks similar to what income distributions usually look like in individual countries. When per capita incomes are expressed in logarithms and arrayed, as in Figure 1.10, on the horizontal axis, for individual countries we visually get a bell-shaped curve (the so-called normal distribution). And indeed for the world now, the distribution, while still slightly elongated on the right tail where top incomes are, looks remarkably close to normal. So, is the world now similar to a single country? Clearly not, and certainly not so politically. But in an economic sense, and particularly if we zero in on Asia and the West, the convergence is unmistakable.

When will China and Asia catch up with the United States/OECD? China's role in shaping the global income distribution was without a doubt determinant since the 1980s. But the very fact that China has, through its advance, reshaped the global distribution means that China's relative position has shifted markedly upwards. Hence its growth can no longer be reducing global inequality as it did in the past. Yet China's growth will continue to have important consequences for the position of Chinese people in the global income distribution and thus indirectly also on the positional displacement or 'downplacement' of the parts of Western populations that are being overtaken by the Chinese.

Before we look at this global 'China effect', it may be useful to start by contrasting income positions of Chinese and American citizens. Figure 1.11 shows the two distributions (with their relative population sizes) along the same income per capita axis. The income

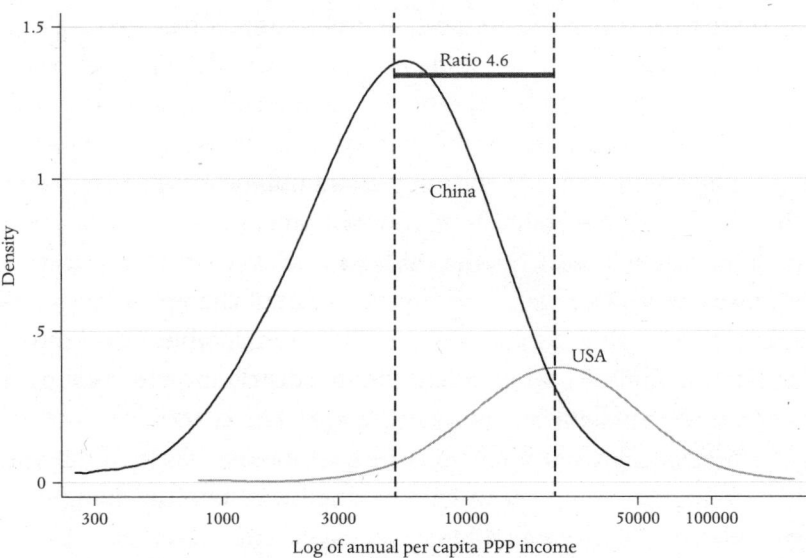

Figure 1.11. Income distributions of China and the United States in 2018[36]

Note: The graph shows income distributions of China and the United States with the areas under the curves reflecting population sizes of the two countries. All incomes are expressed in PPP dollars.

gap between the two medians, shown by the vertical dashed lines, is substantial: US median income is 4.6 times higher than the Chinese (all in PPP terms).[37] But in 1988, the gap was enormous: 18 to 1. The higher growth rate of China, compared to the United States, consequently reduced the gap to its current level.[38] Note also that there is a non-negligible overlap between the two distributions: about 3 per cent of the Chinese (some 40 million people) have an income greater than the US median (by definition, 50 per cent of Americans have an income above the US median), and 4 per cent of Americans have an income lower than the Chinese median.

When might China overtake the US? An important political question can now be asked, couched in somewhat different terms, and perhaps more meaningful from people's point of view than when asked to compare the two countries as a whole: when will China catch up or overtake America? We have seen above that if we look at the total output and technically price each component of that output the same (as PPP dollars do), China has already overtaken the United States. But it has not overtaken it if total output is measured at market exchange rates: there the US, in 2022, still enjoys an advantage of almost 40 per cent. It should be noted again, however, that this advantage (unlike when output is measured in international dollars) depends also on the 'vagaries' of the exchange rates. A cheap yuan will understate China's overall GDP, and accordingly overstate America's. But it might, for example, help Chinese exports and boost Chinese growth. Hence there is a significant ambivalence when using market exchange rates in such comparisons.

When we shift our focus to per capita incomes in PPP terms as here, both the definition and the point of the catch-up change: the question becomes when China's *per capita* income might overtake US *per capita* income. A similar overtake by the United States of Great Britain happened, according to the most recent estimates by the Maddison Project (a database of historical economic statistics), at the very end of the nineteenth century. But regarding the United States and China, the point of the overtake is unlikely to be reached soon because income gaps are still very large. Besides, at that point, when China has the same per capita income as the United States, the global influence of the two countries would be very different as China is likely to have a population about three times greater than the US. So, one could say that at that point in time the US would have already lost global leadership.

Rather than focus on something that is possible only in the very long run (and thus, partly because of that fact, fundamentally hard to predict), a more meaningful question to ask is when there would be as many affluent Chinese as Americans. For the definition of affluence we take US median income. Thus, we ask: when will the absolute number of Chinese people with income equal or higher than the US median income be the same as the absolute number of such Americans? There are currently some 40 million Chinese who fulfil that condition vs one-half of the US population or around 165 million Americans. The calculation of the catch-up is fairly involved and is subject to many assumptions, including the future growth rates of the two economies, changes in domestic income distributions in the United States and China, population growth rates, etc. But the most important among these assumptions is the difference in GDP per capita growth rates between the two countries. That difference was on average 6 per cent per annum in the 1980s, 7 per cent in the 1990s, then rose to 9 per cent in the period from China's accession to the WTO in 2001 to the Global Financial Crisis in 2008, and has since decreased to around 4.5 per cent (Figure 1.12). More recently, the gap has also become more difficult to judge because of the highly idiosyncratic effects of the Covid pandemic from late 2019 onwards. It could be, however, reasonably argued that Chinese growth might decelerate, and that the gap between the growth rates of the two largest world economies might in the next generation range between 2 per cent and 4 per cent per annum. The population growth rates of the two countries may not differ very much even if, currently, the US experiences a higher population growth rate than China (Chinese population is projected to shrink).

Since the US median income is very high (a person with such income is placed at the 93rd global percentile, and we assume that it will stay at that level), our question boils down to asking when the probability of finding an American or a Chinese citizen in the very top part of the global income distribution would be about the same. It turns out that, with the growth gap of 3 per cent per year in favour of China, it would require twenty years; or if the growth gap is less (say, only 2 per cent per year), a decade longer. The power of exponential calculus and a greater size of the Chinese population accelerate things quickly: if the growth gap is 3 per cent per year and extends over thirty (rather than twenty) years, the number of Chinese people in the global top decile would be almost double the number of Americans.

A generation or a generation-and-a-half from now is less than the time that has elapsed from the opening of China to the present. It could be said that China has traversed about two-thirds of the distance that separates it from the US. It is tantalizingly close to something that no one would have predicted when Mao died: that in sixty or seventy years the then impoverished China would have as many globally rich citizens as the United States. It also seems quite achievable: if US per capita growth continues between 1.5 per cent and 2 per cent per year, which has been the case for the past half-century and which is a conventional assumption for countries close to the technological frontier, China will need to grow at 4.5 per cent to 5 per cent: not a growth path inconsistent with its past performance.

It is in this context that we may assess the recent changes in US policies with regard to China that include tighter controls over the technologically sensitive US exports and import restrictions on Chinese goods and investments in the United States. Such policies would in principle negatively affect growth rates of both China and the US. But if, and that is of course a big if, such policies affect the Chinese growth rate more than the US growth rate, then the growth gap would be less. If the growth gap is reduced by, say, half a per cent, the catch-up is postponed by approximately four years. Therefore, American anti-globalization policies *do* have a rational core: which is to provoke a greater deceleration of Chinese growth, and postpone either the overtake or a more serious challenge on China's part to US economic supremacy. In a two-person game where relativities matter, the issue is simply to know whether such policies hurt the competitor more than oneself.[39]

The same calculation can be done by contrasting large Asian countries – namely India, Indonesia, Vietnam, Thailand and Pakistan – with OECD countries. The calculation becomes even more complicated and subject to further caveats because we need to project GDP per capita and population growth rates for many countries (assuming in addition that there are no changes in their internal income distributions). The current gap between the OECD and the combined population of the large Asian countries is much greater than the current gap between the US and China. While the latter median-to-median gap is, as we saw above, 4.6 to 1, the median-to-median income gap between the OECD and the populous Asian countries is more than 10 to 1 (all calculated using dollars of equal

The Rise of Asia

purchasing power and household survey data). This means that the conditions needed to achieve a similar outcome as before – namely, to find out when the total population of the large Asian countries (excluding China) with income equal to or above the OECD median will become equal to one-half of OECD population – are more demanding. Additionally, the growth rate gap between populous Asian countries and the OECD was historically smaller (Figure 1.12), and, in some periods, non-existent. This was not the case with China vs the United States (except in the 1960s). On the other hand, helping the convergence, the Asia–OECD gap was 4 per cent per capita on average between the Global Financial Crisis and the pandemic. Also, the OECD median income is less than the median income of the

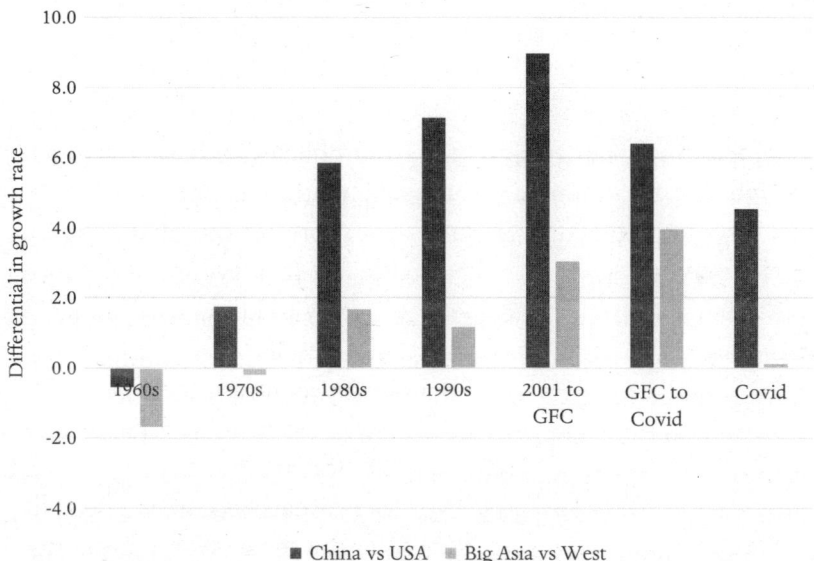

Figure 1.12. Growth gap between China and the US, and populous Asian countries and OECD, 1960–2022 (GDPs per capita in real PPP terms)[41]

Note: Growth gap shows the difference in GDP per capita growth rates between, on the one hand, China and the US (left column), and, on the other, the populous Asian countries (excluding China) and OECD (right column). The growth rates for the populous Asian countries and OECD are calculated for the whole area as a unit. GFC = Global Financial Crisis.

United States, and population growth rates of large Asian countries consistently exceed OECD population growth by 0.7–0.8 per cent per annum. Both make the catch-up easier.[40] Taking all of these complicating factors into account, we find, however, that the Asia–OECD catch-up is unlikely to occur in less than forty years and would require maintaining a per capita growth differential (in favour of Asia) of around 3.75 per cent per annum.

To summarize. In terms of real personal incomes, the point in time when the number of affluent Chinese people may become approximately equal to the number of affluent Americans will take, under the currently reasonable assumptions, between a generation and a generation-and-a-half. A similar catch-up of the rest of East and South Asia with OECD countries may require at least two generations.

Positional decline of the Western middle classes

Another 'translation' from the rather abstract level of countries' GDPs to a concrete level of individual incomes involves looking at the positional change of different countries' populations in the global income distribution. There, we observe what is probably the greatest reshuffle of individual income positions since the Industrial Revolution. The quickly rising incomes across the entire Chinese distribution allowed many Chinese to overtake people from other countries in the global income rankings. This 'China effect', which is the most important component of the global reshuffling, is present in all parts of the global income distribution. It is at its most dramatic, though, around the upper-middle of the global income distribution – where poorer parts of Western countries' populations are located. It is still modest at the very top, that is, at the global top 5 per cent range. This is because not enough Chinese have become so rich as to displace Westerners, and in particular Americans, who have historically 'monopolized' the presence at the very top of the global income pyramid during the past hundred years.

The Rise of Asia

Figure 1.13 (upper left panel) shows the positions of Chinese urban deciles (each decile is composed of 10 per cent of that country's population, ranked from the poorest to the richest) and (upper right panel) Italian deciles in 1988 and 2018.[42] The upward movement (improvement in the position) of Chinese urban deciles amounted to between 19 and 26 global percentiles, meaning that people in a given Chinese urban decile leapfrogged (in real income terms) over one-fifth or more of the world population. For example, a person with the median urban Chinese income was around the 50th global percentile in 1988 but advanced

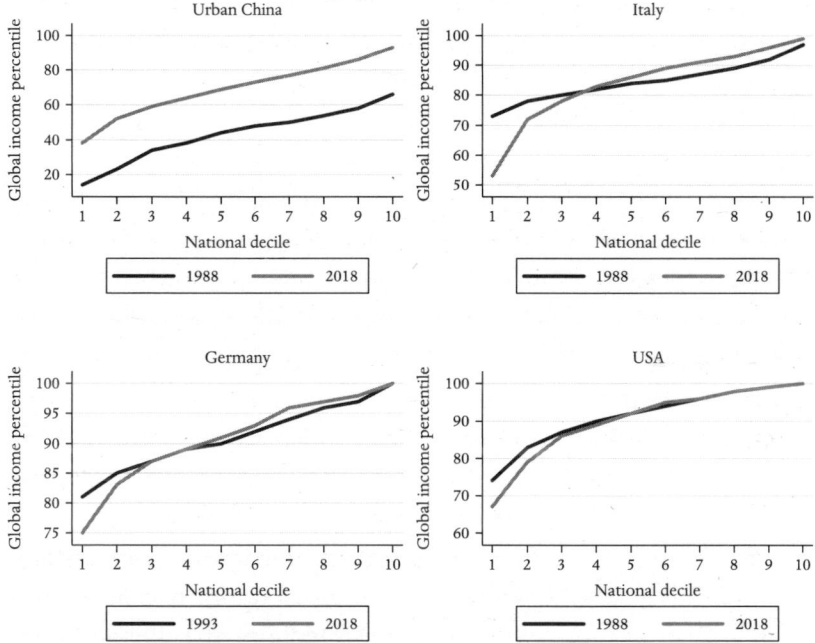

Figure 1.13. Positions of country deciles in global income distributions in 1988 and 2018[43]

Note: The graph shows the global income position of each national income decile (running from the poorest, 1, to the richest, 10) in 1988 and 2018. National income deciles are shown on the horizontal axis. Their global position is shown on the vertical axis. Thus, the fifth Chinese urban decile is at the position of the 50th global percentile in 1988 and at the 70th global percentile in 2018.

to the 70th global percentile in 2018. When keeping in mind the extraordinarily high growth rate of Chinese per capita GDP over that period, this is of course not a surprise. But as the Chinese deciles have gone up in the global income distribution, other countries' deciles, if relatively close to the upwardly moving Chinese, had to go down. This is illustrated first in the example of Italy. The bottom Italian decile has slipped by twenty global percentiles, the second and the third deciles by six and two, respectively. The other Italian deciles were not affected as they tend to be above the part of the global distribution where Chinese influence has been the strongest.

The changes observed in the case of Italy are not unique to that country. The German bottom decile has slipped from the 81st global percentile in 1993 to the 75th percentile in 2018 (Figure 1.13, bottom left panel). The second lowest decile has, like in Italy, also lost its relative position. In the United States (bottom right panel), the bottom decile has moved down by seven global percentiles, and the positional loss – although in some cases minimal – has spread to the bottom 40 per cent of the population. In France (not shown here), the bottom three deciles have lost out, with the lowest once again losing the most, going down from the 73rd global percentile in 1988 to the 69th percentile in 2018.

The populations of rich Western countries, even if income distributions within countries do not get worse, will increasingly be composed of people who belong to very different parts of the global income distribution. Thus, while in 1988 the range of US income deciles was from the 74th global percentile to the 100th (that is, relatively narrow), in 2018, the range was from the 67th to the 100th. (The 100th percentile is the global top 1 per cent.) This is a very peculiar polarization, invisible in national studies of inequality, but visible when looked at globally. Does it matter? Surely not as much as traditional within-country polarization does. Yet to the extent that different global income positions are associated with different consumption patterns, and these patterns are influenced by global fashions and globally determined 'needs', the feeling of increasing polarization in Western countries may become real. To put it bluntly: while in the past both a German metal worker and a German engineer were able to afford a vacation in Thailand (a global good), in the future only the latter may be able to do so. Or to buy the newest type of smartphone or attend the football World Cup.

Relative constancy at the top. Unlike the middle of the global income distribution, the composition of the top has remained more stable. To assess this I look at the composition of country-percentiles that were in the global top 5 per cent in 2008 and 2018. The global top 5 per cent contains between 320 and 330 million people in both years and is more representative of the globally affluent than the more rarified global top 1 per cent.

When one takes twelve countries with the largest absolute participations in the global top 5 per cent in 2008 (they are given in the

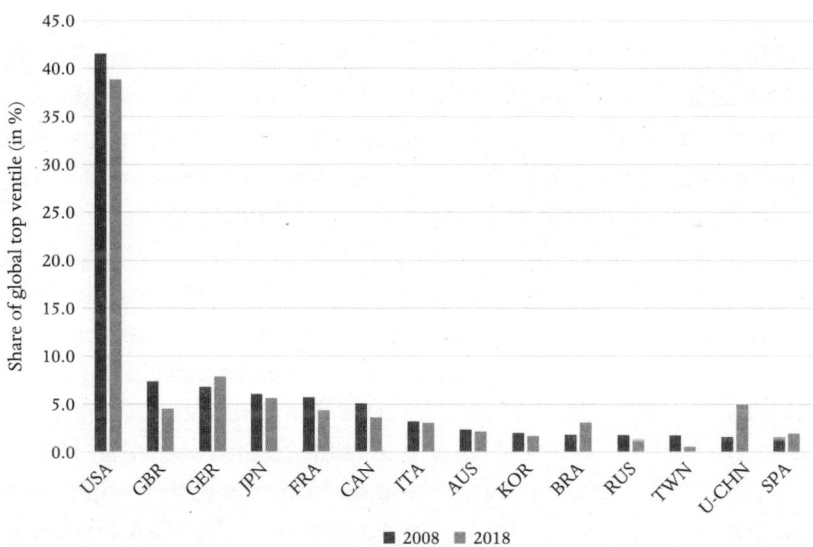

Figure 1.14. The composition of the global top 5 per cent in 2008 and 2018 (in per cent)[45]

Note: Each bar shows the share of that country's population among the globally affluent. For example, about 40 per cent of the population in the global top 5 per cent is from the United States. 'Ventile' means 5 per cent of a given group, similar to 'decile', which means 10 per cent.

first twelve positions, going from left to right, in Figure 1.14), we note that there were only two newcomers in 2018 – urban China and Spain – and, consequently, two dropouts (Russia and Taiwan). Ten out of twelve countries are the same with approximately the same number of people among the globally affluent in both years. The United States is by far the most important. In both years about 40 per cent of the globally affluent are US citizens. The United Kingdom, Japan and Germany come next, with their positions slightly shifting between the two years, each participating by between 5 and 8 per cent among the globally affluent. The newcomers among the top twelve countries are the urban Chinese whose share has gone up from 1.6 per cent to 5 per cent, and the Spanish citizens, going up from 1.6 to 1.9 per cent. The former means that one out of each twenty globally affluent people is currently an (urban-area) Chinese person.

There is, as we have seen, a strong persistence in terms of both countries and the number of their citizens who are part of the globally affluent. The political West has about 280 million citizens among the globally affluent; they account for 86 per cent of the globally affluent in 1988, 87 per cent in 2008 and 83 per cent in 2018. The share of the West among the most affluent has therefore remained preponderant and broadly constant.

Among Asian countries (exclusive of Japan), the Chinese urban population is now the most important. The shares of the Indian and Indonesian urban populations in the global top 5 per cent have also risen between 2008 and 2018: in the case of India, from 1.3 to 1.5 per cent; in the case of Indonesia, from 0.3 to 0.5 per cent; but their numbers are still small.[44] The same is true for the other parts of the world (Africa, Latin America and Eastern Europe) which, with the exceptions of Brazil and Russia, never had a significant numeric participation among the globally affluent.

*

The present and the future: big exogenous shocks, the role of China and Africa

The time when this is being written is unlike any recent period. It is characterized by three large external shocks that are still continuing, and whose consequences are impossible to forecast with any confidence, much less precision. The first was the shock of the Covid pandemic that began in late 2019 and has continued in the years since. It has had important effects on countries' growth rates (e.g., making India's per capita growth rate in 2020 almost minus 10 per cent). It is too early to say how these effects will play out over the medium term since many of the GDP declines were almost immediately reversed in the next few years by the similarly sized increases. However, the decline in global inequality that has been going on continuously since the early 1990s stalled during this period. It is quite possible that the period of Covid (however initially exogenous the event) might presage the end of global convergence and the return to higher inequality between global citizens.

The second important exogenous shock was the deterioration of US–Chinese relations, which, given that these are the two largest economies in the world accounting together for almost 40 per cent of global GDP, is extremely important. In fact, never in recent history (the past sixty years) have the two largest economies accounted for so much of the global output (Figure 1.9). Economic, social (in the area of values) and possibly military conflict between these countries may be devastating for more than just themselves.

The third exogenous shock was the Russia–Ukraine war that so far has not only seriously weakened both economies (e.g., with Ukraine's economy estimated to have contracted by almost a third in 2022) but has affected the rest of the world through economic sanctions, creation of economic blocs, higher prices of energy and food, and in the political sphere the appearance of a de facto global NATO that corresponds to what we call here 'the political West'. This war was 'compounded' by the war in Gaza, which came to be seen in global terms as pitting the political West against the rest of the world.

What can we say regarding global convergence if we abstract from the impossible-to-predict effects of the three large shocks? We can pinpoint two longer-term developments that do not depend directly on the effects of the shocks. They are the changing roles of China, and of India and Africa in the global income distribution.

As we have seen, China's role in shaping the global income distribution was without a doubt determinant since the early 1980s. But the very fact that China has, through its advance, shaped the distribution means that China's relative position has also shifted markedly upwards. Hence its growth can no longer be globally inequality-reducing as it was in the past. At present, Chinese growth is broadly neutral as far as global inequality is concerned.

The end of the benign (pro-equality) role of China on the global stage foregrounds the key roles that will be played by India and the populous African countries in the future. In order for the population-weighted income convergence to continue – i.e., for global inequality to keep decreasing in the future – India and large African countries need to grow faster than the rest of the world, and especially faster than the rich OECD countries. The question has been asked before: can Africa's growth in the rest of the twenty-first century replicate recent Asian (and Chinese) growth? This matters not only because Africa is relatively poor, but because Africa is the only continent whose population is expected to grow in this century and perhaps even in the next.

We obviously cannot answer with any certainty the question regarding the likelihood of Africa's future fast growth, but if we can look at the past and Africa's post-1950 record, and use that as a possible guide regarding the future, we cannot be too optimistic. Only six African countries have succeeded in registering five or more years of consecutive per capita growth of at least 5 per cent. This rate of growth can be seen as a reasonable objective which, if maintained over at least five years, allows a country to achieve perceptible convergence. But it was an objective that, as the data show, was unattainable for almost all African countries. In addition, these exceptional episodes in Africa involved mostly very small countries (in terms of population) and countries whose growth largely depended on one export commodity (oil in the case of Gabon and Equatorial Guinea, and cocoa in the case of Côte d'Ivoire). It is only Ethiopia, itself rebounding from the disastrous effects of the civil war and secession of Eritrea, that was a populous country (with more than 100 million people) exhibiting high growth for a long period of fourteen consecutive years. And that period came to an end with the recent civil war and the Covid crisis. The bottom line is that between 1960 and 2020, there were only sixty-four country/years in Africa that satisfy our criterion (namely, five consecutive years of growth equal to at least 5 per cent per capita) vs 216 for the same period in Asia.[46] The latter of course also involved much more populous countries.

The rise of Asian countries, and China in particular, has set the stage for geopolitical conflict with the political West. The decline in the relative global position of the Western middle classes has lain the groundwork for the emergence of the new elites brought on by neoliberalism and the domestic political turbulence in the West. The next three chapters are dedicated to these topics.

2.

Convergence and Conflict

Economists and political scientists through time have asked whether international trade is more likely to be associated with war or peace, and how desirable income equality is between nations and people. I address these two issues here; they are perhaps the ultimate enquiry of the book. I will consider – through the eyes of economists past and present – the relationship between free trade, *a fortiori* globalization, and peace or war between nations, as well as why income convergence between nations and people may lead to fear and conflict. Whether income convergence, which at first seems a highly desirable objective, might lead to conflict is a deeply pertinent question to ask in the era of globalization and the rise of Asia.

Trade and peace: a synopsis. It is important to distinguish our concern with free trade and its effect on war and peace from general arguments in favour of free trade made on the grounds that, through allowing specialization in production, trade maximizes global output. The argument with which we are concerned here is entirely different: it justifies free trade by arguing that it brings peace; or differently, it disapproves of free trade by arguing that it stimulates war. Logically, of course, one can hold that free trade maximizes global output, while also creating international instability and war.[1]

There is a third relationship to consider: the connection between trade and domestic 'liberty' or what we may call 'agency'. The economist Friedrich Hayek, a key proponent of free-market capitalism in the twentieth century, forcefully argued that the two are related: 'The gradual transformation of the rigidly organized hierarchical [feudal] system into one where men could . . . attempt to shape their own life, where man gained the opportunity of knowing and choosing between different forms of life, is closely associated with the growth of commerce.'[2] Hayek proceeds by providing the examples of Renaissance Italy whose international trade transformed domestic politics in France, Germany, the Low Countries and eventually England. One wonders, however, why the even more intensive trade between the Italian city-states mentioned by Hayek and the Byzantine Empire never produced similar results. This aspect of trade's impact on domestic institutions will appear when we discuss the engagement between the United States and China. The first period of this engagement, from approximately 1978 to the Global Financial Crisis, was thought by many in the United States to be likely to produce domestic, pro-democratization, change in China. That expectation faded later, perhaps in the same way as the oligarchic trading republics of Italy never succeeded in changing the hierarchical and autocratic governance of the Byzantine Empire.

The first sustained argument in favour of free trade was made by physiocratic writers in France and in particular by François Quesnay, the founder of political economy. The argument was that free trade increases the production of agricultural goods which, according to the physiocrats, were the most important for people's welfare. The physiocrats therefore argued against export tariffs that reduced the supply of French agricultural products as well as against different domestic impediments to commerce, like bridge and road taxes and regional customs duties. Their argument had nothing to say on whether free trade would lead to peaceful cooperation between nations. Many modern arguments in favour of free trade are similar: they focus on total increase in output, ignore distributional consequences (e.g., some parties might benefit from trade much more than others) but do not concern themselves with 'external' effects of commerce, on people's behaviour, governance, and peace or war.

The writer who addressed this last question directly was (by his full name, Charles Louis de Secondat, baron de la Brède et de) Montesquieu, a French philosopher who wrote in the first half of the eighteenth century. Like Quesnay, he died before the French Revolution but his ideas influenced the intellectual climate that led to the

Revolution.³ According to Montesquieu, as we shall see in this chapter, free trade is conducive to peace between nations by making people's behaviour and customs more 'agreeable' or softer. This is the idea behind his famous *doux commerce*, the term that Montesquieu invented. Peace arises from the substitution of martial or virile virtues by the more polite or effete virtues of kind behaviour and politeness. (However, since both are motivated by gain, an element of hypocrisy is inevitable in such polite behaviour; and Montesquieu did not fail to notice it.) Peace is not directly achieved by trade. It comes by changing people's calculation: instead of satisfying their self-interest and desire for more property by war and plunder, they realize that by trading non-violently they can achieve the same objectives better, and perhaps with much less risk. The theory will of course appeal much more to physically weaker individuals or militarily weaker nations. But – as Montesquieu could be interpreted – once trading manners become dominant among individuals and nations, even the strong may be persuaded to follow them.

These views, both of Quesnay and Montesquieu, were taken over by Adam Smith, the Scottish economist and moral philosopher who is nowadays considered an iconic defender of free trade. For Smith, free trade was a special application of his general principle of the advantages provided by the division of labour. In the same way in which the division of labour within a single nation increases productivity and output by allowing people to specialize in what they do best, free trade between individuals globally (and indirectly between nations) increases global output by allowing different countries, enjoying different endowments and climates, to specialize in what they can produce more cheaply than others. Our issue (free trade, and war or peace) is addressed indirectly by Smith in an important, albeit often overlooked, passage in *The Wealth of Nations*. Here, he speculates that free trade would lead to similar economic and technological developments in the countries that participate in trade, which would in turn dissuade them from waging war on each other because of their approximately equal military strength. In the world in which Smith lived and worked (the second half of the eighteenth century), he rightly observed that the wars were mostly colonial conflicts made possible by the great inequality in power between European nations and the rest of the world. If unevenness of technological power between nations were reduced by trade, or even better, if their military powers were equalized thanks to trade, that would, in Smith's view, lead to peace. Smith saw the balance of power as a prerequisite for peace, a point that he made as an economist, but which became hotly debated by twentieth- and twenty-first-century scholars of international relations.

Other theories I consider next are very different. They hold, on the contrary, that trade under capitalist conditions tends to lead to war rather than peace. The most important such doctrine was developed in the early twentieth century by the British journalist and economist John Hobson and was expanded during World War I by Marxist economists, Vladimir Lenin, the Russian revolutionary and founder of the Soviet Union, and Rosa Luxemburg, a Polish-German communist murdered in 1919. For them, trade – very differently from the previous writers – means that imperialist nations are focused on the acquisition of raw materials, control of markets in colonies and exploitation of cheap, often coerced, labour. To do so – that is, to conquer a foreign country and impose its government – capitalists harness the military power of their own states. Capitalists and the state thus work hand in hand.[4] But if one country, or rather, if capitalists from one country, desire to achieve all these things, would not capitalists from other countries wish for the same? An attempt to do so by several countries necessarily leads to conflict. Here of course we have an entirely different theory of what trade does: instead of helping people collaborate peacefully, trade sows the seeds of discord because it is basically connected to control, power and acquisition of wealth by all means, including violent ones.

Finally, I consider a somewhat similar theory by Joseph Schumpeter, an Austrian-American economist who in some of his early articles, written in the beginning of the twentieth century, believed that imperialism was a residual of an aristocratic mindset and the product of a feudal or pre-modern class structure. Imperialism and war were not compatible with capitalism: the latter is a rational search for profit, while wars are a way to enrichment through plunder. They are often, Schumpeter believed at that time, irrational because they are driven by the vanity of rulers, not by the cold-blooded gain and loss calculus of economists and traders. However, in his later works, which I will also discuss in this chapter, Schumpeter came fairly close to the theory held by Hobson, Lenin and Rosa Luxemburg. He came there by his own route, however: 'normal' capitalism, according to Schumpeter, was a monopoly capitalism because it was dynamically more efficient than the textbook free-market capitalism, which is composed of small companies unable to influence the market single-handedly. This monopolistic capitalism, Schumpeter averred in his *Capitalism, Socialism and Democracy* published in 1942, exhibited all the features ascribed to it by Hobson, Lenin and Luxemburg. Perfectly competitive capitalism might have been (or might still be) averse to war, but real-existing capitalism is monopolistic and hence warlike. The former is an aberration, or perhaps even an abstract, theoretical construct; the latter, a reality. Schumpeter's insight is increasingly important nowadays because it shows how, from an essentially neoclassical position, one can readily conclude that real-existing capitalism is likely to exhibit conflict among the actors, not only cooperation.

These are the theories that I will consider in this chapter. It is well known that most economists tend to believe that free trade is good for economic growth. They do so on the same basis that Adam Smith believed: that international division of labour improves the allocation of resources and raises overall output. Or going further, they believe that trade is good, basing themselves on British economist David Ricardo's theory of comparative advantage: namely, that countries should specialize in the production of goods which they are not only absolutely better but even only relatively better at producing – which gives to every country a niche in which to specialize. In both cases, justification of trade is basically grounded in maximization in output compared to what an autarkic (or self-sufficient) alternative would produce.

However, even when economists take this sunny view of international trade they have not yet exorcised the ghost of war. As Avner Offer describes in his splendid *The First World War: An Agrarian Interpretation*, the removal of the Corn Laws by Great Britain in 1846, which had previously imposed tariffs and trade restrictions on imported grain, and the acceptance of the doctrine of free trade created the need to ensure that the food which was no longer produced on British soil and had to be imported from North America and Russia would always be forthcoming. That in turn implied 'armed trade', namely the protection of naval routes. Without military naval protection Britain could face famine, particularly dangerous if the country was at the same time embroiled in a war; a famine that the country would not have faced if it were autarkic and produced (expensive) wheat and corn domestically. So here we see how even the very doctrinaire approach to free trade which holds that free trade is good, increases overall output and might even be beneficial for cooperation among peoples might still require a warlike element to make sure that this cooperation between nations does takes place and that there is no possibility of blackmail. We see it today too in the simultaneous US acceptance (at least until recently) of offshoring and geographically complex supply chains and the need to control militarily naval routes through which the goods reach consumers. We see it also, in reverse, in the explosion of the Nord Stream pipeline in order to prevent the transfer of Russian gas and oil to Europe. Thus, free trade and globalization on the one hand, war and peace on the other, have had a complex relationship both in theory and practice. This continues to this very day.

Application of the theories. Next, I ask how we may assess the Sino-American relations in the past half-century through the lens of these theories. Relations between America and China have gone through two different phases in recent history, and these two phases respond to two different ideas about the relationship between trade and conflict. If that is the case then the generality of such a relationship can be questioned, or in other words the element of contingency in explaining the relationship between trade and conflict must be quite important. The contingencies include the type of prevailing international relations, the political power of the trading nations, the power of different groups within the countries and even the role of individuals who represent them.

Multipolarity. Later, I will look at the complexity of the world through the eyes of political philosophers and politicians. How have political philosophers 'organized' the world: what do they see as the main cleavages between different economic and political systems that exist globally, and are these competing systems that draw their legitimacy from different sources compatible with peace or not? In other words, is peaceful coexistence between different types of regimes possible? I consider the work of American political philosopher John Rawls developed during (what I call) the End of History interlude. Its applicability today, when the world is much more fragmented politically and ideologically, is dubious: yet given the historical importance of Rawls's political philosophy, both in domestic and international politics, he is vital to the understanding of how we got to where we are now.

Does international trade lead to peace or war?

People from countries at very different levels of income seldom have much in common.[5] Their daily existences are different, their family lives differ, they listen to different people, have access to widely different levels of resources, watch different movies or read different books. (One may ask oneself how many plays performed in New York or London have as their subject life elsewhere, in a much poorer country, provided it is not in a colonial setting or a Western 'discovery' of a certain country.)

However, when the incomes of countries converge, it must imply other forms of convergence: such as in terms of technology, for countries with different technological levels cannot have similar incomes. It also generally suggests greater trade and personal links between individuals living in these countries, as trade is often conducted between countries at similar levels of development, and personal contacts become much more frequent as the challenges people face and their interests become more similar. Cultural convergence then follows income convergence, and globalization encourages the entire world to become more or less one financial, and cultural, market.

It would then seem that periods of convergence must be periods of peace: people talk to each other, often speaking the same language, their countries trade more, they travel to each other's countries more frequently. And indeed such an optimistic view was formulated first by the French philosopher Charles Louis de Montesquieu in his famous *Esprit des Lois* (*The Spirit of Laws*) published in 1748, and slightly later in a different, more cautious, way by Adam Smith and the authors of the Scottish Enlightenment. Both did so in reaction to mercantilism that saw trade as a war by other means, and neglected the civilizing and peace-promoting effect of trade; in other words, neglected all that was based on us addressing ourselves to the self-interest of the other party, and them doing the same. But out of that bilateral self-interest, cooperation is born, Montesquieu, Smith and others argued.

Such peaceful views of convergence were not the only ones. Convergence, as in the contemporary case we study here, is not a uniform advancement by all countries. Almost always, it is one or two countries that get ahead of the others, and convergence then means that some of the laggards gradually catch up. Thus the United States caught up with Great Britain in production of industrial goods in the late nineteenth century, Germany caught up with (or came sufficiently close to) Great Britain in naval tonnage by the early twentieth century, Japan overtook the US in car production in the late twentieth century, and now China has got ahead of the West in green technologies and electric cars. Thus, in every case, convergence meant also *uneven* development. At first it is a development that favours one side, and then a development that favours the other. That uneven development, the spectre of the catch-up, and possibly of the overtake, creates specific fears for the leader, and far from favouring peaceful coexistence and acceptance of equality, it may do the reverse: awaken the forces of conflict and war. For, if one is used to dominance or primacy and is threatened with being overtaken, and fearful of that fact, how can they stop such a development except by undermining the opponent or, in the last resort, waging war? This is the other, darker side of convergence that, instead of promoting peace, promotes war.

Montesquieu and le doux commerce

What did economists through time make of this question of war and peace? Here, I shall consider four theories, beginning chronologically and with the most optimistic held by Montesquieu, moving to Adam Smith, and then to neo-Marxist theories whose origin lies in the work of John Hobson, and finally to the work of Joseph Schumpeter.

The two most important ideas associated with Montesquieu and trade are stated at the very beginning of Book XX of *The Spirit of Laws*, in the most succinct manner possible, practically indistinguishable from maxims. First, 'that wherever we find agreeable manners [*moeurs douces*], there commerce flourishes; and that wherever there is commerce, there we meet with agreeable manners'. Second, '[t]he natural effect of commerce is to lead to peace. Two nations that trade together become mutually dependent: if one has an interest in buying, the other has one in selling: and all unions are based on mutual needs.' These general principles, ever since associated with Montesquieu, have been repeated, expanded and applied to the modern era by Ivan Bloch at the end of the nineteenth century and Norman Angell just prior to the outbreak of World War I,[6] to such an extent that they had by then acquired almost common-sensical and widely accepted status.[7] But not by everybody. Karl Polanyi, for example, ridiculed them: 'In the curiously credulous atmosphere of the time [before World War I] many took for granted that the solution of the economic problem . . . would not only manage, not only assuage the threat of war but actually avert that threat . . . The writers of that period excelled in lack of realism.'[8] But even in Montesquieu's brief writings on the topic, in the rest of the two books in which he discusses trade (out of thirty-one books of which *The Spirit of Laws* is composed), these optimistic tones regarding *le doux commerce* (the sweet trade) are nuanced and much diluted.[9]

Montesquieu distinguishes trade in ordinary goods (*commerce d'économie*) from trade in luxuries (*commerce de luxe*). Each is associated with a different type of government. Foreign trade in ordinary goods takes place in democracies (governments of many); trade in luxuries is common in governments of one person (monarchies or despotisms). Thus the trade does not change the nature of government; it is rather the nature of government that differentiates the type of trade conducted. The idea can be easily translated into more modern language. In 'polities of many', prosperity is more widespread and the demand for ordinary foreign-produced goods is greater. In autocratic governments, inequality is much greater and only those at the top need foreign luxuries. The rest subsist on domestically produced goods.

But that's not all. Not all countries need to engage in trade, Montesquieu writes. Poland, he thinks, only loses by trade.[10] It has only one exportable product – wheat – and that product is controlled by big landowners. They force peasants into servitude in order to increase the production of wheat and export it.[11] The landowners pocket the entire income from trade. But if Poland had no trade whatsoever, the grandees would have to sell grain to other Polish people at much lower prices than what they get from exports; they might even no longer find it profitable to keep the large domains and might rent them out to peasants to cultivate. Moreover, since the rich always like luxury, they would stimulate the production of such items locally, which, in turn, would put the poor to work and increase output. Autarky would be thus much better. Those who have nothing at home have no reason to trade, says Montesquieu.[12]

Does trade improve morals? Here Montesquieu is again ambivalent: 'The spirit of trade produces in the mind of a man a certain sense of exact justice, opposite, on the one hand, to robbery, and on the other to those moral virtues which forbid our always adhering rigidly to the rules of private interest, and suffer us to neglect this for the advantage of others.'[13] Pursuing the same point, Montesquieu mentions how the spirit of hospitality gradually weakens in more commercially minded societies.

The desirability of trade therefore is not uniform. His original statements on trade and peace – that they go hand in hand, and which, in the way they were made, seem to be comprehensive and brook no exceptions – are altered. Not all countries should trade; trade will not influence the type of government they have, and 'the exact morality' of trade that induces among people some virtues, destroys others.[14]

Adam Smith's equality of power

Adam Smith's positions on trade and its role in facilitating income convergence, peace and cosmopolitanism are not simple. Smith is, in the most common interpretations, taken as a theoretician of free trade. Indeed he was, in principle, in favour of it. To emphasize this point, one can see barter and exchange between individuals, the foundational principles of one of Smith's most enduring contributions to economic science – the division of labour – to be a form of trade. That view of 'trade' with which we shall not be concerned here was seen by Smith to be immanent to humans, and absent among other species.[15]

Concerning the trade between individuals who belong to different nations, and thus trade between nations, Smith largely followed a physiocratic point of view, originally formulated by François Quesnay and his followers. In principle Smith was in favour of free trade between nations and of laissez-passer (i.e., abolition of internal impediments to trade). However, the acceptance of free trade did not come without exceptions, nor were all kinds of trade equally supported by Smith. On the contrary, some types of trade conducted by monopolistic merchant companies such as the East India Company were seen by Smith as fundamentally pernicious and inimical to prosperity. His strongest imprecations are directed at them.

The exceptions to free trade are due to considerations of national defence. The most important, and often cited, example is Smith's praise of England's Navigation Act of 1660, which regulated England's trade with its colonies, on the grounds that 'defence . . . is of much more importance than opulence', and so 'the Act of Navigation is, perhaps, the wisest of all the commercial regulations of England'.[16] Yet later when Smith excoriates mercantilist regulations made by England to help its own producers to the detriment of both foreign and domestic consumers, the Navigation Act will be implicitly included among such nefarious laws.[17] So, while one cannot be sure that Smith avoided all contradictions, to believe that he saw acceptable limits to free trade in exceptional cases is probably an accurate summary of his views.

More important is, I think, Smith's uniformly negative opinion of trading cities and merchant companies. Smith's *bête noire* throughout *The Wealth of Nations* is the East India Company, which not only racked up exorbitant monopoly profits for the sole enrichment of its shareholders, but was utterly indifferent to the fate of the country, India, that in many ways it ruled. Smith writes:

> It is a very singular government [that of merchant companies] in which every member of the administration wishes to get out of the country, and consequently to have done with the government as soon as he can, and to whose interest, the day after he has left it and carried his whole fortune with him, it is perfectly indifferent though the whole country was swallowed up by an earthquake.[18]

Not any better was his view of the merchant republics of Venice, Genoa and Pisa that used military force to extract profits, and which he accused of having unjustifiably benefited from one of the greatest follies in which mankind, driven by avarice and greed, engaged: the Crusades.

> The great armies which marched from all parts to the conquest of the Holy Land gave extraordinary encouragement to the shipping

of Venice, Genoa, and Pisa, sometimes in transporting them thither, and always in supplying them with provisions. They were the commissaries, if one may say so, of those armies; and the most destructive frenzy that ever befell the European nations, was a source of opulence to those republics.[19]

We thus have in Smith two different views regarding the relationship between trade and peace. These views are not contradictory, but they do imply that the link between trade and peace that seemed rather strong to Montesquieu, at least in its most succinct formulation, was not thought as strong by Smith. The violent part could – perhaps too conveniently – be laid at the door of the wrong doctrine of mercantilism. And when criticizing mercantilism, Smith uses exactly this point: 'Commerce, which ought naturally to be, among nations, as among individuals, a bond of union and friendship, has become [under the intellectual leadership of mercantilism] the most fertile source of discord and animosity.'[20] But are all sins committed by trade due to the mercantilist spirit and doctrine?

A trade done by two equally willing parties and under conditions of free competition may be advantageous to both and may, on account of mutual desire to maintain that advantage, lead to peace. But trade conducted by the use of force and under monopolistic conditions is, by definition, violent. Which one is more common? It is difficult to say what Smith thought, and perhaps it is impossible to put numbers on either of the two: are 60 per cent of exchanges done under compulsion, or just 40 per cent, or perhaps only 10 per cent? I think, as I wrote in *Visions of Inequality*, that here too, like in the rest of *The Wealth of Nations*, Smith tacitly contrasts two commercial societies: one as it really exists (and where, in this particular case, trade often goes together with war), and the other that is largely aspirational, and where international trade is beneficial to both parties and leads to peace.

There is, however, another remarkable statement by Smith that, in a most direct way, links the diffusion of economic progress and peace:

> At the particular time when these discoveries [of the Americas] were made, the superiority of force happened to be so great on the side of the Europeans that they were enabled to commit with impunity every sort of injustice in those remote countries. Hereafter, perhaps, the natives of those countries may grow stronger, or those of Europe may grow weaker, and the inhabitants of all the different quarters of the world may arrive at that equality of courage and force which, by inspiring mutual fear, can alone overawe the injustice of independent nations into some sort of respect for the rights of one another.[21]

Using this paragraph and what Smith says elsewhere about the role of trade, we can interpret a causal chain as follows. Economic interaction between countries leads to the convergence in their incomes and technological levels. This, in turn, implies similar military power. And that similar military power maintains peace through mutual fear of destruction. European wars of conquest were (or are, in Smith's time) possible because of huge disproportions in economic and technological power between Europe and the rest of the world. But through economic intercourse such a discrepancy will be gradually reduced and eliminated. And the fear shared by both parties, when nations are of approximately equal power, will keep the peace. In such a complex way, economic interaction is ultimately conducive to peace.

Smith here postulates several hypotheses that have continued to influence our thinking about trade, income convergence and peace for more than two hundred years. Namely, (1) trade promotes income convergence, (2) economic convergence implies convergence in military power, and (3) balance of military power maintains peace. Each of these three propositions remains fundamental in, respectively, economics, political science and international relations. Proposition (1) is entirely economic and has been much studied by economists;[22] proposition (2) is more political; and proposition (3) is entirely within the domain of international relations. It is, I think, quite evident how all three of them can be, rather effortlessly, applied to the current competition between the United States and China if we wish to believe that that competition will remain mostly peaceful because of the fear of mutual annihilation, were it to turn violent. (The MAD – or mutually assured destruction – doctrine, of course, prevented war between the United States and the Soviet Union, but since the two countries engaged in little trade, it is unrelated to our topic here.)

Trade therefore leads to peace, but does so indirectly by creating equivalence of military power which, in turn, through mutual fear, makes the trading nations peaceful. Ultimately, it is not mutual trade interdependence and its stimulation of sweet virtues of accommodation of other people's wishes that makes the world peaceful but the harsh reality of military balance of power.

Finally, let us consider briefly Smith's cosmopolitanism. It is unambiguously stated in *The Theory of Moral Sentiments*:

> The wise and virtuous man is at all times willing that his own private interest should be sacrificed to the public interest of his particular order of society. He is at all times willing, too, that the interest of this order of society be sacrificed to the greater interest of the state or sovereignty of which he is only a subordinate part. He should, therefore, be equally willing that all those inferior interests should be sacrificed to the greater interest of the universe, to the interest of that great society of all sensible and intelligent beings, of which God himself is the immediate administrator and director.[23]

That cosmopolitanism – the notion that all human beings on the planet are part of a single community – can be readily translated into the utilitarian doctrine where the benefits of a greater number of people matter more than the benefits of fewer (as the quote below explicitly states). But Smith was also aware that such cosmopolitanism is not a popular attitude to take in real life, and that there is necessarily a contradiction between it and what may be called patriotism or nationalism. 'In the great society of mankind . . . the prosperity of France [because of its larger population] should appear to be an object of much greater importance than that of Great Britain. The British subject, however, who upon that account, should prefer upon all occasions the prosperity of the former to that of the latter country, would not be thought a good citizen of Great Britain.'[24]

Hobson, Lenin and Luxemburg's imperialist competition

The most important feature of the hypothesis of imperialist competition is that it links purely domestic developments to international economic relations, and, ultimately, to inter-state political conflict. British economist and journalist John Hobson, German Marxist and politician Rosa Luxemburg and Russian Marxist and revolutionary Vladimir Ilych Lenin are considered the originators of the hypothesis of imperialist competition, to which they came individually but not independently.[25] The Hobson-Lenin-Luxemburg hypothesis, as it has come to be known, was formulated by the three thinkers on the eve and during the first years of World War I. It takes one specific channel as crucial: high inequality in incomes makes domestic consumption insufficient, which in turn leads capitalists and entrepreneurs to seek investment opportunities abroad, where presumably their profit is higher. There is, however, no reason to believe that exactly the same channel would hold under different circumstances today. The hypothesis can be made more general by highlighting that Hobson, Lenin and Luxemburg focus on how strictly domestic economic developments (like the lack of domestic demand) influence international economic relations, and create a possibility of conflict. This maintains the main ingredient of the original hypothesis – the domestic origins of conflict – and preserves the relevance of the hypothesis's key claim: the spillover of domestic economic problems into the international arena.

During World War I, inter-imperialist competition reached its high point, both in terms of theoretical importance as well as in what actually happened 'on the ground'. The war was probably the most momentous historical event in the past hundred-plus years. The possibility of the outbreak of war among major powers was discussed extensively in the period before 1914. Left-wing economists, many of them Marxists, saw the forces leading to war in the increasing power of monopolies and cartels, whose needs for a wider 'field of action' – that is, for control of the sources of raw materials and cheap labour, as well as their influence over their governments – led countries to engage in foreign conquests.[26] Such policies pursued by several countries at once would, in their view, end up provoking conflict. A number of episodes, most notably the Anglo-French conflict in Fashoda in Sudan in 1898, the two Moroccan crises that pitted Germany against France and the UK in 1905 and 1911, and the two Balkan crises that opposed Russia to Austria-Hungary and Germany in 1912 and 1913, seemed to justify this point of view. Imperialist competition was seen to arise from domestic economic conditions; it was brought about by the economic interests of the elites.[27]

Not everybody in the early 1900s agreed with the ineluctability of the conflict, though. As we have seen in the writings that extended the Montesquieu school (like Bloch and Angell), the very opposite was believed: that under the conditions of economic interdependence, wars would be so ruinous for everybody that they would never be undertaken. Polanyi in *The Great Transformation* ascribed the same beliefs to *haute finance* in Europe: small and limited colonial wars may be fought, they may even be profitable, but a war between major powers in Europe would be calamitous.[28] Schumpeter, as we shall see below, thought that rational capitalists would never agree to a war; the more capitalistic the society, the less likely it is to go to war. For us today, with the world experiencing very similar forces as on the eve of 1914, it is a sobering experience to realize that smart people, using the same methodological approach (capitalists are rational, they pursue profits), would come to the polar-opposite conclusions regarding the relation between globalization and conflict.

What was the exact logical chain of imperialist competition theory? A view that became the origin of left-wing thinking on imperialism was formulated by John Hobson in *Imperialism*, published in 1902. Hobson explained imperialism by the search for new and more profitable investment opportunities by the elites, caused by the major economies' surplus of investable funds. The surplus was created because of high inequality and insufficient domestic aggregate demand. If inequality were less, Hobson argued, there would be greater domestic demand and no need for the rich to look for investment outlets elsewhere.[29] This is, of course, based on a well-known economic regularity, later used by Keynes, that poorer people consume a greater proportion of their income than the rich.[30]

Hobson's hypothesis was later incorporated, fully or in parts, by Vladimir Lenin and Rosa Luxemburg and it remained influential for a long time among Marxist economists, even as the war was going on, and, later, as it ended. Karl Polanyi clearly subscribed to it in his *Great Transformation*:

> Economic imperialism was mainly a struggle between the powers for the privilege of extending their trade into politically unprotected markets. Export pressure was reinforced by a scramble for raw material supplies caused by manufacturing fever. Governments lent support to their nationals engaged in business in backward countries. Trade and the flag were racing in one another's wake.[31]

As Marxist influence in economics waned and different types of war took place (World War II and the Cold War), less attention was paid to the hypothesis and it was never tested empirically. It should be noted, though, that neoclassical economics has no *economic* theory regarding the outbreak of World War I, which, given the methodological 'imperialism' of economics as a science and the fact that the war broke out in the midst of full-scale globalization, is rather odd. This makes Hobson-Lenin-Luxemburg the only extant economic theory that seeks to explain the origin of World War I and thus the 'mould' from which other, similar theories that connect trade and conflict have developed.[32]

Revival of the theory. The theory of imperialist competition has been experiencing something of a revival recently because of the Global Financial Crisis in 2008 and trade tensions between the United

States and China. Atif Mian, Ludwig Straub and Amir Sufi have shown that rising income inequality in the US since the 1980s has produced a savings glut; these excess savings led to a search for potential investment opportunities that were excessively risky (the amount of savings was too high to be accommodated by sufficiently safe investments).[33] Mian, Straub and Sufi thus link the 2008 Global Financial Crisis to the mechanisms that are similar to the ones in the imperialist competition hypothesis. But the consequences stay within the nation-state. They do not argue that the surfeit of US savings is behind US investments in China, nor that such investments would exacerbate political tensions. In fact, if anything, investments should reduce tensions because American citizens who own Chinese assets do not have an incentive to promote conflict. Neither do Chinese holders of US government debts who currently own more than $800 billion in US Treasury bills. Obviously, such Chinese assets could potentially be targets for freeze or seizure in the case of a more serious Sino-American conflict; so they can hardly wish for such a war. However, we can note the similarities between the Mian, Straub and Sufi hypothesis and Hobson, Lenin and Luxemburg's ideas.

The political scientist Ilya Matveev has gone further and argued that the current US–China conflict has all the standard features of imperialist economic competition.[34] In his view, the destabilizing actor in the rivalry is China, whose model of growth requires expanding foreign markets to export to and invest in. To do so, it needs to squeeze out other imperial powers. The root cause of the conflict with other nations lies again in the domestic disequilibrium. If China (whose consumption as a share of GDP is extraordinarily low[35]) could increase domestic consumption, it would not need to go after foreign markets and would not be engaged in inter-imperial competition. This approach raises the question of why China is unable to increase domestic consumption. We have seen that in the Hobson-Lenin-Luxemburg theory the ultimate cause of war lies in domestic inequality. The governments could not, especially not under the conditions of the early-twentieth-century capitalism, do much about it short of engaging in massive redistribution of wealth that was politically unfeasible, and was never considered. But China, as a country of political capitalism where the state's role is much greater, should be able to increase domestic consumption. The question then becomes: why not? There are several possibilities. Perhaps the reason lies in an inflexible model of export-led growth that has made the country rich and cannot be easily changed; or in the power of state-owned enterprises (SOEs) that see the expansion to foreign markets as the way to grow and acquire political clout at home; or perhaps because the elite of the Communist Party of China (CPC) regards China's economic projection of power abroad as a worthy geopolitical objective. This new maldistribution of income is not, like the old one, grounded principally in inequality of incomes between individuals, but rather in inequality of economic power between the sectors: state vs private, manufacturing vs services.

A variant of inter-imperialist competition and of the destabilizing factor being China's pattern of growth is advanced by Matthew Klein and Michael Pettis in their book *Trade Wars Are Class Wars*.[36] Chinese underconsumption is due, they argue, to high government-directed and subsidized (via low interest rates) investments. In order to finance such investments, SOEs' profits have to be high and thus wages and consumption are squeezed. If such high SOE profits were distributed to the population through greater social transfers, the problem of underconsumption would be solved. But they are not distributed; instead they are used for additional investments, including abroad through the Belt and Road Initiative. The cause of China's underconsumption, according to Klein and Pettis, thus lies in the power of the state to transfer resources to the SOEs, creating in the process higher inequality and a surge of investments locally and abroad. The latter enter into a strategic competition with investments from other countries. This is true for Africa where there is a tacit imperial competition between the United States and China. Why does the Chinese state do it? Probably because it sees foreign investments as a policy tool that increases its international power.

It should be noted that while both Matveev's, and Klein and Pettis's mechanisms are similar to the classic Hobson-Lenin-Luxemburg theory whereby domestic imbalances create an international problem, the source of maldistribution of income is different. In the original hypothesis, maldistribution was due to a capitalist system functioning in such a way as to squeeze wages; in the current hypothesis, it is due to the state repressing the wage share and consumption to create resources for foreign investment.[37] The latter is a wilful policy, the former, an unintended outcome of the capitalist system.

Schumpeter's trade vs atavistic imperialism

Joseph Schumpeter was an Austro-American economist who, perhaps with Keynes, was one of the most influential economists of the inter-war period. His theory on whether trade leads to war or peace is interesting for several reasons. It was formulated at the same time as Lenin and Luxemburg's theory during the end of World War I, clearly with the knowledge of the two, and reacts to the same events. The key text for Schumpeter's theory is 'The Sociology of Imperialisms' (note the plural) published in 1918–19 – a very long essay of some eighty tightly printed pages in its English translation.

For Schumpeter, imperialism, most purely defined, is 'objectless': namely, it is not directed against something or somebody that can be shown to impede one's interest. It is thus not rational: it is a simple will to power.[38] The canonical examples, according to Schumpeter, are the Assyrians, Persians, Arabs and Franks.

In Schumpeter's view, imperialism is atavistic and in contradiction with 'normal' rational capitalist routines, whose objectives can be much better achieved in peace and by peace. By 'atavistic' Schumpeter means that the roots of imperialism lie in the 'old-fashioned' ideas of glory, honour, jealousy, pride, etc., to be distinguished from modern capitalist ideas that are based on the balance of pecuniary gains and losses. We should thus expect imperialism to diminish as capitalism becomes stronger. The least imperialistic nations are the most capitalistic ones, such as the United States and the United Kingdom.[39]

This is the usual reading of Schumpeter. However, an alternative interpretation is possible, based on his entire writings and his view of dynamic forces that propel capitalism.

In 'The Sociology of Imperialisms' Schumpeter allows that imperialism can appear in capitalistic societies. But there 'we ... must evidently see [imperialistic tendencies] only as alien elements carried into the world of capitalism from the outside, supported by noncapitalist factors in modern life'.[40] However, if a capitalist system is not one of perfect competition and free trade but a capitalism of monopolies, Schumpeter allows that 'organized capital may very well make the discovery that the interest rate [i.e., a capitalist's income] can be maintained above the level of free competition if the resulting surplus can be sent abroad'.[41] 'Organized capital' may realize that it has a lot to gain from having colonies or controlling other countries. Schumpeter continues, 'they can use cheap native labor ... they can market their products ... at monopoly prices; they can, finally, invest capital that would only depress the profit rate at home and that could be placed in other civilized countries only at very low interest rates'.[42] In conditions such as these, the metropole 'generally pours a huge wave of capital into new countries. There it meets other, similar waves of capital [from other countries], and a bitter, costly struggle begins but never ends. In such a struggle ... it is no longer a matter of indifference who builds a given railroad, who owns a mine or a colony.'[43]

In this description of the role of monopoly capital in fostering colonization and imperialism, Schumpeter is hardly a hair's breadth away from Lenin and Luxemburg. Perhaps so, but these are, according to Schumpeter, special conditions of monopoly (or 'trustified') capitalism that cannot be identified with 'normal' or 'usual' free-market capitalism.

Is this true? Not if we go by what Schumpeter says in *Capitalism, Socialism and Democracy*. There the point is forcefully made that the key feature of capitalism (i.e., what makes it grow) is innovation and that innovation is possible only if capitalism is monopolistic; or if it is not, innovation itself will lead to the creation of monopolies (a phenomenon that we can observe today just by looking at Google, Microsoft, Amazon, etc.).

> The introduction of new methods of production and new commodities is hardly conceivable in perfect competition from the start. And this means that the bulk of what we call economic progress is incompatible with it. As a matter of fact, perfect competition is and always has been temporarily suspended whenever anything new is being introduced . . . even in otherwise perfectly competitive conditions.[44]

Further, since monopolistic competition is, according to Schumpeter, dynamically more efficient than the textbook free-market capitalism, the former will come to dominate and indeed become the normal form in which capitalism will exist and prosper.

Now, if the normal form of capitalism is monopolistic, the 'normal' form of behaviour of such capitalism is as forcefully described in 'The Sociology of Imperialisms': trying to keep the rate of profit above the 'natural' level by exporting capital to other countries, aiming to control cheap labour and resources there, and thus likely running into a conflict with other monopolized national capitalisms. So this is the normal modus operandi of capitalism – according to Schumpeter. And this is how capitalism increasingly looks today.

The contention that perfect competition and free trade are incompatible with imperialism becomes irrelevant: even if the contention is valid. It refers to a textbook case of capitalism that, Schumpeter tells us, is bound to lose out and yield to a more dynamic and innovative monopolistic capitalism – which in turn always leads to imperialist competition.

Putting these two things together not only reformulates Schumpeter's theory of imperialism – which comes exceedingly close, nay practically becomes identical to, neo-Marxist theories of imperialism in its emphasis on the low domestic rate of return.[45] It also gives us a new view of capitalism: one where the conflictual nature of trade is an opinion not confined to neo-Marxists, but held more broadly by thinkers like Schumpeter, who see monopoly capitalism as the 'normal capitalism' because it is the only type of capitalism compatible with innovation and economic efficiency. Bringing Schumpeter into the frame of the twenty-first century, where monopolies grow in strength by the day, we can learn that – irrespective of our political position – we should expect ever more conflict and perhaps even wars. For monopolistic capitalism, in Schumpeter's view, is inextricably linked with a violent, competitive, imperialist mindset. It is a very similar view as recently expressed by the French historian Arnaud Orain who sees capitalism as cyclically moving between, on the one hand, a liberal and free-trade version, and, on the other, a monopolistic and mercantilistic mode.[46] When it is in its latter mode, capitalism exhibits all the traits described by Schumpeter: violent competition for the control of the sea and land and creation of vertically integrated monopolies (i.e., large monopolies that cover the entire production chain, from raw materials to the final product).

Recent Sino-American relations: from doux commerce to imperialist competition

None of the four theories linking trade and international relations considered here explains Sino-American relations in their entirety. But each of them does elucidate a period or a phase in the relationship. The first phase, from the late 1970s to the mid-2010s, can be seen as the period of the *doux commerce* between the United States and China, driven by political and economic interests on both sides. The second phase, that of imperialist competition – still ongoing – is obviously a reversal of the first phase and is caused by the domestic economic problems of one rival (United States) and the type of economic growth followed by the other (China).

Doux commerce *under the shadow of the Soviet Union*. The combination of the *doux commerce* and the acceptance of the different bases of political legitimacy, i.e., the peaceful coexistence of states with different political systems, are features that can be readily associated with the period of US-Chinese relations after the diplomatic ties were re-established (January 1979) up to the mid-2010s. During these years, not even a murderous crackdown on demonstrators at Tiananmen Square nor the heavy-handed suppression of the Falun Gong sufficiently perturbed the relationship. The explanation made for this in American circles is, somewhat self-servingly, that the US did not want to pressure the Chinese side too much – because the logic of economic development and Chinese espousal of state capitalism were bound to lead ultimately to the democratization of the country, and to China accepting domestically the same democratic norms as America. This was indeed a radical application of the modernization theory, and it had some foundation in the reality of East Asia, when applied to the evolutions of South Korea and, later, Taiwan. But a more likely reason why the US continued to enjoy a honeymoon with China was that the *doux commerce* was proving extraordinarily profitable to many US companies, and the likelihood of greater profitability was ever more tempting – as the immense Chinese market became even bigger with economic growth and at the same time also more open. On the political side, the honeymoon and the accommodation of different systems of government was helped by the triangular nature of the relationship between the US, China and the Soviet Union. America's opening to China was always part of this geopolitical equation, and as long as the Soviet Union was a strong US competitor, having the Chinese on its side, or at least not having China on the Soviet side (as was the case between 1949 and 1956), was in the American national interest.[47]

It is in this context, as has been noticed many times before (by Giovanni Arrighi, Julian Gewirtz, Martin Jacques, Isabella Weber and others), that we have to look at the initial Chinese reforms. When, after Mao's death, the Chinese leadership went in search of a model of growth it could emulate, it was natural that it would look first at other communist countries that had introduced elements of market economy. Yugoslavia and Hungary were the most interesting, and rather obvious, choices.[48] On closer inspection, however, as in the early 1980s both countries were going through an economic crisis caused by their difficulties in repaying foreign loans, their models were found wanting. The Western loans were contracted precisely in the initial stages of their reforms – the point at which China stood then – based on the idea that they would help relaunch growth and exports to the West. The loans would basically, it was thought, repay themselves. But the reality was entirely different. Hungary and Yugoslavia had major difficulties servicing the debt and, in order to repay it, had to go further in accepting Western countries' and creditors' demands: to adopt price liberalization, deregulation and wholesale privatization. The reforms, which began in the 1960s, thus showed their manifold weaknesses in the 1980s, precisely at the time when China went looking for an economic model. Therefore, the results of partial reforms of semi-planned economies did not exactly suggest to the Chinese that such reforms should be imitated.

Had Chinese economists and leadership followed that path, they would have had to implement at least the following three policies: (1) foreign borrowing; (2) large and quick deregulation of prices; and (3) privatization of many enterprises. This was indeed the Big Bang shock that all East European economies adopted in the mid- to late 1980s (and Russia, in 1992, after the dissolution of the Soviet Union). Quite sensibly, China opted against such an approach, and decided to follow the examples of geographical (Japan and South Korea), and not ideological, proximity. Instead of borrowing (1), it preferred to encourage foreign investments and technological upgrading brought by foreign companies; on prices (2), China followed for decades a dual system with one part of the market fully liberalized and the other part state-controlled. Only gradually were the two markets unified. And on privatization (3), the reduction of the relative size of the state sector took place through the creation of de novo private companies, and Township and Village Enterprises that mushroomed in rural areas and whose property structure was the most unusual (state, communal, local and private property were combined).[49] The share of the non-state sector increased through faster growth of such companies, not through the forced conversion of state assets into private hands. Only much later (in the mid-1990s) was the state sector directly reduced through limited privatizations. So on all three key issues, Chinese reformers did the opposite of what East European reformers did.

As in South Korea and Japan, the strategy included the expansion of exports. For the strategy to work, or even for the strategy to begin to be adopted, the prerequisite was normalization of political relations with the United States. The US was the only country that could provide both the investment China needed and the market to which China could export. Thus without political accommodation with the US, the entire Chinese (and more broadly, the East Asian) model would have been unthinkable.[50] It is in this political context that we have to situate China's keenness, under Deng Xiaoping, to develop political and economic relations with the United States: politically, to counteract the Soviet pressure on China; economically, to develop. Likewise, American keenness to engage with China was twofold: politically, to weaken the Soviet Union's international role; economically, to make money.[51] Henry Kissinger's *On China* explains the concordance of interests from both sides and its expected outcome: 'The reward for Sino-American rapprochement would not be a state of perpetual friendship or a harmony of values, but a rebalancing of the global equilibrium that would require constant tending and perhaps, in time, produce a greater harmony of values.'[52] It is only in such a context that the *doux commerce* could flourish.

These are the reasons why both from the American and the Chinese perspective the first period of the relationship between the two giants was characterized by cooperation, by the emphasis on the sweet nature of commerce, and by the lack of questioning of the political differences that existed between the countries.

The antechamber to change. The transition to the second period of the US–China relationship began, at first slowly with the Global Financial Crisis, and then more openly with the 2016 electoral revelation of American domestic problems. Globalization did not help the Western middle classes in the way that was expected. As long as these classes did not play a significant political role or could be mobilized at four-year intervals by being given 'the red meat' of false ideology in order to be used as a voting machine, the problem was either not obvious or was solvable. That is, as long as the economic unhappiness of the malcontents – those parts of the electorate who felt left behind by globalization – could be assuaged at four-year intervals without producing political earthquakes, their unhappiness was not a political problem. But when the twin rule of centrist Democrats and centrist Republicans (by themselves interchangeable in many respects, so much so that many people argued that the US is ruled by one party composed of two branches) became threatened and the outcome of elections unpredictable, with Donald Trump relying on the long-ignored malcontents, the US political elites soured on globalization.

This was only the antechamber to the second phase in China–US relations, the period based on imperialist competition or geopolitical rivalry. That geopolitical rivalry could not be, by itself, based only on America's fear of losing the upper hand in Asia, for China did not yet threaten US dominance in the region. To explain it, we have look to something more locally palpable and important: the loss of political control by America's elite that came with the rabble-rousers à la Trump being supported by the losers of globalization. As a result, either globalization as we knew it or the elite's power had to go. Without this domestic pressure in America, the geopolitical rivalry between the US and China would have come much later, or perhaps never. But now, the threat to the domestic political hegemony of the elite was identified as lying in the globalization that favoured China and depressed the incomes of American middle classes.[53] In order to eliminate a domestic threat, foreign policy had to be utilized, and changed. In short, the 'pivot to Asia' did not happen simply because the US foreign polity establishment suddenly discovered the 'China threat' to its Asian hegemony. The pivot to Asia and the tensions with China came because the elimination of the 'China threat' was needed in order to regain domestic stability, or more exactly, to try to ensure that the rabble-rousers never again got close to power. Thus came the following chain: low economic growth among the middle classes → political discontent → appearance of Trump who mobilized that inchoate discontent → threat to the elite rule → anti-China policies → geopolitical competition with the ultimate (elite) objective being to alter the rules of globalization, improve the position of US middle classes and end the electoral 'insurgency'.

Thus, in the second period of China–US relations the stakes changed significantly. In fact, if we look carefully, every single element of the relationship underwent a transformation. The demise of the Soviet Union changed the triangular relationship. Instead of being a very useful counterweight to the USSR, China became a potential rival. The importance of this possible new rivalry increased not only on account of the disappearance of the USSR but, independently, because of China's economic success. As we have seen, from a country that produced 2 per cent of global output, China became a country that produces almost one-fourth of it. The consequences of China's growth were twofold. Thanks to its economic and technological weight, China became a formidable strategic competitor of the United States, affecting America's economic conditions, polarizing its population into those who lost their jobs or whose incomes were reduced because of Chinese imports, and those among the US capitalist class who continued to profit from investments, the outsourcing of American jobs and general economic cooperation with China. Trump's 2016 administration, because it was elected to a large extent by those who Hillary Clinton called the 'deplorables', was the first to raise issues with China whose origin was entirely in the domestic economy. At first such issues were ignored, or ridiculed by the more centrist, standard establishment. The US seemed almost destined to sign the Trans-Pacific Trade Treaty that was in the spirit of the continuation of policies that characterized the neoliberalism of the first period. But once the opponents of China zeroed in on it, not only was the signature of the treaty rejected by the candidate Trump, but eventually the entire establishment shared the same opinion. So much so that even Hillary Clinton, in the run-up to the 2016 election, while originally very much in favour of the treaty, decided to campaign against it.

The domestic origin of geopolitical tensions. The second phase of the Sino-American relationship can therefore be seen much better in the light of imperialist competition, not simply as a battle for foreign markets (although in Africa we see that too) as the traditional theory of imperialism assumes, but fought to a large extent on the domestic economic field over the fate of the American middle classes. As in traditional imperialist competition theory, the root of the problem is not in international relations, but in domestic economics. It spills out from domestic economics into domestic politics and thence into the international arena.[54] This is exactly what happened with Sino-American relations politically after approximately 2016, although the economic issues were known since at least the Global Financial Crisis. And more recently, similar domestic woes (low consumption) in China have exacerbated the conflict.

As Figure 2.1 illustrates, US growth has been deeply unequal in the past generation and a half. It favoured the top classes whose relative (percentage) gains vastly exceeded those of the upper-middle, middle and lower-middle classes. These larger relative gains translated into even greater absolute gains since the initial (starting) levels of income were much higher for the rich. The top 1 per cent, followed by the next several high income percentiles, benefited the most (as we also saw in Chapter 1). The figure here gives the data for the thirty-year period from 1986 to 2016, but one could pick at random any year after 1980 and before the Covid crisis, and find exactly the same pattern of the curve: about equal growth (20–30 per cent over thirty years, which gives less than 1 per cent per person annually) for almost all of US households, and then sharply increasing growth as we get closer to the richest 1 per cent.

When the data for the United States and all other countries in the world are put together, as was done in the well-known 'elephant chart' for the period of High Globalization 1988–2008,[56] it becomes apparent that the Western middle classes that were around the 70th–80th global percentile have had a period of disappointing growth, while the Asian middle classes (even if poorer than the Western ones) and the global top 1 per cent registered much higher real growth. The slowdown of the American middle-class growth was attributable to a significant degree, although it is hard to determine

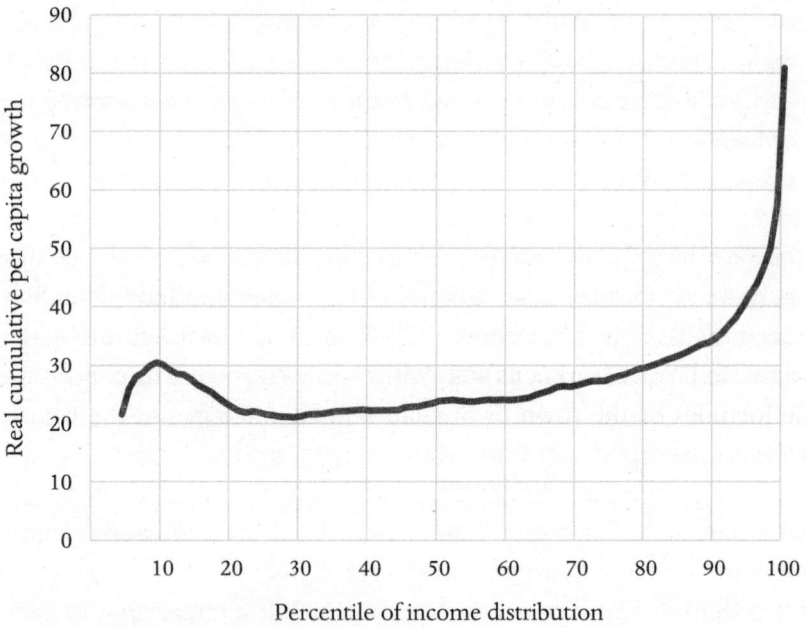

Figure 2.1. United States 1986–2016. Cumulative growth of real per capita disposable income across income distribution (in per cent)[55]

Note: The graph shows real (inflation-adjusted) growth of per capita disposable (after-tax) income in the United States between 1986 and 2016, across all percentiles of income distribution. The graph shows that the top 1 per cent's real income increased by 80 per cent whereas income at the median increased by only 23 per cent.

exactly how much, to imports from China and outsourcing to China. There were two possible responses to the 'China challenge' to the Western middle classes. One was to change the rules of globalization so that it no longer hollows out Western middle classes; the other was to improve the income position of the middle by taxing more the domestic rich and redistributing income from the top to the middle. The latter approach could have substituted for the anti-China stance. But that policy found many opponents among the rich, and the difficulty of raising taxes in societies with already high tax rates became manifest. Instead, the permanent election-season promise to reduce taxes was seen as a way to woo donors and voters.

Had Trump in 2016 decided to run on a plank of higher tax rates instead of a trade war with China he would have lost many donors, and would not have gained even the lower-middle class who preferred to regain their jobs 'stolen' by China rather than depend on the magnanimity of the rich. Perhaps one needed a Polanyi to explain that the issue was not mere money. It was self-respect, having a job, knowing what to do in the morning, serving as a role model for the kids, not having to depend on other people's money.[57] It is indeed the issue of self-respect and optimism about the future that we find in Daniel Markovits's *The Meritocracy Trap* when he contrasts the fortunes of the town of St Clair Shores, Michigan in the 1950s and early 2000s.[58] And it is the loss of the feeling of self-respect that fed the opioid crisis and created 'the deaths of despair' as so eloquently described and analysed by Anne Case and Angus Deaton in their influential book *Deaths of Despair and the Future of Capitalism*.

Taxation rather than the trade war would not have found favour with the national security establishment either; they were not particularly interested in the travails of America's middle classes but rather looked at the Sino-US relationship through a strategic and military lens. All of these reasons made a refashioning of globalization (and thereby the anti-China policy) much more attractive. That position, to be consistent, had to question the domestic bases of the Chinese government's legitimacy. Thus both the *doux commerce* and the political accommodation of a different system were jettisoned, and US policy took the turn consistent with ideologies of international competition where the domestic set-up of the rival power is challenged in order to weaken it.

Similarity between the hypothesis of imperialist competition and the current US–China conflict. As this chapter has shown, there are remarkable similarities between the core of the neo-Marxist hypothesis of imperial competition and the dynamic that is observed during the second phase of US-Chinese relations. It may be best to visually compare the 1914 hypothesis with current developments (Table 2.1). The similarities lie in the original problem, which is the maldistribution of national income (i.e., too high inequality) and foreign investment that

Hobson-Lenin-Luxemburg hypothesis	2020s US-Chinese developments
	The effects of globalization on the US middle class
Maldistribution of national income (high inequality) for domestic reasons	Increased maldistribution of national income (high inequality) due to international and domestic causes
Surplus of investible funds	Surplus of investible funds
Foreign investments	Foreign investments
Need to protect investments and access to cheap labour in foreign lands	National political discontent because of lack of good jobs and hollowing out of the middle class
	Threat to the elite rule
	Change the rules of globalization to Chinese detriment
Conflict with other imperial powers that do the same	Conflict with China

Table 2.1. The logical chains of the imperialist competition in 1914 and today

Note: The table should be read from the top to the bottom (within each column) as an approximate description of the logical and chronological chain of events.

is propelled by a combination of a domestic glut of savings and superior foreign returns. The conflict occurs internationally in both cases although the arenas where it is fought are different. In the pre-World War I period, the conflict involved imperialist powers competing with each other on 'foreign terrain' (i.e., in colonies and semi-colonies). Nowadays, the conflict involves the two largest world economies, the US and China, and the field of conflict concerns the rules that would obtain in international economic relations. For sure, some of the conflict spreads to other countries (most notably, to countries in Africa, where the Chinese Belt and Road Initiative clashes with American attempts either to torpedo the initiative or, failing that, to imitate it), but these are secondary effects. On a more abstract level, even if phenomenologically the two conflicts are different, one can say that both the pre-1914 conflict and today's conflict are clashes over economic primacy. For a country to win in the pre-1914 world, it had to control trade with a given colony; for a country to win today, it has to set the rules of globalization and have sufficient power to change them when they are no longer to its advantage.

Why did the nature of the relationship change? How do we explain the change in relationship between economic integration and war or peace that has occurred between the United States and China? It is indeed not the first time in history that relations based on interdependence and even amity evolved into competition and enmity. The very fact that this happened is sufficient to dispel the general idea that economic collaboration is associated with only one type of political outcome, whether it be leading to war and competition, or to peace and mutual collaboration. Contingencies play a big role and whereas the underlying factors may fashion the overall relationship, the exact character of the relationship depends on multiple factors. I thus do not think that we can have a deterministic explanation of the relationship between trade and international conflict. At times, trade leads to similarities in incomes and preferences, as it did in Europe's long road from the Coal and Steel Community in 1952 to the monetary union in 1999. But at other times, as between the US and China now, it is conducive to conflict. The difference seems to depend on the political set-up and political objectives of the actors.

Why are we afraid of convergence?[59]

The background. It is useful to think of the current changes in incomes between different parts of the world within the framework provided by the Industrial Revolution. Why? First, we can regard the manufacturing rise of China as a delayed spread of the Industrial Revolution to Asia. Second, we can see it is a mirror-effect of what the original Industrial Revolution implied for the income positions of Europe and Asia. While the original Industrial Revolution made Europe rich, deindustrialized parts of Asia (e.g., Indian cotton production precipitously declined under the onslaught of cheaper British exports) and created large real income gaps between people in Europe and those living in Asia, the current technological revolution is undoing these original effects. It is leading to the industrialization of China, the deindustrialization of Europe and North America, and reduction in income gaps between people in the West and people in Asia. Thinking of the recent changes on the *grande échelle*, or on the world stage, we can see them as bringing the dispersion of economic activity across the Eurasian continent to a point not dissimilar from where the dispersion of economic activity was around the middle of the second millennium, when real incomes in the Italian peninsula and China, or England and India were similar, or at least did not differ by more than a factor of 2 or 3 (i.e., double or triple).[60] Within this type of *longue durée* thinking, the original Industrial Revolution appears as a temporary aberration that produced extremely high differences in the standard of living between the early adopters and the parts of the world, like China, India and the African continent, that failed to grow for the better part of the nineteenth century and the first half of the twentieth century. But once China, India and the rest of developing Asia set on a path of economic growth, the enormous advantages of the West began to be eroded.

These dramatic changes had repercussions on the level of global income inequality and its composition. Figure 2.2 shows both the level of global income inequality (defined as inequality in real incomes between all individuals in the world) and its decomposition in two parts: (A) the aspect of global inequality that is due to inequalities *within* individual countries, and (B) the aspect of global inequality that is due to inequalities *between* mean incomes of countries. The higher B is, the more dissimilar are countries' mean incomes and, all other things being equal, the more unequal the world. Another way to look at B is to see it as what global inequality would be if all within-national inequalities were zero, in other words if all citizens of the United States earned the mean income of the United States, all citizens of Nigeria earned the mean income of Nigeria, etc. B thus highlights a very different issue from A: while A reflects national inequalities, B shows us how unequal the world is because of different levels of development between countries.

As the graph shows, in the early nineteenth century, after the

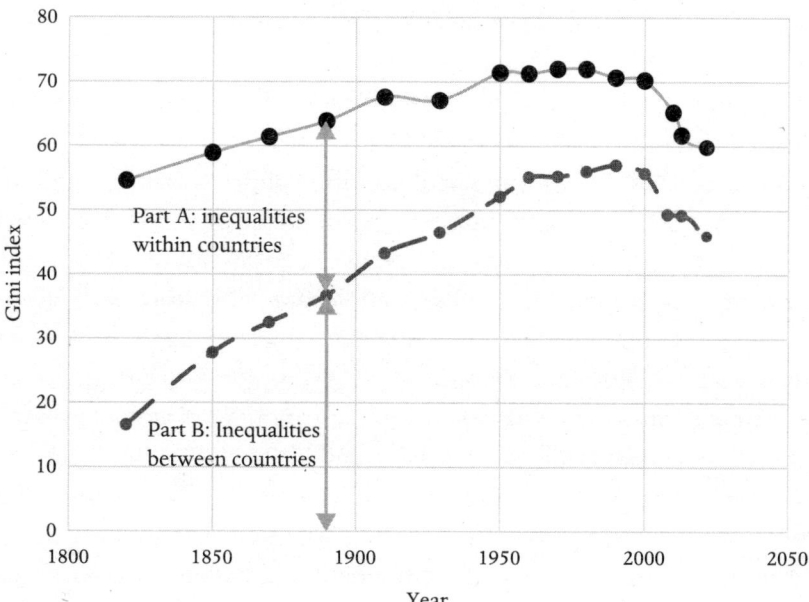

Figure 2.2. Within-national and between-national income inequalities (together equal to global inequality) during the past two centuries, 1820–2018[61]

Note: The graph shows global inequality and its two components: inequality due to the differences in incomes within countries (i.e., among individuals belonging to the same country; part A) and inequality due to differences in mean incomes between countries (part B). The latter is equal to total inequality in the world that would exist if all people in a given country had the mean income of that country, that is, if national Gini coefficients were zero. A + B = total global inequality between individuals.

Napoleonic wars, the estimated global inequality, shown by the top line and measured by the Gini coefficient – a measure of inequality that ranges from 0 (everybody has the same income) to 100 (one person has the entire income of a group)[62] – was relatively low, with Gini around 55. It then started its more or less steady rise for the next century and a half. But that increase was a very particular one: it was mostly driven by the *between* component, that is by the widening gap between mean incomes of the countries. As can be seen in the graph, it was the rise of part B that was behind the increase in global income inequality over the past two centuries. While in 1820, less than a third of global inequality (17 Gini points out of a total 55 Gini points) was due to income differences between nations, the rise of the West, by creating the income wedge with the rest of the world, pushed up component B and thus global inequality too. In some simple or intuitive terms, global inequality could be seen during that period as essentially determined by the movements of real incomes in the West, China and India, since the three taken together accounted then (as today) for approximately half of the world's population and income.

Changes in within-national income distributions played an important but secondary role in increasing global inequality. For example, within-national inequalities in the US and the UK increased in the 1800s and peaked in the UK around the last quarter of the nineteenth century and in the US in the early twentieth century or around the Great Depression.[63] Thus higher within-national inequalities contributed to the rising global income inequality as well, but, to the extent that we know their evolution in the nineteenth century (since the data for many parts of the world are fragmentary), rising within-national inequalities were not the main driving force.

Something similar is happening today, in the period that we can approximately date to the turn of the twenty-first century. As shown in the graph, the decline in global inequality is occurring thanks to the shrinkage of component B, as real incomes in China and India catch up with the West, *despite* rising within-national inequalities in many large countries. Thus, in the recent period, the forces included in component A (rising inequality within nations like the United States, China, Russia, etc.) are working against the forces included in component B (convergence of real incomes between Asia and the West, that is higher growth rates in relatively poor than in rich countries). The former forces (rising national inequalities) are to some extent offsetting the latter, but they have not, so far, been sufficiently strong to reverse the effects of strong economic growth and thus income convergence unleashed by Deng Xiaoping's reforms in China in the 1980s, the Đổi Mới economic reforms in

Vietnam in 1986, India's economic liberalization in 1991 and more recently Modi's reforms over the last decade, and other economic developments in the rest of the 'emerging' or 'resurgent' Asia.

What happens to global inequality today is therefore not determined by what happens to within-national inequalities that currently dominate the headlines, but rather by the forces of cross-country economic convergence. In the past quarter-century, the effects of economic convergence have been dominant, but nothing guarantees that they will continue. Unless other parts of the world (notably Africa) begin to grow faster, at rates double or triple those achieved in the West, the forces of economic convergence may weaken and eventually peter out (as discussed in Chapter 1).

Interdependence between global convergence and national inequalities. While we can for analytic purposes discuss what happens to within-national and between-national inequalities separately, it is clear that the two developments are not independent of each other. It could be argued that the rise of China, the main factor behind the convergence and the shrinkage of component B, caused the widening of income differences within rich nations.[64] In other words, while fast growth of real incomes in China helped reduce income gaps between countries and global income inequality as well, it might have also led to the stagnation of real wages, loss of jobs and the emergence of the precariat in the West – all the phenomena that have widened income disparities in rich countries. But note again that this interdependence of the between and within components is very similar to what happened during the first Industrial Revolution: then, the take-off of England and Western Europe created income gaps between those countries and the rest of the world. In addition, it widened national income distributions elsewhere – for example, by gutting artisanal cloth production in India, transforming the Indian self-employed sector into a 'reserve army of labour', or making landless many African farmers who previously used commonly owned land.

It is important to keep very clearly in mind the distinction between components A and B. They are very useful for analytic and political purposes, but we must never lose sight of the fact that the two components are interdependent. Thus, if we allow ourselves an optimistic take on future developments in the world – namely, to hope for further shrinkage of component B to drive global inequality down and lead to the creation of what may be termed 'the global middle class' – this perhaps desirable development by itself may produce wrenching effects on income distributions *within* individual nations, and exacerbate political instability. Imagine a world in which the current massive income gaps that exist between countries of the European Union and Africa are dramatically reduced to the extent that an average citizen in Mali has an income that is not very different from the income of an average Italian. This would be, undoubtedly, considered by many as a desirable development that would not only eliminate absolute poverty as we know it today but also create a 'global middle class'. However, such a development may be accompanied, or may even be made possible, only by the widening income gaps between those in the currently rich countries who are able to take advantage of global integration and people whose jobs might have been lost because of African competition. Thus, a 'globally positive' development may produce undesired effects nationally and lead to national political turbulence.

We can thus easily grasp that the achievement of a Utopian-like world of affluent societies across the globe will not be (nor can it be) achieved without profound economic and political shifts in power between countries, and within most countries. Or, to put it in more formal language: to get to the Utopian point U, the world will have to pass through a number of politically difficult states that may derail the whole process and make the achievement of point U impossible. This is of course due principally to the fact that the world is now, and for the foreseeable future, politically organized into nation-states, and thus 'globally desirable' changes such as the catch-up of Asia and Africa, if associated with 'locally undesirable' outcomes such as wage stagnation and unemployment in the West, may be considered politically unacceptable by the national electorates.

Migration. The very high level of component B, or inequality between countries, despite its recent shrinkage due to Asia's catch-up, has an added political implication. Its size also reflects the scale of advantages that an average person in a poor or emerging economy can expect to reap through migration to a richer country. In conditions of globalization, where the knowledge of such income differences is widespread and the costs of transportation are low, differences in country incomes cannot exist without provoking structural migration flows. By 'structural' migration I mean that migration is driven by large earning gaps, not by individual preferences for, say, a different climate or way of life. But 'structural' migration is embedded in the existence of income differences: there cannot be an offsetting migration of people who desire to have lower incomes.

Thus we face a trilemma: at any one time we cannot have globalization, high differences in mean incomes among countries, and no systematic or structural migration. If, as today, we have globalization and high differences in mean incomes, as for example between Spain and Morocco, Germany and Turkey, Italy and Libya, the US and Mexico, we cannot *not* have migration flows. We can, of course, shut down these flows by reversing globalization. Creation of border fences and walls is doing this: its objective is to limit globalization to the movements of capital, goods and technology, but to stop migration of the other factor of production (notably, labour). I do not think that this is, in the longer term, a feasible solution, because the forces of one's 'own betterment of life' (to use Adam Smith's term) that underlie migration are too strong to be stopped in a permanent fashion by walls and fences. On the other hand, greater equality of incomes between Europe and Africa, or North and Central America, which would diminish structural migration, is a long process that, even when assuming rather optimistically that African and Central American countries are able to significantly accelerate their growth rates, would take at least a century.

African and to some extent Asian migrations into Europe are a process that cannot be stopped (even when extreme measures such as those of the Trump administration in the US are applied) and will not be reversed for a very long time. The European Union's policies towards migration should move from the stop-gap measures used currently, to an overall thinking that would combine the ability of foreigners to move on a temporary basis to Europe (so-called circular migration) with policies designed to accelerate growth in poor countries, principally in Africa. The situation is similar in the United States as the political backlash against migration, and the building of the fence along the border with Mexico (which has continued regardless of what party is in power in Washington) show. Non-documented immigrants in the US are indeed a group whose path to citizenship is unclear or impossible. They are not, however, who I have in mind under the temporal or circular migration, which is an entirely legalized process where migrants enjoy legal protection, equal conditions at work, including pay, and access to health care and insurance, but do not have an open path to citizenship and, in principle, have to return to their country of origin after a given number of years (four or five).[65] This is not an ideal solution, but it has the advantage of being a 'middle' solution, such that it avoids a total ban on migration that is becoming increasingly supported by large groups of citizens, opinion-makers and political elites in the United States and Europe, and the unrealistic idea of full freedom of movement.

The change in global income positions, or the reshuffling of global income distribution. As shown in Chapter 1, we are living in the period of the greatest reshuffle of individual incomes since the Industrial Revolution. The rise of China, India and other large Asian countries means that the relative income positions of many people in the world have changed within a relatively short span of time equal to one or two generations. Most of the people from the rising Asian countries improved their positions in the global income distribution, and for many people from the slower-growing Western countries, their global income position slipped. Among both groups, the improvement or deterioration were continuous, as shown in Figure 2.2 for respectively the 9th urban income decile in China and the persons with a median income in the United States. The consequences of the reshuffling go beyond simple (and, at first, largely unknown or hard to observe) increases or decreases in one's global income position. They eventually appear quite visible in the ability to access goods or services that are priced internationally and are easily affordable only to people with a certain level of income. As mentioned before, foreign vacations, travel to international sports events and purchase of the newest clothing or communication equipment are their outward signs. Many of these goods are 'positional' goods (also called Veblen goods): they are purchased primarily for the message of affluence that their ownership conveys. But this precisely means that one's position in the global income distribution matters and is visible, and hence deterioration would be visible too and thus personally felt.[66]

The key conclusion that can be taken from the study of global income inequality is that even desirable economic outcomes that may be thought to unambiguously increase the overall amount of 'happiness' in the world are normally associated with local (national) income

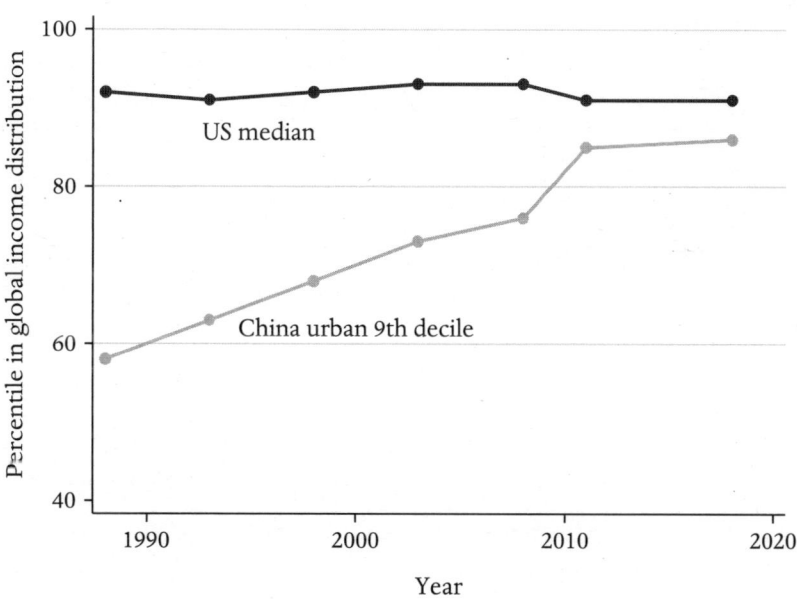

Figure 2.3. The global income positions of a person with US median income and a person at urban China's 9th decile, 1988–2018[67]

Note: The graph shows on the vertical axis global income positions (percentile) of individuals who have income placing them at the US median and those who have income placing them at China's 9th (second highest) decile of urban population.

and 'happiness' losses that in turn, through their impact on politics, may derail such globally advantageous changes. It is an illusion to believe that what is good for the world must be good for everybody.

Complexity of the world

Rawls's End of History Law of Peoples

In 1999, American philosopher John Rawls published a seminal work in political philosophy for the era of globalization, entitled *The Law of Peoples*. His objective was to propose the rules that should govern the relations of countries whose governments' bases of legitimacy are not the same. The 1990s were the years just after the end of the Cold War when the unquestioned and widespread belief in the advantages of liberal capitalist democracy meant that it was expected that all countries would eventually become liberal democracies, and thus the legitimacy of all governments would become identical. Rawls's attempt to sketch how the world of politically different nations might function was therefore a brave endeavour, and even deemed by some to be unnecessary, given that many believed that the world had reached the 'end-point of history' with only one political system in existence or on the horizon.

In this short volume Rawls turned his attention away from how a single nation should be organized (as in his 1971 book *A Theory of Justice*) to how the world should be organized. It had to be done at an abstract level, yet not so abstract that the real world of the 1990s would be unrecognizable. The configuration of the world, however, has changed greatly in the past thirty years. The abstract sketch made by Rawls is no longer compatible with what we see today and thus the recommendations that he drew from that sketch are not especially relevant – and I shall explain why. However, not only does Rawls's thinking, both in its domestic and international visions of how the polity should be ordered, remain deeply influential, but we also lack an alternative political vision that might challenge him and be more reflective of today's conditions. This is why engaging with Rawls today is still important. Perhaps one could say that by seeing defects in Rawls's observations, we can also grasp more easily the extent to which geopolitics has changed in the past quarter-century, as well as seeing more clearly what a new political philosophy of the world needs to include.

In *The Law of Peoples*, Rawls defines five types of societies: liberal societies (the same ones with which his *Theory of Justice* was concerned), consultative hierarchical societies, 'burdened' societies, outlaw states (notice: not societies) and benevolent absolutisms.[68]

Both liberal and consultative hierarchical societies are deemed 'well-ordered' societies because they observe human rights and allow for some, more or less meaningful, role for people in running public affairs. They also respect each other and accept the difference in the principles upon which their governments are based. One can imagine that the liberal societies are the liberal democracies of the West, Japan and South Korea (what we called 'the political West'), while the consultative hierarchical societies may be countries like Jordan and Morocco where the ruler shares power in many matters, except diplomacy and the military, with an elected parliament, even if the elections themselves may be biased towards some parties and all but rule out others. The two types of well-ordered societies coexist in peace and do not try to impose their internal order on each other. We can term this 'the Rawlsian accommodation'. The third group, the 'burdened' societies, are prevented from becoming well ordered by their poverty. Here we may imagine countries like Eritrea, Sudan or Chad, which are held back politically because of their extreme material poverty.

The well-ordered societies, though different in their internal structure, can coexist in peace because they respect each other. Liberal societies do not try to impose their norms on consultative hierarchies so long as consultative hierarchical societies 'behave' well. Rawls allows for economic coercion or military intervention, but only in exceptional cases.[69] What these exceptional cases are is never defined or impossible to tell exactly, but it is worth highlighting that the rules of non-interference in domestic affairs, enshrined in the UN Charter and so strongly insisted upon by the proponents of the New International Economic Order, are not accepted by Rawls. One can also ask, what happens in reverse: that is, are consultative hierarchical societies allowed, under some special circumstances, to interfere in the domestic affairs of liberal societies? The fact that Rawls does not even entertain this possibility indicates that he is – despite an attempt not to appear so – imagining a hierarchy of different forms of government where liberal societies are at the top. They are assumed to be internally capable of sorting out their affairs so that no one from without is allowed to interfere with their type of governance. Interference goes only one way.

Liberal societies have a duty to help burdened societies (that is, poor countries) but only as far as it is needed for them to become well ordered. Becoming well ordered does not require, in Rawls's view, being rich. It can take place at a very low average level of income. After that point, even huge differences in incomes between countries, but within the group of well-ordered societies, are immaterial and there are no grounds for the continuation of international aid. Aid is thus bounded in time. Relative unimportance of wealth is a theme reprised from *A Theory of Justice*.[70] There, too, the role of income as a primary good is not consistently upheld and, in a lexicographic ordering, more income cannot be substituted for less freedom. In other words, freedom cannot be traded away. According to Rawls, the desire for higher income is not an objective of liberal societies, but only of some groups like businessmen.[71]

If formerly burdened societies wish to become richer, they can easily do so, Rawls believes, by borrowing money from what he calls 'the Society of Peoples' (perhaps an equivalent of the World Bank).[72] It is somewhat strange to read Rawls repeating in the international arena the point with which he disagrees in the domestic setting, and that is often made by conservative economists: that poor people can become rich by pulling themselves up by their bootstraps and borrowing money for worthwhile projects. Somehow, what Rawls finds implausible nationally becomes quite realistic internationally.

The prospects for economic convergence, already reduced by the very restrictive role assigned to international aid, are further diminished by Rawls's stance on international migration. Migration is neither an individual right nor an acceptable way to alleviate global poverty or inequality. Countries have a duty to open their borders to those who want to leave, but they are also allowed to close their borders to those who want to move there. There are no open borders in a general sense. Countries (that is, organized peoples) have full control of their territory and they alone decide whom they want to accept. Liberal societies should accept refugees who flee political or religious persecution but not economic migrants. Immigration is limited to the 'duty of hospitality' to those whose lives are threatened in their own countries, not to those who are poor there.

This is the sketch of the world under globalization: liberal societies reaffirm their liberal principles daily; they live in peace with consultative hierarchical societies; they do not export democracy except in extreme cases of misbehaviour by other societies; they help only the poorest countries moderately and over a limited time-horizon; and they do not allow economic migrants. Income convergence among countries is not important and we are unsure if it would even take place or not. As Rawls clearly writes, the levels of wealth among the well-ordered societies will differ. National inequalities are governed by the well-known difference principle enunciated in *A Theory of Justice*: namely, that all inequality has to be justified by making the poorest better off in an absolute sense, but global inequality between individuals is indeterminate. Even if all countries were to observe the difference principle nationally, this would tell us little about global inequality since the latter is predominantly determined by the differences in mean country incomes (see Figure 2.2) which, according to Rawls, are immaterial.[73]

Rawls's worldview is now out of date. Since the End of History era, in the past three decades, several seismic changes have occurred on the world stage that have also changed global geopolitics.

Liberal democracies no longer affirm the principles of liberalism, as Rawls expected, neither domestically nor internationally. It would be inconceivable for Rawls, if liberal societies were working well, that they would generate a third or more of 'malcontents' who clearly do not believe in liberal principles nor are willing to affirm them in their daily lives. This, plus the pervasive role of money in electoral politics, lower tax rates for capital than labour and neglect of public education, imply that liberal societies are domestically very far from the idea of political liberalism.[74] The very first domestic principle of justice, namely that 'irrespective of economic and social class, people have roughly equal chances to influence political decisions',[75] is falsified by manifest differences in citizens' political power, themselves derived from large differences in wealth. The difference between liberal societies as they truly exist today and the way they are described in *The Law of Peoples* and *A Theory of Justice* is so great that it goes beyond the expected difference between an abstract idea and reality; the two belong to entirely different species. In foreign policy, the subject with which *The Law of Peoples* is directly concerned, liberal societies often act like outlaw states, as shown by the Iraq war. They break the fundamental rule on which the international community is founded: absence of wars of aggression. Truthfully, therefore, it is not clear if liberal societies do peacefully accept other countries with different bases of legitimacy (as Rawls expected them to do), except in very special circumstances where such countries are useful for ulterior purposes. Thus, sufferance of others is not, as Rawls wanted to have it, an integral part of the international order, but a flaw expected to be fixed.[76]

The benign consultative hierarchies that Rawls had in mind probably in order to fit Islamic societies into his scheme of the world[77] are, with the exception of a couple I mentioned, practically non-existent. The Middle East is either in total chaos (Iraq and Libya, both due precisely to the interventions of liberal societies) or in the grip of absolutist dictatorships as in Egypt, Saudi Arabia and the Gulf sheikdoms. They are not well-ordered societies in Rawls's terms.

There is no place in Rawls's taxonomy for multi-country non-state organizations like ISIS. A general theory that has no place for organizations that do not accept current state borders is clearly incomplete. This is an issue on which Rawls is especially weak. He takes borders as given, which is, as he wrote in the wake of the break-ups of the Soviet Union, Czechoslovakia, Ethiopia and Yugoslavia, rather odd. And today, with the war of Russia against Ukraine, Israeli settlers encroaching on Gaza and the Israeli army fighting the population there, and Azerbaijan expelling several hundred thousand Armenians – all of them wars over borders and thus land – the absence of any discussion about what the 'just' borders are is a glaring omission.

There is also no place in Rawls for what is now called illiberal democracy, namely a society that has most of the political accoutrements of a liberal society (elections, political parties, NGOs), and yet where only one party or one leader ever wins elections and where the media and the judiciary are directly or indirectly controlled. Further, the systems of two among the most economically successful countries in the world (China and Vietnam) are not mentioned. How can one discuss the international context of today's globalization without China?

Migrations, driven by economic reasons and thus by global inequality, do not have a place in Rawls at all. But large economic migration does exist in a globalized world. Economic migrants from Africa and Asia into Europe or from Mexico and Central America into the United States number millions.

Finally, as was already clear in *A Theory of Justice*, Rawls grossly underrated the importance that people attach to income and wealth for their happiness. This misjudgement is particularly striking in the era of globalization when income differences between individuals and countries have become starker, more visible, better known, and hence more important as motives for action or invidious comparison.

Thus, Rawls falls short of defining not only a compelling, but a moderately realistic political philosophy that reflects multiple types of political systems that exist today, and are likely going to exist in any multipolar world. By not providing a realistic theory Rawls also fails to address the essential question that motivates his work in principle: to provide theoretical underpinnings or the rationale for peaceful coexistence of countries whose political systems differ. For a more realistic view of the political division of the world, we have to turn to politicians.

The ideational political divisions of the world: how is the world divided and classified?

How is the world actually seen by politicians as opposed to political philosophers? Tables 2.2–2.4 represent an ideational picture of the divisions of the world as it was perceived by different political sides during the three different periods with which we are concerned here: the Cold War, the End of History era and the Struggle for a Multipolar World. Such classifications represent various ideological views of the world, which give us an insight into how different states, politicians and their ideologists conceive of the world, and of its different 'poles'.

The Cold War view of the world. Table 2.2, covering the period of the Cold War, is rather uncontroversial. It shows how the world was viewed by the four blocs: communist, capitalist, Maoist and the

Communist	Capitalist	Maoist*	G77/Non-aligned
		Hegemonic superpowers (US and the Soviet Union)	
Capitalist countries	Democracies/developed countries	The second world (developed western countries) and socialist revisionist countries	First world (developed capitalist countries)
Socialist countries	Totalitarian countries		Second world (socialist)
Decolonized countries to whom socialist countries are 'natural' allies	Developing nations	The Third World (including China)	Third (non-aligned) world (Africa, Asia and Latin America)**

Table 2.2. The Cold War view of the world

* As defined by Mao Zedong. Internationally, it gained prominence after it was enounced by Deng Xiaoping at his UN speech in April 1974 when the People's Republic of China was reintegrated into the United Nations.
** With China's position being ambiguous, most of the time ignored.

developing world. The 'divisions' of the world as seen by communist countries and the developing world (G77 or the non-aligned movement) were fairly similar, with the exception that the developing countries in the communist nomenclature were seen solely as countries in the process of decolonization, which made them the 'natural' allies of the socialist bloc. Meanwhile, the G77 or non-aligned world did not consider themselves to be 'natural' allies of the Soviet Union and the socialist bloc (even if attempts to make them so were made from time to time).

The particular classification of the world held by communist countries goes back to the 1920 Comintern meeting where Lenin, in a departure from orthodox Marxism, put the emphasis on combining the domestic struggle of the working class in rich countries with decolonization, i.e., the struggle for independence from the main capitalist powers, even when the latter struggle was headed by national bourgeoisies (and not by workers' parties). Lenin then proposed a division of the world shown in Figure 2.4 that, with minimal

Figure 2.4. The division of the world in 1920 as a result of World War I (according to Lenin)[78]

Note: The vertical axis shows the population (in millions, around 1920) that belongs to each of the three categories.

corrections, remained the guiding principle of how the Soviet Union and the socialist bloc officially viewed the world.[79]

The rich capitalist countries looked at the world essentially through a political lens. They preferred it to the economic perspective that was adopted by the socialist and G77 groups, because politics highlighted their advantage: namely, their democratic systems. It is notable that the term 'capitalism' was seldom used by the rich countries to describe themselves in official arenas. Things changed only in the 1990s.[80] Adopting their political lens, these countries, which may have otherwise been called the First World, saw themselves as democratic countries with high levels of income. Socialist countries were regarded as totalitarian countries, again emphasizing their political rather than their economic set-up. Finally, the developing nations were defined by their low level of income only, as their political regimes were deemed to be too diverse to allow classification.

Mao's view of geopolitics was quite different from the other three systems. He put the US and the Soviet Union on the top, in a special group as hegemonic superpowers who were trying to rule the world, or at least to tell the rest of the world what it must do. The Second World comprised developed Western countries whose position was, according to Mao, contradictory. On the one hand, they were the former colonial powers that exploited and continued to exploit the Third World. But, on the other hand, they were dependent on the hegemonic power of the United States. Their margin of manoeuvre was slim. Similarly, socialist bloc countries outside the Soviet Union were in a contradictory position: they were ostensibly independent but in reality ruled by the Soviet Union.[81] After 1956, China refused to be a part of that bloc, or, to use a rather picturesque description by Deng Xiaoping, to be a 'gem in the Soviet necklace made of barbed wire'.[82] It is worth noting that Raymond Aron in his monumental 1960 book *Peace and War* divides the world into almost exactly the same groups as Mao. Each of the two blocs is led by a hegemon (and thus the two hegemons stand apart), and within each bloc, the member-countries optimize between the desire for greater sovereignty and the need for protection by the hegemon, or fear of the hegemon's ire.[83]

According to Mao, the Third World was inclusive of China. Lin Biao, the Vice Chairman of the Chinese Communist Party, even went a step further by thinking of the Third World as the countryside that would, like in the Chinese Revolution, overthrow the cities of the world (i.e., the First and the Second Worlds). China's classification of the Third World differed from the definition by the G77 and non-aligned movement. According to the latter, China was not a part of the developing world since it did not belong to any of the organizations or movements – namely, the non-alignment movement, G77 and New International Economic Order – that were created by the countries of Asia, Africa and Latin America.[84]

It is notable that both communists and capitalists viewed the developing nations as somewhat not fully 'realized' variants of themselves. The communist world saw the Third World as having the potential to become fully fledged socialist countries. They were, it was implicitly held, unable to resort to the dictatorship of the proletariat and to have workers' parties in power because of the weakness of the working class and low levels of ideological development. But with time, the growth of the economy would create more jobs and more workers, and better education would make religion and other prejudices obsolete. Thus, the Third World could not fail to accede to socialism. The capitalist world, however, saw the Third World as a group of developing nations that, provided they managed to generate sufficient savings and economic growth, and protect private property, would be on the path to becoming democracies. The examples justifying each side's views come easily to mind. Algeria, Tanzania and Vietnam were very much in the mould that the socialist bloc desired; South Korea, Taiwan and Kenya seemed to validate the Western point of view. W. W. Rostow's *The Stages of Economic Growth: The Non-Communist Manifesto* (published in 1960) probably best captured the Western position of seeing economic growth as making 'the world safe for democracy', and, it was understood, safe for capitalism.

Thus, in the late twentieth century, neither the communist nor capitalist blocs saw developing countries as having agency or freedom to become something different from what the two blocs wished them to be. Developing countries were seen to be in the process of 'acceding' to a superior form of civilization, whether that be socialist or capitalist. This mindset has survived to this day among the elites of the political West and is often the cause of misunderstanding between the West and the rest of the world.

The End of History view of the world. After the fall of communism in the late twentieth century, the stadial or Whiggish theory of history – that is, the view of history as a linear, progressive force – remained standing, or was even reinforced among the countries of the political West, whereas others gave up pretending or believing that their systems contained lessons for the rest of the world. In fact, their posture was ideologically defensive. Their ambition in struggling to create a multipolar world was to be accepted with the political and economic systems they had, and not to propose their systems as desirable for the others to emulate. This unipolar moment after the End of History dramatically simplified the views of the world (Table 2.3).

The Western-preferred classification changed only in the sense that liberal democracies were no longer limited to West European countries, North America, Japan and South Korea, but now included East European former communist countries and potentially the entire globe. The end of history (i.e., liberal capitalism) applied to all. Perhaps, it was thought, some countries might not yet have become democracies but they were striving to be. The aspiration to become a liberal capitalist democracy was considered to be universal. It was a huge simplification of the world: history no longer existed because it was irrelevant. Whether a country was poor or rich, whether it had

Western/globalist	Chinese
Liberal democracies	Developed capitalist countries
Dictatorships	Socialism with Chinese characteristics
	Developing countries

Table 2.3. The End of History view of the world

this or that religion, a complex ethnic make-up or not, ultimately did not matter. Everybody could – and should – it was thought by the West, become a liberal capitalist democracy. Even low country income was no longer considered a serious impediment. The End of History ideology that became popularized by and associated with Francis Fukuyama, author of the eponymous book published in 1992, was a voluntaristic ideology, not different in its messianic undertones from early communism.[85] To some extent, perhaps it makes sense that once communists were defeated, the anti-communists who shared similar chiliastic views of the world would become intellectually dominant.

The only other category of nations that existed during the End of History era were dictatorships, which due to the stubbornness and ruthlessness of their leaders refused to accept the Zeitgeist. This elementary classification with just two categories influenced, as we saw above, the American political philosopher John Rawls to write *The Law of Peoples* in 1999 which proposed a more nuanced classification. At least Rawls acknowledged that poverty might represent an obstacle to instant democratization.

Meanwhile, the Chinese abandoned the Maoist schema, but did not accept the new universalist Western classification. They introduced one where a special place was reserved for China (note that there was no special place for China in the Maoist classification). It was a socialist country, but as almost all socialist countries had collapsed, China had to be a socialist country with (unique) Chinese characteristics. Hence collapse was excluded.

I did not include among the End of History views any classification coming from the developing nations, because at that point their ideologies were muted on the geopolitical stage. They accepted the views held by Western centres of power even when they were not democracies; they could not, for political reasons, claim that their objective was not ultimate democratization. They were non-democracies *faute de mieux*, that is, their lack of full democracy could not be ideologically presented as desirable on some other grounds. Iran might have been the only exception.

And indeed, the only 'odd man out' during that period were Islamic regimes that were neither democracies nor dictatorships. This is why Rawls created for them a special category of consultative hierarchical societies. These countries, however, did not themselves produce a classification they believed in, or which explained how *they* saw the world. The same is true for the Islamic Movement, although the 'extenuating circumstance' here was that it was headed by non-state actors – and the classifications we have in mind tend to be 'produced' by states or by the organizations of states. This could not be done by disparate and diffused non-state actors even if they shared a religion. ISIS's idea of the khalifate is the closest they came to the definition of an ideological division of the world, with the khalifate of course applying only to Muslims and unifying them in one single polity.

Unipolar or multipolar world. The simplistic End of History classification 'exploded' with the changes in the world that happened after the 2008 Global Financial Crisis, Covid and Russia's invasion of Ukraine. The Western view changed too. While on the top are, as before, liberal democracies, they became geographically circumscribed to what we have called 'the political West'. The 'liberal democratic world' is now more geographically and narrowly

Western	Russian	Chinese	BRICS*
Liberal democracies (the political West)	Liberal democracies (the 'collective West')	Developed capitalist countries	The political West
Illiberal or hybrid democracies	Sovereign democracies	Socialism with Chinese characteristics	
Autocracies			
	World majority		Global South (principally BRICS)
Developing countries		Developing countries	Other developing countries

Table 2.4. Current view of the world

* Refers to the association first composed of Brazil, Russia, India, China and South Africa. Currently, it has ten official members.

defined than at the time of the End of History when such a realm was open-ended, and it was held that every country bar dictatorships was, or aspired to become, a liberal democracy.

New regimes that are neither fully democratic nor dictatorial have emerged. This has given rise to the idea of illiberal or hybrid democracies. The term comes originally from Hungarian Prime Minister Viktor Orbán who called Hungary an illiberal democracy. Afterwards, it spread to many other countries, and became a popular term whether it was used affirmatively as Orbán did, or pejoratively as many commentators do. It is noticeable again that the Western classification avoids the economic side of the matter but focuses on how the politics are organized. Finally, on the bottom of the West's classification are autocracies and developing countries. Autocracies is also a new category. They are not like the totalitarian regimes of yore, given that they do not attempt to control the entire public sphere. The appellation is etymologically correct in the sense that autocracies are indeed ruled by one person (in all cases, one man).

Post-Yeltsin Russia always sat uncomfortably in the End of History classification – even when it was a member of the G8. Since the mid-2000s Russian ideologists have introduced a new category that they called the 'sovereign democracy'. The name was invented by the political strategist Vladislav Surkov who worked both for Yeltsin and later for Putin. It was used for the first time in 2006, and incidentally, or perhaps not incidentally, just a year before Putin's famous speech at the Munich Security Conference that is now considered as marking the beginning of the split between Russia and the West. The appellation is very interesting because (like Orbán's) it does not rule out democracy, but qualifies it. The qualifier 'sovereign' was created precisely with an international, and not domestic, political idea in mind, that is, to indicate that Russia (and other countries to whom the term may apply) refuses to be dragged into the 'liberal democracy' camp hierarchically structured around the United States as a leader. So, 'sovereign' meant 'politically independent in international affairs'. By itself, it had nothing to do with domestic politics.

The Russian government and its ideologists have also recently begun to use a new term that largely covers BRICS and other developing countries allied to BRICS. It is 'the world majority', a term devised to stress the combined size of population of such countries. The term is used very much to highlight the incongruence of the Western-used phrase 'international community' that in practice includes only the political West and a few other select countries, and that, in terms of the population it represents, is inferior to 'the world majority'.[86]

The Chinese classification continues as before. The new one which in some sense is an inheritor of the non-aligned classification appeared among BRICS countries. I am not thinking here of China and Russia, which were already mentioned with their own classifications, but other large countries such as Brazil, South Africa, India, Egypt, Ethiopia and Iran (all members of BRICS). One can add to them large developing countries that are not official members of BRICS (say, Nigeria or Indonesia). The BRICS distinguish between the political West, the politically emerging countries of which BRICS are the largest association, and other developing countries. The latter may be similar in many respects to BRICS but are not members, and are not as important by population and GDP as BRICS. All of them together represent the Global South.

The fact that the world currently has at least four reasonable views as to what types of political civilizations different countries belong to is itself, first, a testimony of the end of the End of History ideology with its much narrower view of political and economic systems, and second, an indication that we have entered the period of the struggle for multipolarity. It is thus not surprising that the supporters of a multipolar world (China, Russia, large BRICS countries, including India) have come up with their own ideological schemes. There are, of course, other possible schemes like the Iranian one that divides the world into Muslim and non-Muslim parts, but these classifications are limited to individual countries and do not have much traction or recognition among the rest of the world.

The current classifications, like the others, represent an ideological view of the world. They also illustrate a return to a more diverse view of the world similar to what existed during the Cold War. The Western ideational classification of the world moved away from the binary division into democracies and dictatorships as during the End of History period. Both autocracies and illiberal democracies are the new post-Cold War categories. The communist classification morphed into the Russian view of the world, and the Chinese classification changed with the end of Maoism. The Third World classification, although related to what used to be the non-aligned movement and the NIEO, evolved as well because it recognized the much more important global role played by large developing world actors. And the terms 'developing countries' or the 'Third World', even if still used, lost much of their power and relevance compared to the period of the Cold War. The developing countries themselves split into those that were on their way to strong growth and development (the rise of Asia) and others that, as we have seen in Chapter 1, failed to converge. The very idea of a developing world, which in the past implied similarity of incomes and political outlooks, is now questionable. And perhaps such a world no longer exists.

3.
The Elites

The past forty years have created new ruling classes in America and China. While some of the features of the new elites in both countries have been studied, including by myself (see *Capitalism, Alone*), their key characteristics have never been clearly spelled out using empirical data. This is the objective of Chapter 3. Using the data from the US Current Population Survey, I show that an increasing share of the richest Americans are both labour-income and capital-income rich. This phenomenon is termed 'homoploutia', meaning that such people are equally ('homo' or same) rich ('ploutia') in both factors of production (labour and capital). This is a new development in capitalism, sharply at variance with classical capitalism where people who had assets (and thus derived large incomes from capital) seldom worked. The new elite is also 'meritocratic' as shown by the fact that they have high labour incomes, and thus have highly skilled jobs, and, in the majority of cases, attended prestigious and expensive schools. The new elite thus combines ownership of assets with credentialism of high levels of education. This elite represents about 3 per cent of the American population, and a similar percentage in other high-income countries around the world.

China has even more thoroughly transformed its elite. Using the data from Chinese Household Surveys, I show that the composition of the elite (the richest 5 per cent by income) has entirely changed between 1988 and 2018. While in the beginning of the period most of the elite depended on the state for their income, whether as government or Party functionaries, or managers and highly skilled workers in state-owned enterprises, the picture, thirty years later, is very different. Fifty-seven per cent of the elite are either small or large capitalists (the latter category was almost non-existent in 1988) or the professional-managerial class (half of whom are working in private companies). But those who are the richest, even by the standards of the elite (*la crème de la crème*) are large capitalists who are also members of the Communist Party of China. They have higher incomes than other members of the top 5 per cent, and they – like the elite in the United States – also have the credentials; in this case the credential of CPC membership. They account for 1.5 per cent of the Chinese urban population.

Why focus on the US and China? Because the two giants are paradigmatic of a global shift in who elites are, and how they operate globally. And, of course, these superpowers – by the nature of their scale and influence – shape the world we live in. As we come to the second half of the book, we focus on these two countries to describe how their national shifts in wealth and economic policy are changing the future of the world.

America's new ruling class: homoploutia with credentials

Inevitably, the definition and the analysis of the American ruling class begins with US philosopher James Burnham's *Managerial Revolution*.[1] Published in 1941, it has set the terms under which we see the ruling class in the United States. Burnham's original formulation was different from the class formulations that took place in the 1960s, and is yet different from the one that we find today encapsulated under the title of the professional-managerial class. But all of the ways we have understood American elites in those intervening years relate to, and are in fact derived from, Burnham's 1941 work.

Burnham's managerial class. It is therefore important to go back to Burnham's book. His key idea was that the capitalist system was being gradually replaced by 'managerialism', a new social system where private capital is nationalized and the ruling class is composed of state-appointed or state-approved managers of companies. Capitalists, if they still exist, play a purely passive role. The ideology of sanctity of private property gradually becomes weaker and ultimately disappears.

His analytics are entirely Marxist. Burnham begins with a very simplified analysis of what capitalism is and how it has developed within the womb of the feudal society. He then discusses the Marxist notion that the system that would replace capitalism would be socialism. In everything that touches on capitalism itself, Burnham is fully in agreement not only with Marx but with Lenin and the Third International. He uses historical analogies highlighting the similarities between the way capitalism was born within a feudal society, and managerialism is being born within the capitalist society. The idea of a new system being born *within* the previous system is very important for Burnham, as it was for Marx. Its function is to show that systemic changes happen because the new ways of organizing production are more efficient than the old. The new ways of organizing production create a new ruling class that promotes them and economically benefits from them. Burnham thus rejects voluntarist notions of a 'new society' being created consciously, *ab ovo*, or from the beginning, as Leninists did.

Where Burnham dramatically departs from Marxism is in his view that the system that would replace capitalism will not be socialism but 'managerialism'. Socialism is defined, quite reasonably, as a (i) classless, (ii) free and (iii) internationalist society. Burnham observes throughout his book and especially in the chapter written about the Soviet Union that none of these three features holds true for the Soviet Union. It is (i) a class society where managers and Party functionaries have political power, control instruments of production and have a preferential position in the distribution of national output.[2] (ii) People are not free but subject to a totalitarian system. Soviets are politically irrelevant, toothless façades. (iii) There are almost no traces of internationalism because the managerial ruling class is interested in national aggrandizement and national power. Thus the Soviet Union is not a socialist, but a managerial society. It is, in fact, Burnham argues, the first managerial society in history, built on economically underdeveloped foundations; yet a society that is already (at the time of his writing) followed by the other nascent managerial societies of fascist Italy, Nazi Germany and New Deal's USA.

As mentioned, Burnham rejects the idea that socialism would replace capitalism. Workers cannot run complex economic systems nor can the ideals of socialism be attained so long as the level of economic development is not sufficiently high. But even what is *sufficiently* high may be forever unreachable. Burnham holds the view that human wants and needs are not limited. Hence the abundance upon which socialism and ultimately communism are predicated is simply not around the corner, nor may it ever be. (If needs are not limited, abundance is impossible.)

Socialist internationalism (socialism's third formal characteristic according to Burnham) would imply a world government, which is impossible given the enormous variety in incomes, religions, value systems and beliefs that exist between nations. Consequently, neither abundance nor internationalism can be achieved. Therefore, socialism is a utopia. Additionally, we cannot show that it springs endogenously from within the capitalist society as Marx thought; it was, on the contrary, the product of voluntarist 'construction of socialism'. This further delegitimizes it as an inheritor of classical capitalism.

But what is not a utopia and will replace classical capitalism is managerialism. Burnham devotes a significant part of *The Managerial Revolution* to explaining how managers gradually displace capitalists in the running of large enterprises, how they see capitalists (who spend most of their time in Florida playing golf) as parasites. All short- and long-term business decisions are made by managers, with capitalists playing almost no role. Thus managerialism naturally rises within capitalism.

Capitalists' abdication is not voluntary, though. When they tried to run companies according to the principles of profit, Burnham writes, they ran companies and countries aground. They created mass unemployment,[3] large piles of money that were never invested, low growth and recurrent economic crises. Capitalism, according to Burnham, is showing itself unable to solve economic problems in complex modern societies. Public discontent with the economic system is rising, and unwillingness to fight for it is shown, among other things (Burnham wrote in late 1940), by the very low rate of voluntary recruitment in the British and US armies at the beginning of World War II.

The only way to prevent the economic collapse is to bring in the state. Burnham here discusses Keynesianism, nationalization of various segments of the economy and the introduction of sectoral planning. An increasing share of the economy is run by different government bodies. Burnham mentions a bewildering array of newly created outfits under the Roosevelt administration: 'BLRB, SEC, ICC, AAA, TVA, FTC, FCC, the Office of Production Management (what a revealing title!)'.[4] He notes that Roosevelt in his 1940 re-election campaign never used the terms 'businessmen', 'owners' or 'bankers', replacing them with 'technicians in industry' and 'managers'.[5] What is really happening, writes Burnham, is a gradual replacement of the private-property-based rule of capitalists by the rule of government technocrats, creeping nationalization, or at least the introduction of strong constraints on the use of private property. The New Deal United States is moving towards managerialism, joining there the more advanced managerial societies of the USSR, Germany, Italy, Japan and France (after its defeat in June 1940).

The picture presented by Burnham is very powerful. This is written, as mentioned, in 1940–41, after the Ribbentrop–Molotov pact, the partition of Poland and the defeat of France, and Burnham's ideas seemed to align well with the reality as the three countries discussed (USSR, Germany and the US) displayed strong economic similarities. In all of them, the importance of private property of capital, compared to what it was before World War I, was significantly smaller and the economic and political power of capitalists much weaker. In the Soviet Union, both the private property and capitalist political power were eliminated entirely; in Nazi Germany, private property was broadly protected (but only if we disregard the vast extra-legal seizures of Jewish property) but its remit was

The Elites

restrained by ever expanding state power, and politically capitalists mattered little. The US under Roosevelt might have not been as 'managerially' advanced as the Soviet Union and Germany, but it was clearly following the same path. The addition of Italy, France, Japan and many smaller European countries whose systems were similarly structured (say, Poland and Spain) provides additional plausibility to Burnham's thesis.

Although Burnham's thesis of managerialism as a new system is perhaps the best known, it was not entirely original. Very similar ideas about the inevitability of socialism, looking very much like managerialism, can be found in Joseph Schumpeter's *Capitalism, Socialism and Democracy* published only a year after Burnham's book. One can see them also in Hayek's *Road to Serfdom*, written in the 1940s and published in 1944. In most key economic aspects Hayek hardly differs from Burnham. He acknowledges in Chapter 4 of *The Road to Serfdom* that technological progress (economies of scale, greater efficiency of monopolies, almost necessary conversion of successful competitive companies into monopolies) may render free competition obsolete or require planning, but he argues that such gains from standardization of large-scale production are temporary and one cannot be sure that they would hold in the future.[6] The important difference, however, was that Hayek's book was partly normative, in the sense that the greater role of the state was seen as something intrinsically malign. Burnham, on the other hand, took great pains to insist that his analysis is value-free and that he is simply discussing the way in which different economic and political systems succeed each other. Any ideas of inserting moral judgements in historical evolution are unscientific. Moreover, in Burnham's view (which gives it added relevance today) it was not the state as such – a largely unaccountable machine – that defines the new system, but, very importantly, the new managerial class that controls the state.

History did not move the way Burnham thought it would. His prediction that World War II would lead to the division of the world in three large areas, ruled respectively by the United States, Germany and Japan, did not come to pass. In effect, when we look at the changes in the world in the past eighty years the very opposite of what Burnham expected happened. Not only did the Soviet Union and the United States get together in order to defeat Germany, Italy and Japan, but the United States by the 1980s reverted strongly to capitalist ideology and sanctity of private property, jettisoning many elements of what Burnham called 'managerialism' or what may also be called the New Deal order.[7] Then, after a protracted Cold War, the conflict with socialism was resolved to the advantage of capitalism, and formerly socialist economies turned capitalist. They too joined ideologically, and also in *fact*, the capitalist world. Even China became economically capitalist, and the world became 'unified' in terms of the real-existing economic practice.

It is worth mentioning here that the ideological reversal regarding the importance of private property and private initiative is something that Burnham explicitly ruled out, as he believed that both private property and the ideology that justified it were on their way to extinction.[8] The ideological reversal, begun in the 1980s, was moreover, in many ways, even greater than when proxied by the effective reduction of the role of the state. Government spending as a share of GDP remained broadly constant in almost all Western countries because even the most adamant proponents of neoliberalism found it politically difficult to dismantle all institutions 'inherited' from the period of the welfare state. But the anti-state and pro-private property ideology that almost by definition regards the state as wasteful and the private sector as efficient took hold across a remarkably wide swathe of the political establishment, opinion makers and even the general public.

Thus, if one looks at the situation of the world since 1989–90, Burnham has to be seen as wrong in practically everything: managerialism did not replace capitalism, capitalist ideology is triumphant, the three great powers did not divide the world among themselves. And yet . . .

And yet the situation nowadays may be thought as validating some of Burnham's predictions. Burnham's ideas can be 'repurposed' to explain the rise of the professional-managerial class, by arguing that this class – *pace* Burnham – does not arise in opposition to the owners of capital, and thus, as it were, creates a new managerial society, but rather that it accomplishes a fusion with the top members of the capitalist class, and creates a *new capitalism*. The professional-managerial class and the top of the capitalist class compose the new elite. As I will show, the new class is not rich only in terms of labour income (as it would be under Burnham's managerial society) or capital income (as it was under classical capitalism), but also in terms of both labour and capital incomes. So its key features depart from what we knew of capitalism before, and from what various proponents of the managerial class (not only Burnham) thought of societies that would succeed classical capitalism.

Moreover, this 'adjustment' (in reality, this empirical evidence) explains also the revival of pro-capitalist ideologies during the past forty years and their accompanying features: higher income inequality, lower inter-generational mobility and the rising share of income from capital in GDP. They all demonstrate the greater power of capital owners since the Thatcher/Reagan revolutions in the early to mid-1980s, and especially so after communism – as a potentially competing social system – was defeated.

The new capitalism: homoploutia. Thus, while Burnham thought that the rise of the managerial class must be accompanied by the irrelevance of capital owners, 'withering' of private capital, greater power of the state and de-emphasis of the profit motive, the current reality in all these aspects is quite different. Nevertheless, a credentialled or meritocratic managerial class has been created and has expanded. It is different from the one Burnham saw coming because it does not arise in opposition to the capitalist class, but, on the contrary, directly in support of it. Additionally, and importantly, such a managerial class becomes part of the capitalist class, and at some point might become its majority. Its existence is therefore reflected in the rising phenomenon of 'homoploutia' in the United States and advanced Western economies.

Homoploutia means that the top of the income distribution is not composed, as in classical capitalist societies, of people whose entire, or almost entire, income is derived from ownership of capital, but increasingly of people who receive high incomes from both labour and capital, and thus not only belong to the top income class, but are among the highest wage-earners and among the richest capitalists. This is an entirely new phenomenon.[9] It is not equivalent to the fact, noted before (see, e.g., Piketty in *Capital in the Twenty-First Century*[10]), that the richest groups today have a greater share of labour income than in the past. This is, of course, true. But what was not noticed, and what the concept of homoploutia highlights, is a triple coincidence: (i) the richest people are also (ii) the highest paid wage-earners and (iii) the richest capitalists. For the sake of convenience, we shall define as members of the 'homoploutic' new class those who are in the top decile by labour income, capital income and total income.[11]

Figure 3.1 contrasts the situation in the United States against that of a less advanced and more 'classically' capitalist country like Mexico, or that of Spain and Sweden. About 30 per cent of people in the highest US income decile are the people who are also among the richest decile of capitalists and the richest decile of wage-earners.[12] The US homoploutic elite therefore consists of 3 per cent of the US population. That proportion has shown a steady increase since the early 1980s, which coincides with the time when US income inequality began to increase and inter-generational mobility to go down (see, e.g., Atkinson, Piketty and Saez 2011; Piketty and Saez 2006; Corak 2013). Homoploutia is much lower (under 10 per cent) in Mexico where, consistent with classical capitalism, the richest capitalists do not normally also work for a wage, and equivalently, not many among the highest paid wage-earners have enough property to accede to the top capital-income decile. Similar results obtain for other Latin American countries (Brazil, Peru, Colombia). Richer OECD countries such as Spain, Italy, Germany, the Netherlands, Italy, etc. are between the US and Mexico, with, on average, 20–25 per cent of the top income decile being homoploutic (as can be seen in Figure 3.1).

What would happen if the percentage of homoploutic households among the top decile increases further? Suppose that almost

The Elites

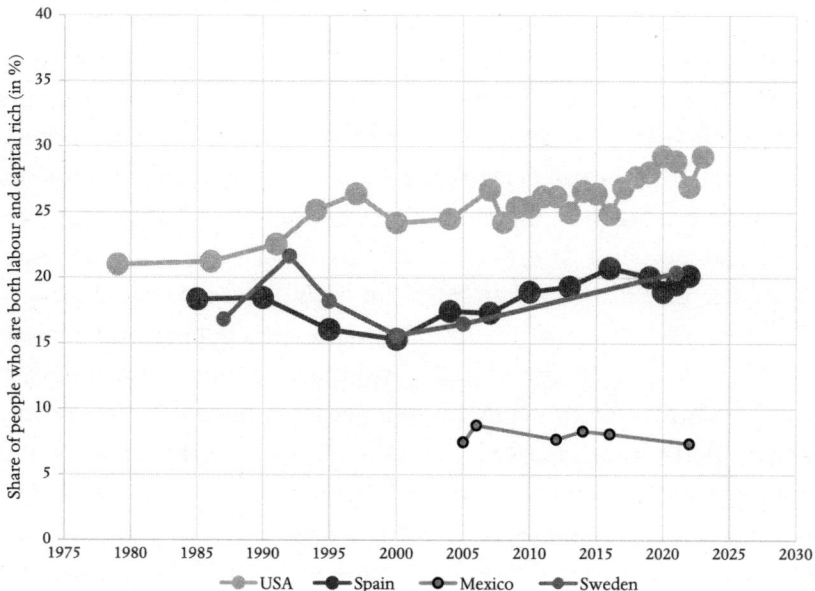

Figure 3.1. Homoploutia in the United States, Spain, Sweden and Mexico: percentage of people in the top income decile who are both top capitalists and top wage-earners[13]

Note: The graph shows that an increasing share of the top income decile consists of people who are both rich capital owners (belonging to the top decile of capitalists) and rich wage-earners (belonging to the top decile of workers). The top income decile is defined as the richest 10 per cent of a country's population by disposable (after-tax) per capita income.

all those who are in the top decile by total income are also in the top decile of capitalists and workers. This would be an impregnable elite; it would be invulnerable to the fluctuations of the labour market since it has assets and capital income to fall back on; similarly, gyrations of the stock market, fluctuations in profits and interest, can be cushioned thanks to high-paying jobs. Being rich in both factors of production is a new development that has, at least for the homoploutic elite, solved the perennial conflict between capital and labour. It is arguably the only development in modern capitalism that would surprise Marx.[14] If such a homoploutia could be extended along the entire income distribution, with everybody becoming in equal measure a capitalist and a worker, class conflict would also be eliminated. In addition, the increase in the share of capital in total income that has occurred during the past thirty years in most rich countries and that may be exacerbated (as some economists believe) by the deployment of artificial intelligence in the future would have no impact on income inequality. With the same shares of capital and labour along the entire income distribution, an increase in capital share raises everybody's income by the same percentage and leaves (relative) inequality unchanged.[15] But this development, along the entire income distribution, would require 'people's capitalism' where many more people than today own property. This, as we shall see next, is quite improbable given the current numbers. What seems more plausible is the expansion of the homoploutic upper class: instead of only one-third of the top income decile being homoploutic, it could become one-half or two-thirds or even more. This would cement its position at the top, and help it transmit its advantages across generations through an ability to ensure better and more expensive education for its offspring, and endow them with more capital through inheritance.

To put the meaning of this new top class that defines the new capitalism into better perspective, we should note that in advanced capitalist countries 60 per cent or more of the population have almost no financial income from property.[16] This is shown in Figure 3.2. In fact, income from capital is extraordinarily heavily concentrated, with its Gini approximately twice as high as Gini of disposable (after-tax) income. Thus while in 2022, 60 per cent of US households had zero or quasi-zero income from capital, the richest capitalists (people in the top 1 per cent by capital income) had a capital income of almost $100,000 per person per year, which for a conventional household composed of four people implies an annual family income of $400,000 from financial assets alone.[17] The homoploutic class, that is, those who are in the top decile by disposable, labour and capital income, also have large income from capital: $20,548 per person annually, which, with an equivalent

The Elites

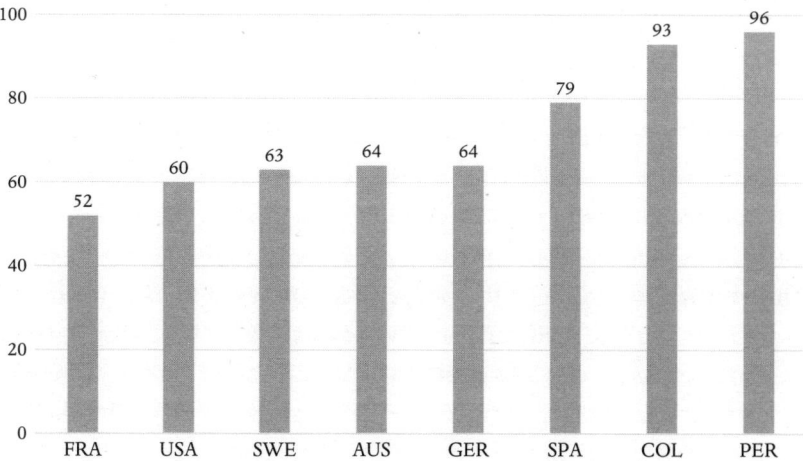

Figure 3.2. Percentage of country's population that has zero or negligible annual income from capital ownership[18]

Note: The graph shows the percentage of population with zero or less than $100 per person in annual income from property. The data refer to the latest year for which the country-level information is available in the Luxembourg Income Study; this (at the time of writing, spring 2024) ranges between 2018 and 2022.

assumption about the average family size, yields more than $80,000 per family.

The origin of the homoploutic class and its effect on income distribution. At the most general level, homoploutia can come into existence through high parental income (at some point transferred as inheritance or inter-vivos transfers to offspring) that enables individuals to attend expensive schools and then get highly paid jobs; or differently, through good education, luck, hard work and a high salary that over one's lifetime allows for substantial savings and thus high capital incomes. The first path is what we call 'fusion' with the old capitalist class, the second is 'self-fusion'.[19] There is little doubt that in reality a combination of both processes is at work. Yonatan Berman and I have looked more closely at the association of rising homoploutia in the United States with other simultaneous distributional changes (increasing capital share and more unequal distributions of both capital and labour incomes).[20] The correlation between homoploutia and rising inequality of labour income is by far the strongest. That would suggest a possible causal channel that goes from rising earnings inequality that has made high savings possible; or, perhaps less likely, through greater attractiveness of working for the individuals who already have high capital income (say, a trust-funder who is no longer indifferent to the increase in income he or she can make by working). The likelihood of this channel is reinforced by the fact that top wage-earners (often the top executives) are paid partly in company shares. These shares, when paid out, are considered as ordinary labour income – in the same way that fringe benefits paid to workers are considered as in-kind labour income. But in the following periods, income derived from them (dividends or interest) counts as capital income. This creates homoploutia. The particular path whereby homoploutia came to be so important deserves much more analysis, and is, of course, hard to study because it requires longitudinal data (i.e., the data that follow particular households or individuals over the years).

How important was homoploutia in raising income inequality in the US since the 1980s? Yonatan Berman and I try to answer that question by looking at the actual share of the richest decile in total US income and at its counterfactual share if homoploutia had not become as prevalent. We find that greater homoploutia accounts for about a fifth of the increase in the top decile share between 1986 and 2020.

The fusion of what may be called the original or simple professional-managerial class with capitalists proper, or more commonly through their own transformation into capitalists (in which case the 'fusion' is not realized across individuals or families but, as it were, within oneself), is a new moment in the evolution of capitalism. I believe that it defines the new ruling class in advanced capitalism. The new ruling class or the new elite has, mirroring its capital and labour incomes, two parts: a capitalist side, which we just discussed, and a credential, or meritocratic, side to which we turn next.

The new capitalism: credentialism. The meritocratic side has been much discussed, but perhaps its best recent exposition is in Daniel

Markovits's *The Meritocracy Trap*.[21] The credentialled class feels superior because of its educational achievements (and thus ultimately because of self-perceived intelligence and skills), and tends to ignore the fact that these educational achievements often depend on family wealth and status, access to 'privileged' information regarding the rules used by schools and universities in their acceptance policies, and not the least that it relies on an often enormous expense of money needed to attend the top ranks of schools all the way from pre-kindergarten to graduate degrees. By the time children of the rich leave graduate school, Markovits calculates that the cumulative difference between parental investment and subsidies provided by the elite schools, and investments along the similar path made by the parents of the children of the middle class, is an astronomical $10 million.[22]

Markovits argues that 'what is conventionally called merit is actually an ideological conceit, constructed to launder fundamentally unjust allocation of advantage'.[23] The system is relatively easy to explain by writing it as a modification of Marx's famous M-C-M' scheme (invested money → production of commodities → more money). Here it is M-E-M' where E stands for production of children's education. The moneyed elite, itself well educated and hard-working, dedicates large amounts of effort and money to place its children through the most expensive, elitist and competitive education system in the world that begins with pre-kindergarten and ends with graduate school – in order to make sure that children earn ever higher incomes and stay on top. 'Meritocracy' is thus just another way to create and maintain a de facto ruling class, where the birth advantage (fundamental to its power) is concealed by educational credentials.[24]

Through their belief that the advantages they enjoy are fully merited, and accordingly, through their contempt for the poor (what Markovits calls 'a conservative virtue'[25]), meritocrats have created a deep chasm within the US polity between themselves and the rest, most notably between themselves and the middle class (the political influence of the poor in America has never been strong). Not only in income, but in consumption patterns, beliefs and health outcomes, the gap between the meritocrats and the middle class is wider today than the gap between the middle class and the poor.[26]

The economic and cultural divide that has opened between the meritocrats and the middle class feeds the cultural and political wars in the United States. As Markovits writes, the middle class that was left behind does not resent billionaires and entrepreneurs; it resents meritocrats and their supercilious attitude towards the 'deplorables'. We shall return to the political consequences of this gap in Chapter 4.

Combining credentialism and homoploutia. The capitalist aspect of the ruling class is, as we have seen, reflected in the rising homoploutia. In fact, if the ruling class were not combining meritocratic and capitalistic elements, it would be very highly placed in the wage distribution, but not in the distribution of income from ownership. It simply would not own enough private property to be placed that high. This was indeed the standard situation of the credentialled or meritocratic middle classes during most of classical capitalism; their members were educated, often part of liberal professions, but almost never had sufficiently high incomes from ownership of assets to be placed alongside the top decile of capitalists. Similarly, top capital owners seldom had any labour income, and even more seldom *high* labour incomes. This dichotomy is still easily observable today in less advanced economies like those in Latin America, where, as we have seen, the share of the homoploutic class is much smaller than in the richest Western economies.

The path to homoploutia can, in the two polar cases, come through inheritance or alternatively savings from high labour incomes. As already mentioned, both paths are probably involved for homoploutics. Relatively well-off and well-educated parents provide information and money necessary for 'credentials'; credentials lead to highly paid jobs; these jobs enable individuals to save; with these savings they buy financial or real assets thus becoming capitalists, and ultimately (if they manage to accumulate enough assets) derive sizeable incomes from property. Moreover, as it has often been noted (Philippon and Reshef 2012; Smith et al. 2019) – but proper conclusions have not been

The Elites

drawn – high-paying jobs that involve payment in company shares, that is, in financial wealth, automatically 'unite' in the same person high labour and high capital incomes and produce a homoploutic top class (i.e., 'the self-fusion'). This is another instance illustrating the fact that, contrary to what was thought by James Burnham and Joseph Schumpeter in the 1940s, and by Raymond Aron and John Kenneth Galbraith in the 1960s, the professional-managerial class owes its income and power not to opposition to capitalists, but to its *alliance* with capitalists, and its acceptance of the capitalist mode of production. It is not the state that creates the managerial ruling class, but its symbiosis with capital.

In conclusion, (1) the new ruling class in advanced capitalism (and even more strongly, in the United States) is a class that was successful in uniting the old-fashioned managerial class with top capitalists. (2) That fusion does not take place only or mainly through a similarity of material interests, or similarity of positions in the process of production of the two classes (managerial and capitalist), which, in principle, might not rule out the possibility that the two classes may move apart, or that their interests may diverge. (3) On the contrary, the new ruling class is created by fusion, as it were 'within', which implies a concordance of material interests. Highly credentialled individuals acquire capital, or rich heirs acquire the best education and then high-paying jobs. Interests of the professional-managerial class thus become intertwined with the interests of capital. The old-fashioned capitalist class might still maintain its position at the fringes, but is clearly destined for extinction, even in the cases where their members may have inherited wealth but neglect to obtain educational credentials.

There are three features characteristic of the new ruling class: the sociological one as seen in what we call the fusion of 'meritocrats' with capitalists; the economic, as seen in the data on increasing homoploutia; and finally its ideological aspect seen in the unquestionable acceptance of the importance and role of private property. That acceptance is not solely a 'passive' ideological predilection for private property and the profit motive, but is grounded more solidly in one's own material interest. The new class has thus become as committed to the defence of private property and to the limits of the role of the state as was the old-fashioned capitalist class.

Difference between the homoploutic ruling class and the technocratic professional class. The new homoploutic ruling class is a different and financially richer version of the professional-managerial class as proposed originally by Burnham, and then retrieved to some extent in the 'system convergence' literature of the 1960s and 1970s by John Kenneth Galbraith,[27] Daniel Bell[28] and Raymond Aron,[29] which held that socialist and capitalist systems, by being both modern and technocratic, must ultimately produce the same class structure. Galbraith and Aron wrote about the modern industrial societies where the type of ownership (state or private) was less important, and where managers run the system, determine prices and quantities, and eventually take full control.[30] Shareholders are either fooled or ignored by the company boards and managers. According to this view, industrial societies, whether of the Soviet or American type, required the same type of management. Andrei Sakharov, the famous Soviet physicist, expressed similar ideas around the same time. Technocracy in the language of the 1960s, and not bureaucracy, must rule for economic progress in Soviet-type economies to continue, and the rule of a technocratic or professional class in both systems will ultimately lead to systems' convergence. Although the trajectory whereby socialist and capitalist systems end up with a similar class structure was different in Galbraith and Aron from what Burnham had in mind, there are also strong similarities in at least two aspects. First, the rule of professionals is made inevitable by the requirements of modern technology, and the need to run it efficiently;[31] second, the ideology of technocrats is not capitalistic, nor do they care much about private property. This latter is by definition true for the technocrats in socialism, but it is true, Galbraith and Aron averred, in capitalism as well. One could think of iconic managerial figures, both East and West, from the mid-twentieth century who indeed distinguished themselves by managerial efficiency but were probably indifferent about the ownership structure of the companies they ran and the security of private property more broadly. Robert McNamara ran Ford Motor Company, but he applied the same managerial skills in his government jobs as US Secretary of Defense and then as president of the World Bank. Enrico Mattei was one of these unmatched business leaders managing the Italian state-owned petrochemical company ENI. Aleksey Kosygin, the Soviet prime minister from 1964 to 1980, was considered to have been a supreme technocrat in his original jobs when tasked with moving Soviet industries east during World War II and heading the State Planning Commission. It is clear that this mid-twentieth-century managerial class is of an entirely different type from the homoploutic ruling elite with which we deal today. The technocrats were equally happy to run efficiently and technocratically companies that could be state- or privately owned, and they seldom, or never, acquired wealth that would transform them, or their children, into rich capitalists.

Difference between the homoploutic ruling class, Burnham's managerial class and the 'wokist' professional-managerial class. The idea of the professional-managerial class (vaguely related to Burnham) has seen something of a revival recently in right-wing intellectual circles. They argue that such a class, 'armed' with its credentials and ideologically liberal mindset to the extreme, has conquered in the United States and elsewhere in the West the machinery of the educational institutions and the government and has in a way created a 'deep state' within the state. Such a state is impervious to democracy in the sense that it controls all the levels of effective power regardless of who might get elected to the highest office.[32] The deep state may manipulate information, present biased conclusions, or simply fail to implement what it is asked to do. Polish philosopher Ryszard Legutko is one of the main ideologues of this view.[33] It should be noticed that the 'deep state' in this understanding of the term differs from its original usage that was common in Turkey and Pakistan to indicate the lack of government oversight and control over parts of the military or intelligence services. Here the deep state is not limited to the military or intelligence apparatus, but spreads to all parts of government administration.[34] It gets to these positions not through some giant conspiracy but because its ideology is extensively adopted by all institutions of higher learning that provide credential bureaucrats who run the government. It thus holds the lock on knowledge-creation and thereby also on how things are seen and presented by the media, non-profit institutions, think tanks and ultimately government.

This was the point recently made by N. S. Lyons, a conservative American analyst, in his essay that forecast the United States converging onto the Chinese model.[35] The convergence, however, is defined only in ideological terms. Lyons sees 'woke' ideology – loosely, an awareness, and according to the critics exaggerated awareness, of social and racial injustices – as a form of elite thought-control that is not different from that exercised by the Communist Party of China. This is an interesting idea highlighting the similarity in credentialism and ideological 'control' between the two systems, which I will say more about later.

However, whatever we make of 'wokeism' as the ideology of the professional-managerial class, the idea that the US is moving towards a managerial society that has any resemblance to what Burnham thought of is entirely wrong, as our short sketch of Burnham's ideas, and more importantly as the description of the way the new ruling class is being created, show. Similarly, the connection between Burnham's managerial class and today's idea of the professional-managerial class is entirely fanciful. Burnham grounds the definition of both capitalist and managerial societies in the relations of production ('The instruments of production are the seat of social domination; who controls them ... controls society, for they are the means whereby society lives'),[36] not in the ideology that is, in the contemporary right-wing discourse, completely dissociated from the production side. The managerial society, according to Burnham, can exist only when the ownership of most means of production is vested in the state, and the managerial class plays the dominant role in managing these instruments of production. None of it is true in the United States today, and Lyons's attempt to enlist Burnham and the 'managerial society' to his point of view is either a misunderstanding of Burnham or a misappropriation of his ideas. As argued before, the American dominant class is imbued by a strong capitalist ethos, it defends its property and controls the government. While Burnham clearly locates the origin of the managerial class in the relations of production, Lyons's professional-managerial class is implausibly 'rooted' entirely in the sphere of ideology. In thus being entirely idealistic, the professional-managerial class definition differs also from the 1960–70s theories of technocracy, where the power of technocracy was based on its providing superior economic performance, that is, on real phenomena, not just ideology. In Lyons's repurposing of the professional-managerial class, its ideology seems to spring out of nowhere, or rather bizarrely to stem from the ideology spread by the centres of higher learning without an explanation as to how such centres have stumbled upon, and been able to impose, the ideology of 'wokeness'.[37]

With the empirical data that track the concentrations of income from both labour and capital, we can now clearly see the existence of a homoploutic ruling class. With its deep links to modern-day capitalism and defence of private property rights, which is indeed inherent in the fact of homoploutia, we can see why the new ruling class has defended its own financial interests. Moreover, it explains why the new elite did not reject the principles of private profit (as most authors thought it would), but rather espoused it as strongly as the classical capitalist class did.

China's new ruling class: capital ownership with CPC membership

The enormous economic changes in China in almost fifty years since the economic reforms of 1978 are mirrored by a significant change in China's top income groups. Chinese GDP per capita in 2018 was, in real terms, 7.5 times greater than in 1978. This is according to data from the Maddison Project, a database of historical economic statistics; Chinese official data show an increase of thirty times. Even when taking the much more conservative, and likely underestimated, Maddison Project data of a 7.5-fold increase, it still took

Britain just short of two centuries to multiply its 1800 GDP per capita (the assumed beginning of the Industrial Revolution) by as much.[38] Even if all classes in China benefited from this phenomenal growth, not all of them benefited equally (Figure 3.3). In both rural and urban areas, richer groups gained proportionately more (and, of course, in absolute terms, their gains were even more lopsided). Inequality thus increased in cities and the countryside, and even more in China as a whole, because the gap between the average urban and rural incomes soared.

The speed of economic change was reflected in the speed of transformation in the top socio-economic groups. Similar changes

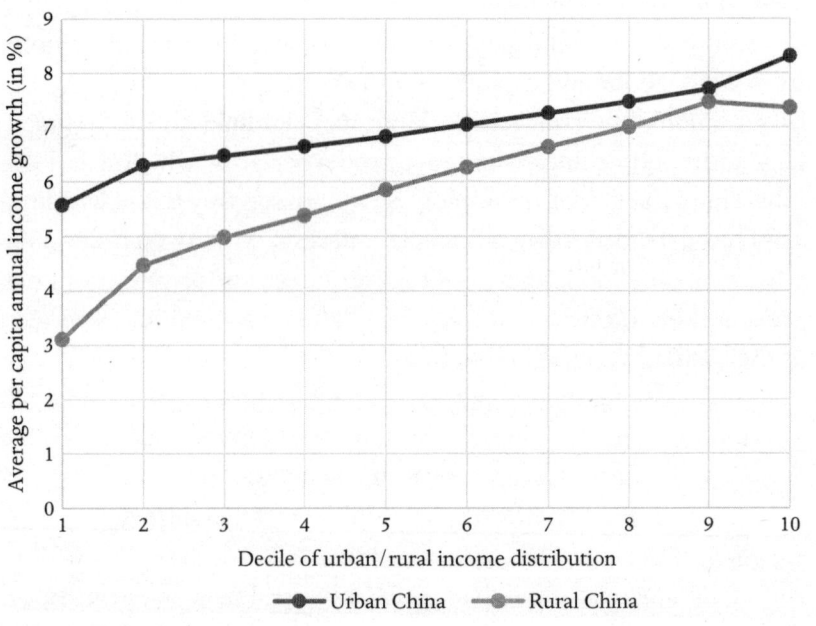

Figure 3.3. Income gains among Chinese urban and rural populations, 1988–2018[39]

Note: The graph shows the average annual real (inflation-adjusted) income growth among Chinese rural and urban income distributions. The upward sloping line implies that the richer deciles' income increased more in percentage terms. Data from Branko Milanovic, 'The three eras of global inequality, 1820–2020 with the focus on the past thirty years', *World Development*, vol. 177, May 2024.

happened in England during the Industrial Revolution, but not at the same speed. In his research on this period, the British economic historian Bob Allen found that in England and Wales it took capitalists almost two centuries to more than double their share in the total population, passing from 3.4 per cent in 1688 to 7.8 per cent in 1867, while their average income remained at the level of about two-thirds of that of landlords.[40] One can view this as a capitalist expansion by 'extensive margin', that is, by expanding the importance of the capitalist class in relative size while keeping broadly unchanged its relation to the income of the richest group.[41] As we shall see, in China capitalist expansion proceeded both by 'extensive margin' (there are simply many more large- and medium-scale owners) and by 'intensive margin', or by relative wealth, as capitalists' incomes grew faster than those of other classes.

What happened to China's urban elite in recent decades? Using nationally representative household surveys, Li Yang, Filip Novokmet and I documented the change in the composition of the elite between 1988 and 2018.[42] The elite is defined here as the richest 5 per cent of the Chinese urban population. While in 1988, more than two-thirds of the elite were, for their income, dependent on the state, whether through employment in various government and CPC organizations at different administrative levels or by being employed by the state-owned enterprises, thirty years later, more than one-half of the elite was composed of people whose income was made in the private sector. They were the owners of large or small capitalist enterprises and the professional-managerial class employed in private companies.[43]

As Figure 3.4 shows, in 2018, almost one-third of the elite were capitalists; either as large business owners or those whose private businesses employ fewer than eight workers (including, of course, those who may be self-employed).[44] These two groups were entirely marginal in 1988 and 1992, accounting for 2 and 5 per cent respectively. One-fourth of today's elite belong to the professional-managerial class. Thus, together with capitalists, they account for more than half of the elite (32% + 25% = 57%). While before the urban reforms

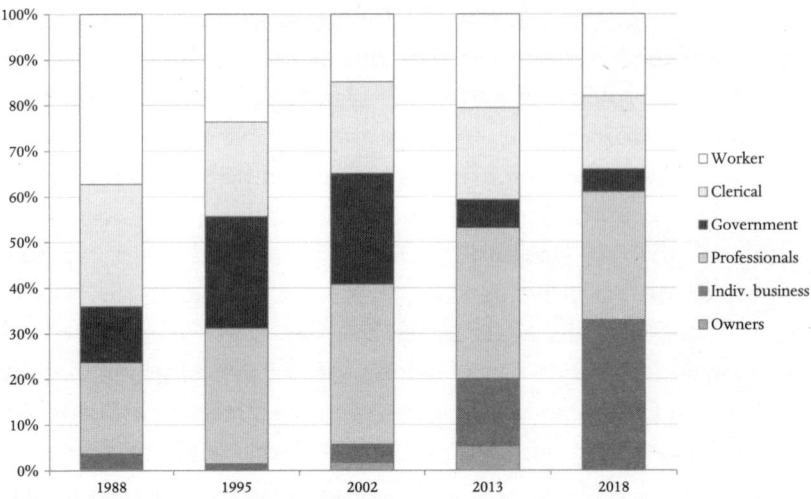

Figure 3.4. Social composition of the urban elite in China, 1988–2018 (percentage of individuals)[45]

Note: The graph shows the changing social composition of the richest 5 per cent of urban Chinese. For example, the professional class's participation rose from 20 per cent in 1988 to 28 per cent in 2018. Individual businesses have fewer than eight hired workers. Owners (or capitalists) employ over eight workers per company. These two classes are combined in 2018 data.

in the early 1990s, the Chinese urban elite was overwhelmingly composed of skilled workers, clerical staff and government officials, by 2018, it had become an elite where professionals and business owners were in the majority. The increase, among the elite, in the importance of the social classes whose livelihood is not related to the state is perhaps the most dramatic reflection of deep changes undergone by urban China in the past thirty years.

Instead of looking at the number of people from different classes in the elite, Figure 3.5 looks at the elite's share of total urban income (the height of the bar) and sources of that income. Income share of the elite increased from 13 per cent to more than 20 per cent of total urban income, which is consistent with the increase of inequality in urban China. More interestingly, private sector income sources that for the elite were almost negligible in 1988 (about 1 per cent of total

The Elites

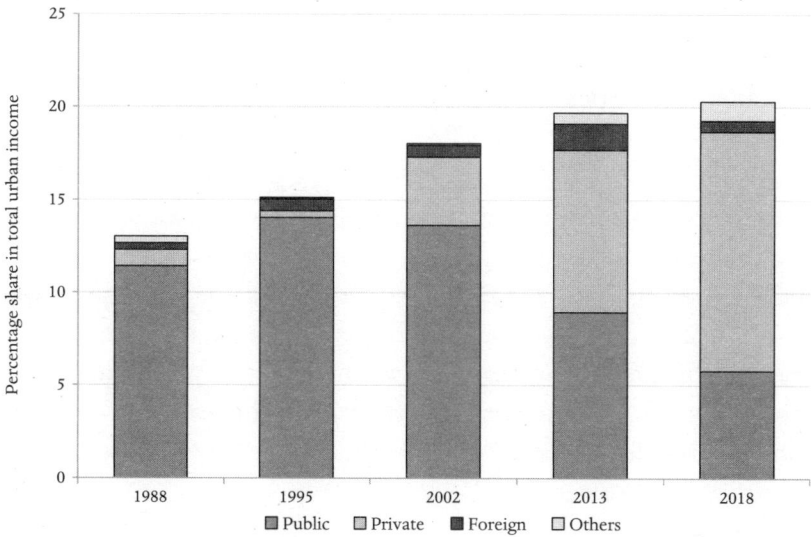

Figure 3.5. Income sources of the elite, by sector of ownership, 1988–2018 (in % of total Chinese urban income)[46]

Note: The graph shows the composition of the top 5 per cent of China's urban income. The height of the bar gives the income share of the top 5 per cent in total urban income.

urban income) expanded to account for the largest source of the elite's income today. The expansion is particularly clear since 2002. By now, private sector income accounts for two-thirds of total income of the elite. Simultaneously, public sector income has shrunk. In short, public and private sector incomes have switched places as the principal elite income source over the past thirty years.

CPC credentialism. The next question is whether in a de facto single-party system political influence or connections help increase income.[47] It is especially intriguing in China, where the ruling party is officially committed to looking after the interests of the poorer and less educated sections of the population but where the observed changes clearly paint a picture of the rising importance of well-educated professionals and rich capitalists.[48]

The share of CPC members among the elite in 2013 was about a third, and among the top 1 per cent around one-fourth (Table 3.1).[49]

These are significantly lower shares than in the past: at its peak, in 2002, CPC membership in both top groups exceeded one-half (among the top 1 per cent it reached almost 60 per cent). This is not surprising given the change from a state-based to private sector-based elite.

In 2013, the income premium to CPC membership (after controlling for other factors like gender, age, education, experience and social group[50]) across the entire urban population was 5 per cent (Table 3.1). In other words, everything else being the same, CPC membership added 5 per cent to one's income. The premium can be thought, in the most direct fashion, to reward the membership by allowing people who are Party members to accede to positions of

	Frequency of CPC membership (in %)	Returns to CPC membership (in %)*
Total urban population	~20	+5
The elite (top 5 per cent)	33.1	---
Top 1 per cent	24.2	---

	Within the 5 per cent elite	
	Frequency of CPC membership (in %)	Returns to CPC membership (in %)**
Owners of large private sector companies	14	+34
Small private sector owners and self-employed	5	0
Professionals	31	0
Government and SOE officials	45	0
Clerical staff	43	0
Workers	13	--

Table 3.1. CPC membership and its advantages (in 2013)[51]

* Calculated from a regression across the entire urban population and controlling for other observable characteristics like age, gender, education, experience, etc.
** Calculated from a regression across the top 5 per cent and controlling for all other observable characteristics and with the omitted category being a worker, i.e., the CPC premium is calculated for a large private sector owner, a professional, etc., compared to what the premium would be for a worker. The results show that for all elite members except for large private sector owners, CPC membership provides no statistically significant additional benefit.

greater authority and hence to have higher income. The premium may also be due to unobserved individual characteristics like hard work or ambition (which, in turn, may be correlated with the desire to be a Party member).

The result acquires additional significance when combined with the finding that in a regression analysis undertaken across the elite (the top 5 per cent), private sector businesspeople who are also CPC members tend to receive a very large premium from membership (34 per cent compared to an equivalent person without CPC membership).[52] This premium for private businesspeople is in contrast with all other social groups to whom CPC membership, once they are elite members, is not financially important. It is also noteworthy that there is no evidence of such a large CPC membership premium for private sector businesspeople in the years before 2013. Capitalists and the self-employed represent, as we have seen, about a third of the elite; consequently, we are considering here about 1.5 per cent of the total urban population (a third of the 5 per cent). They combine sizeable ownership of assets with Party membership.

Like the path that unified high labour and capital incomes in the United States, the transition between the CPC nomenklatura and private sector entrepreneurships can happen in different ways. The membrane between the two may be thin. Party functionaries have become entrepreneurs (the so-called *xiahai* entrepreneurs) and entrepreneurs have been co-opted into the Party.

These advantages are confirmed when we consider the top 1 per cent of China's urban population. Figure 3.6 shows that CPC members who are in a given elite group (either the top 5 per cent or the top 1 per cent) are not better off or worse off than the non-CPC members of that elite group. But this is not true for private sector businesspeople who are in the top 1 per cent. There, the Party card combined with being a capitalist, whether large or small, displays its full advantage. That particular group has significantly higher income (+29 per cent) than either other CPC members who are among the top 1 per cent, or non-CPC members who are also in the top 1 per cent.

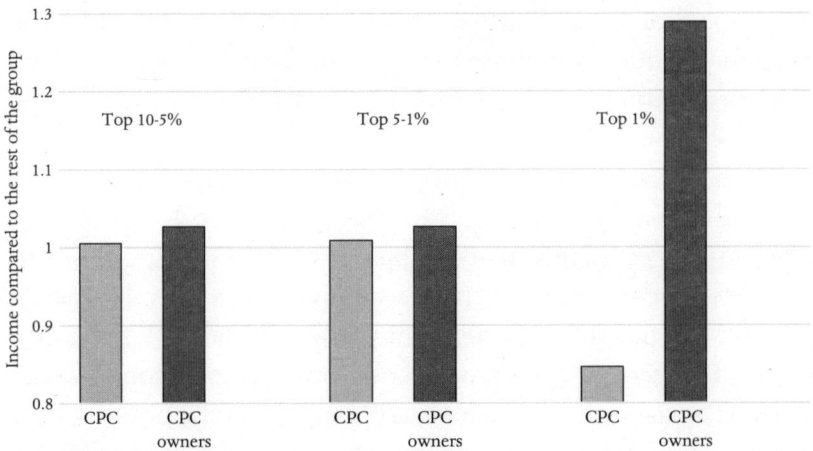

Figure 3.6. Relative income of CPC members and CPC members who are 'owners' (self-employed or large owners)[53]

Note: The graph shows the average relative income of CPC members (*CPC*) and CPC members who are self-employed or large owners (*CPC owners*), who are part of percentiles 91 to 95 (left), percentiles 96 to 99 (middle) and the top percentile (right) relative to the mean income of that group. Value of 1 indicates that the average income of a specific group is the same as the average income of the given percentile. All values refer to 2013.

What it means is the following: CPC membership is generally useful – the average premium from the membership as opposed to non-membership is about 5 per cent. But once a person is within the top income groups (for whatever reason), CPC membership no longer provides additional gain *except* in the case of large-scale capitalists, for whom that advantage varies between 29 and 34 per cent.[54]

The ranking of those who are members of the top 1 per cent is then as follows: the richest are capitalists with CPC membership, the second richest are non-CPC members, and the least rich (among that very elite group) are CPC members from other (non-capitalist) social classes. One can therefore conclude that CPC members who are very rich are now fewer in number (their participation in the top groups is less than in the past); they are also, at the very top, equally rich compared to their non-Party peers *except* when they combine CPC membership with private sector ownership, and the larger that ownership, the more valuable the membership.

This is, I think, the key conclusion. CPC membership is a credential. But it does not help one to do better equally, irrespective of one's social groups. The value of the credential is particularly high for the individuals who own businesses. This is the essence of the new ruling class in China: CPC membership provides a (political) credential, akin to educational achievement in the West, and that credential is particularly valuable when combined with one's own capitalist or entrepreneurial position. For the people who live in a world of concepts, and not reality, the fact that the membership of the Communist Party of China is especially valuable for capitalists might seem like a contradiction in terms. But in a de facto one-party system of state capitalism, membership in that one party (whatever its name) is important for business. However, as I will argue in Chapter 4, this feature may not be liked by all. It might present distinct dangers for the regime and there may be good political reasons for the rulers to curtail it.

Elite corruption. An important insight into the economic and political power of the new elite in China is provided by the anti-corruption campaign that began in 2012 with Xi Jinping's assumption of presidential power at both state and CPC level. The anti-corruption campaign targeted not only petty corruption (the so-called flies) but also the richer and more powerful, especially those with high positions in the Communist Party (the so-called tigers). Thanks to the centralized nature of the anti-corruption campaign and publication of individual data regarding the accused, we can get a unique glimpse into the actual incomes of the elite that include both their legal and illegal sources.

The campaign is conducted by the Central Committee's Directorate of Inspection (CCDI), which is a permanent organ of the Communist Party of China's Central Committee. In some ways, the CCDI can be seen as the modern successor to the censorate institutions of the Ming and Qing dynasties.[55] The CCDI's top officials are selected for five-year terms to coincide with those of the Central Committee members. Inspection and control are its permanent functions, but over the last decade the CCDI was put into action more than ever before. By May 2021, a total of over 4 million cadres and officials had been investigated, with 3.7 million of them having been found guilty and punished.[56]

The campaign attracted attention by political analysts worldwide not only because of its size but because people who were previously considered 'untouchable' were found guilty of bribery or misutilization of funds and put in jail. The most important examples include Zhou Yongkang, member of the Politburo's Standing Committee (consisting of seven people only), and Xu Caihou, Vice-Chairman of the Central Military Commission. The campaign was also questioned because of its possible political use by Xi Jinping as a way to sideline or punish opponents.

Utilizing the data systematically compiled from individual conviction cases and regularly updated on the CCDI website, a database of senior Chinese officials found guilty of corruption during the period 2012–21 was created by Li Yang, Yaoqi Lin and myself.[57] The dataset includes detailed information for 828 cases of crimes of corruption referring to 686 convicted individuals (some individuals are accused and convicted of more than one crime).

The accused and convicted (the two are interchangeable because all individuals included in the database have been found guilty) are categorized by the CCDI in order of importance, as Centrally Managed Cadres, Provincially Managed Cadres and Central-Level Cadres. Centrally managed cadres are the most senior officials (e.g., central- or provincial-level ministers). They may be considered as a national-level CPC nomenklatura. Provincially managed cadres are the same except at the level of provinces (they may be mayors or CPC city secretaries), and the third group includes somewhat less important officials, mostly those working in, or managing, SOEs and state institutions (hospitals, schools and courts). They can be, for simplicity, referred to as respectively national, provincial and local/SOE nomenklatura. It should be noted that centrally managed cadres can be, and generally are, appointed to the positions of authority at the provincial or lower level. There is thus a difference between the cadre level and the administrative level at which a cadre operates. For example, a national nomenklatura member can be appointed to be a minister in a province. All are, however, 'tigers' in the language used in the anti-corruption campaign.

The CCDI provides detailed information on each accused, with their demographics (name, gender, age, birthplace), education level and major of studies, employment information (geographical location of the workplace, the year of initiation and termination of the most recent job, administrative level of the job) and Party-related information (year of CPC membership, attendance of the ideologically oriented Central Party School).

There are several crimes of which defendants are accused. Here I focus only on the accusations (and convictions) for corruption, which include bribery, embezzlement of public funds and dereliction of duty in order to make material gain. The amounts of money or the overall monetary equivalent that was embezzled (because some of the illicit gains were made in the form of gold, paintings, jewellery, etc. and are converted into yuan) are provided for each individual defendant.

Not surprisingly, the amount of corruption increases with the cadre level. Members of the national-level nomenklatura have been convicted of embezzling more than 4.5 times as much per case as members of the provincial nomenklatura, and more than three times as much as those of the local nomenklatura (inclusive of SOE managers for whom corruption seems to be especially lucrative). To provide an idea of the amounts in question: the centrally managed cadres were accused, on average, of $14.1 million of corruption, provincial nomenklatura of $2.8 million and the local nomenklatura of $4.3 million (all expressed in 2018 US dollars and using the 2018 exchange rates). While by the share of the number of cases of corruption, the provincial nomenklatura dominates (two-thirds of corruption cases are due to them), much greater amounts of corruption per case for the national nomenklatura mean that almost two-thirds of total corruption, measured in money terms, is attributable to the centrally managed cadres (Figure 3.7).

The median age of the person convicted of corruption is fifty-eight, and the median number of years of CPC membership is thirty-four. There is a noticeable absence of older people (many of them are retired, and less likely to be troubled by investigation even if they might have been involved in some corruption in the past) and younger people whose positions are probably not high enough to 'deserve' (or attract) much corruption. The distribution by age is also reflected in the year when the defendants joined the CPC: 75 per cent of defendants joined the Party before 1988, and 87 per cent before, and including, 1992. This means that 13 per cent (100 minus 87)

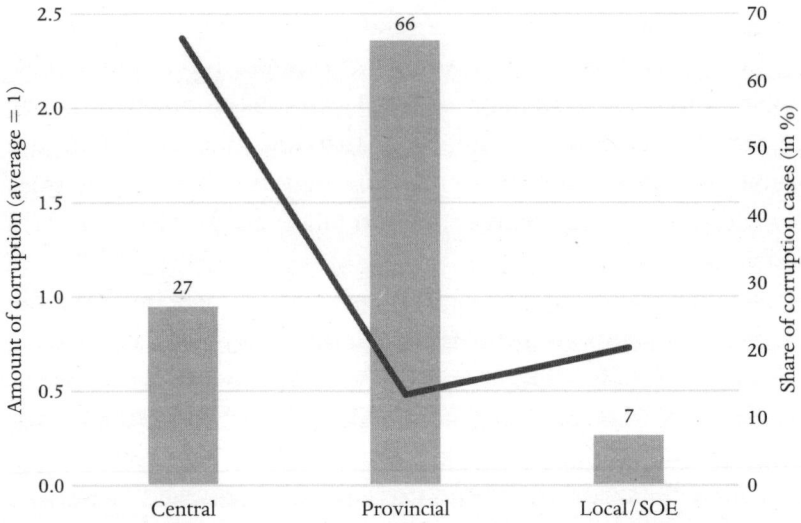

Figure 3.7. China: average amount of corruption (line) and the percentage of cases of corruption (column) by CCDI classification of cadre level[58]

Note: The graph shows the amount of corruption per case (on the left vertical axis) normalized by the overall mean. Thus the value of almost 2.5 for the nationally managed cadres means that the average amount of corruption of which they are accused is almost 2.5 times the mean. The right vertical axis shows the percentage of cases of corruption. That number is also displayed on the top of each column.

joined the Party during the leadership of Xi Jinping's two predecessors. Practically nobody among the defendants joined the Party after 2012 when Xi Jinping became the President of China and head of the Party.

The fact that there is relevant individual information (which is compatible with the information provided in Chinese household surveys) allows us to estimate the legal income of those convicted of corruption. With their legal income alone, they belong to the higher parts of the Chinese urban income distribution: more than half of them would be in the top 5 per cent of urban earners; 6 per cent would be among the 'top 1 percenters'. The person with the median legal income among the defendants has an income that is 3.2 times greater than the Chinese median urban income. We can thus confirm that our sample deals with rich urbanites, or the 'tigers'.

But because the amounts of corrupt income are so large, defendants' total income is, thanks to corruption, at the median, between four to six times greater than their legal earnings. The defendants thus climb to the very top of the urban income distribution. When illegal income is included, 82 per cent of them are among the urban 'top 1 percenters' and almost all are in the top 5 per cent.

The amounts of corruption are themselves heavily concentrated, much more so than earnings or disposable income. The top 10 per cent of cases account for 58 per cent of total corruption; the equivalent share for the top decile of disposable income in urban China is 33 per cent. The concentrated nature of corruption and the fact that it further benefits the people with the top urban incomes shows that corruption, in its revealed part, is an important contributor to Chinese urban inequality.

To give an idea of the actual incomes of the elite compared to the rest of the urban population, and compared to those who do not engage in corruption, let us summarize the findings: if the median urban income is denoted by 1, the median legal income of corrupted CPC 'tigers' is 3.2, and the median overall (legal plus illegal) income of such individuals is between 13 and 19. As mentioned, 82 per cent of corrupt officials are in the top 1 per cent. Indirect evidence from the anti-corruption campaign thus shows that the top of the Chinese income distribution is much richer than what appears from surveys or tax data. We must also take into account the fact that CCDI data cover only CPC cadres; if a private entrepreneur, whether a Party member or not, engages in corruption, such information will not be included in the CCDI database. Thus, the extent of corruption and its contribution to inequality is almost surely greater than what we can establish using CCDI data only.

Why the elites matter. The power of the new elites in the United States and China is reflected in the many indicators we have considered in this chapter. But it may be worth showing what it seems to imply for social mobility. Indeed, if the elites are strongly established and desire to transmit their advantages across generations, we can expect that social mobility will gradually be reduced. The elites will reproduce themselves. In recent research, economists Roy van der Weide and Ambar Narayan have indeed found declining relative educational mobility in both countries. Comparing the generations born in the 1950s, 1960s, 1970s and 1980s, their results show that mobility was high among the 1950s generation in China that came of age during the Cultural Revolution (Figure 3.8). This is not surprising, given how turbulent those times were (nor is high educational mobility under such circumstances necessarily good). Afterwards, educational mobility steadily went down, reaching for the generation born in the 1980s the level of mobility of the 1950s generation in the US. American mobility similarly declined for each additional cohort from the levels of the 1950s, but not as much as it went down in China. In the latter, as the graph shows, it virtually plummeted. Elite dominance was translated in both countries into a stronger connection between educational attainment of parents and children and thus in inter-generational transmission of elite privileges.

Some evidence of an inter-generational elite connection is provided by a quick look at the very top of the political pyramid in the two countries (Figure 3.9). In the past forty years, in the United States, a son of a president became president himself (together they ruled for twelve years). Another president's wife (Hillary Clinton)

The Elites

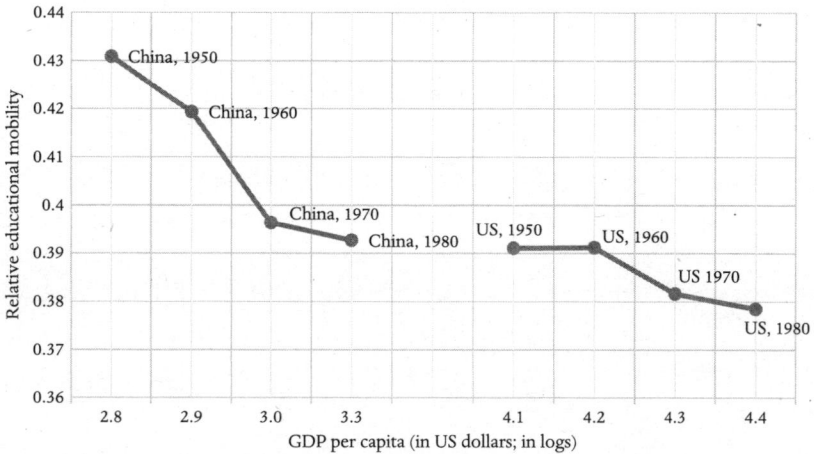

Figure 3.8. Educational mobility in China and the United States[59]

Note: The figure shows relative educational mobility (the expected rank of a child, in the child education distribution, whose parents are in the bottom 50 per cent of the parents' education rank distribution) on the vertical axis, and the level of GDP per capita (in logs) on the horizontal axis. Value of (say) 0.4 on the vertical axis means that the child is located at the 40th percentile of income distribution.

became Secretary of State, New York senator and (unsuccessful) presidential candidate. The current US president used to share the same social circle with the Clintons (to the extent of being invited to the wedding of their only child) and was a significant donor to the senatorial campaign of Hillary Clinton, whom he later, and unrelatedly, defeated in the 2016 presidential election. In China, the two most important competitors for the top CPC position in 2012 were both 'princelings', with fathers (Bo Yibo and Xi Zhongxun) who had direct connections to Mao, and with both fathers being purged during the Cultural Revolution. Yet, the fathers' friendship with Deng Xiaoping was crucial to them being reinstated to high positions in the 1980s. Deng also knew both sons. Xi Jinping's father was moreover friends with Jiang Zemin, President of China and head of the Party for ten years, who also helped Xi Jinping's career. We thus notice here too an extremely tight relationship that, like in the United States, combines nepotism with belonging to the same social circle.

The Great Global Transformation

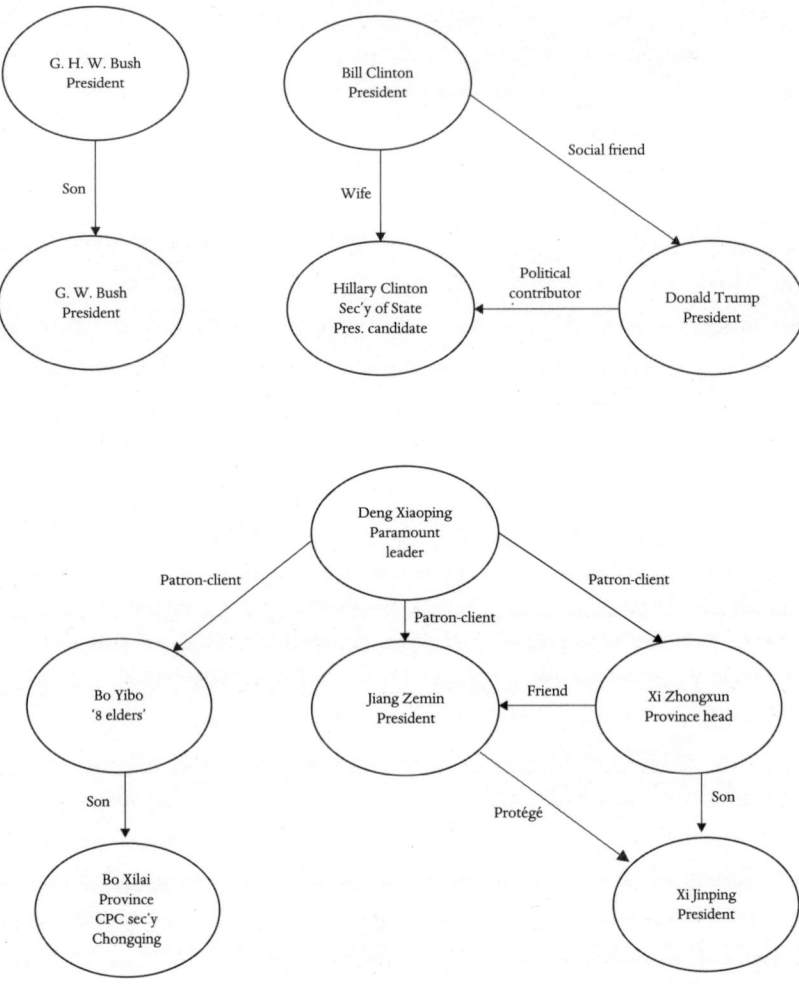

Figure 3.9. Political elite interrelationships in the United States and China

The career relationship of Bo Xilai and Xi Jinping is structurally very similar to that of Hillary Clinton and Donald Trump. Both duos knew each other for at least several decades: Bo and Xi from their early years when they lived in the special compounds in Beijing reserved for high bureaucracy; Hillary Clinton and Donald Trump from their more mature age when they socialized in New York. Both then turned against each other and fought for the highest office in the land; one lost – in the Chinese case the loser ended up in jail (after a big scandal including bribery and possible murder), in the US case, in political irrelevance and bitterness. This difference of fates summarizes a difference in the political systems, although precisely what that difference is can be for the reader to judge.

The folksy nature of elites. When we look at the two most important elites in today's world – American and Chinese – we see not only how they have changed in the era of globalization, by having become richer than their average compatriot (which has been noted many times and is evident from a simple observation that measures of inequality like the Gini coefficient have risen in both countries), but also how the origin of their incomes and their position in the system of social reproduction has evolved. They are both new elites, in that they epitomize the new capitalism which is in some respects more elitist than traditional Western capitalism, and in the case of China, obviously more elitist than the Communist Party nomenklatura of the Maoist era that went through many perturbations. The top class is now more elitist and its position more impregnable because it has, in the United States, 'diversified' by being very rich in terms of both labour and capital incomes. Similarly, in China, it includes rich capitalists and many from the professional-managerial class. Chinese homoploutia, even if less than in the United States, is significant and rising.[60] In both countries, high incomes go together with credentialism: educational status in the United States, membership of the CPC in China. The coupling of high income and credentialism imbues the elite with a significant dose of self-confidence. It comes from the feeling that their position in society is reflective of their higher intellectual and moral worth. It makes them similar to the aristocratic elites that likewise combined high income with credentialism of aristocratic titles, and conviction of one's own superiority. The bases of these new classes' superiority, like their monetary bases of wealth, are different, but the feeling of deserving the wealth is not. Since the new elites do not shun labour and value work as an indicator of intellectual superiority, they are at the same time more 'folksy'. They do not shy away from working seventy hours a week, or, if needed and in order to garner publicity, from doing some menial labour. The abhorrence of manual labour that was common to the traditional elites, both in the West and in Asia, is alien to them. They work hard, boast of working hard, believe they could work even harder, and find in work both pleasure and a sign of having been chosen.

4.
National Market Liberalism

The goal of this chapter is to look at the forces that are trying to check the rise to power of the moneyed elites in the United States and China, and to some extent in Russia. The rise of these new elites since globalization began was, as argued in Chapter 3, connected with global neoliberal policies that not only resulted in higher inequality and accumulation of various advantages by the same people, but also emphasized ideologically the acquisition of wealth as the main objective of human activity. Wealth, therefore, became an implicit indicator of personal worth or virtue. Such neoliberalism has, in the West, led to a score of nefarious social outcomes: lower middle-class social mobility, higher rates of mortality and morbidity among the poor and the middle class, low economic growth for most, absence of spread of property among the middle classes, precariousness of jobs. But the rise of the new elites is present – and resented – in many parts of the world, not only in the West. The resentment of the wealthy, or the reaction to the fear of their excessive power, manifests itself worldwide in different ways. In the West, it is associated with the rise of populism; in China, with the strengthened role of the Communist Party; in Russia, with the rule of the security services. But in each of these cases, which to a casual observer seem so disparate, the goals of these new directions are the same: to push back against the accumulated power of the elite.

It is in this context that we should look at the politics of Donald Trump, Xi Jinping and Vladimir Putin. Their policies try to stem or control the rise to complete economic and political dominance of the moneyed elites, and to curb or reverse globalization seen as causally linked with their rise. In a word, their governments represent an attempt to reverse global neoliberalism. In the United States and many countries in Europe, this takes place through the so-called populist reaction. It manifests itself electorally by votes obtained by the right-wing 'populist' parties and their coming to power or playing a much more important political role. Their electoral and ideological base is composed of people who are excluded from the internationalist or liberal circles of the elite, and to whom globalization has brought little economic gain, while socially it lowered their position globally (Chapter 1) and, perhaps more importantly, lowered it subjectively, in their own eyes. In China, the anti-rich reaction took the form of the reinforcement of the power of the Party's bureaucracy over the new capitalist class whose importance, both in size and relative income, has expanded spectacularly (Chapter 3). Xi's turn to the left is directed against the policies of his two predecessors who admitted more capitalists to the top decision-making bodies of the Party. Instead of the Party setting limits to what capitalists can do, the opposite became a real danger: the Party could be used as the instrument of control by the rich. To stop that, Xi Jinping began an anti-corruption campaign (Chapter 3) and unambiguously restated the leading role of the Party. Finally, in Russia, the reaction against the wealthy oligarchs took the form of the re-establishment of control by secret services over the moneyed elite that arose in Yeltsin's Russia. The objective of Putin's famous 'reinforcement of the vertical of power' of the early 2000s (i.e., concentration of power at the top) was to rein in the oligarchs. Some of them were exiled, a few assassinated, but all got the message that their enrichment was acceptable only if it was approved by the state, which increasingly meant the security services. During the war against Ukraine, Putin also began a large anti-corruption campaign that principally affected the notoriously corrupt military establishment, but spread to various federal and local officials. It is rather unusual to proceed to purge the military establishment in the midst of a war, but Putin probably believes that the losses through demoralization of the top cadre can be compensated by having a leaner and less corrupt war machine.[1]

National Market Liberalism

Despite their many differences caused by their different backgrounds, and the conditions of the countries they rule (or where they make their political career) – or even their own subjective perception of what they are doing – Trump, Xi Jinping and Putin internally followed the same logic: check or break the new globalized elite. These policies, depending on the country, have different ideological components. In the United States, populism has a strong anti-liberal, anti-elite, anti-migrant and at times racist strand; in China, it is a (mild) return to Maoism tempered by nationalism; in Russia, it is nationalism with conservative ideological elements plucked from tsarist Russia and Stalin's rule. But in all cases, the objective is the same: constrain, push back, break the moneyed elite and reverse its ideological hegemony. This is why the struggle has not only economic and political aspects but also an ideological goal. Trump speaks of bicoastal elites, Xi gives examples of communist discipline and self-abnegation, Putin targets 'traitors'.

It is worth pointing out that Trump, Xi Jinping and Putin were themselves, as individuals, the products of the neoliberal era and each of them did very well in the atmosphere that held sway throughout the 1990s and the early 2000s. Trump was an entrepreneur who made money, often under dubious legal circumstances, in New York working in the three markets that had never been associated with probity: real estate, Miss Universe competitions and casinos. Xi Jinping made his career under the previous leaders (whose legacy he is now trying to overturn) and became powerful thanks to being a 'princeling' and thus enjoying the advantages he received from his father who was high up in the CPC hierarchy.[2] Putin came to power thanks to the oligarchs and in particular to Boris Berezovsky who believed that Putin, with his shy behaviour, sad eyes and downcast gaze, would be their malleable puppet. Putin gave them all the right indications that he would be, and in the most foul climate of Yeltsin's decomposing Russia, he was awarded the top post by the grace of some of the most corrupt people among the oligarchs. Thus, each of these three leaders came from within the system of wealth accumulation and power of the rich they are now fighting to control. And each of them, like Moses in reaction to the Pharaohs, lashed out at those who brought him to power, not only for personal reasons but because he found a willing audience that would follow him and yield him power. Trump, accidentally, found his audience in the nationalistic xenophobic wing of the Republican Party; Xi Jinping found his audience in the conservative elements of the Communist Party of China; Putin found his audience in the secret services of Russia. Each of these constituencies reacted and fought against the new and seemingly unstoppable rise of the elite: liberal in the US, capitalistic in China, oligarchic in Russia. In this chapter I will discuss the broad outlines and meanings of Trump's and Xi Jinping's policies, showing that they should be seen as part of the same 'counter-revolution' against global neoliberalism and the excesses of elite enrichment during the 1980–2006 era.[3]

The goal of the challengers. The current changes taking place in the world, both domestically and internationally, should be seen as a reaction to decades of domestic impacts from global neoliberalism and the domination of unipolarity. These two components defined the world from the end of the Cold War to approximately the Global Financial Crisis in 2008 or most definitely until Trump's election in 2016. The domestic component was attacked not only by Trump, Xi Jinping and Putin, but by many leaders of smaller countries. At the international level, the 'counter-revolution' translates into the attempt to put an end to the unipolar world and create a multipolar one. The multipolar world is not just the same neoliberal world with several geopolitical poles. Multipolarity, in the view of these leaders and ideologues close to them, includes not only a greater dispersal of global power, but – and this is key – the acceptance of the difference in the domestic bases of legitimacy. To put it clearly, this is a rejection of liberal democracy as the only acceptable principle according to which societies ought to be organized. And similarly, also rejected is the idea of a unipolar dream world where all countries are liberal democracies and there is a single hegemon. Global unipolar neoliberalism is thus being challenged in both of its defining features: the acquired power of the elite is to be curbed and different political systems are to be accepted as legitimate. Externally, unipolarity is to be replaced by multipolarity.

The question is whether this challenge will succeed. It is important to realize what this challenge is not. It is not an attempt to replace global neoliberalism by another global system that would apply to all. The challengers are defensive. Their goal is that they themselves be allowed to practise a different system domestically and to have a say in international councils. They are aiming at the 'Rawlsian accommodation': obliging the neoliberal regimes to accept challengers' domestic legitimacy and to negotiate with them internationally. It is therefore wrong to assume, as some commentators do, that the so-called Autocracy Inc. has an objective similar to global neoliberalism: namely, to extend its rule across the globe. The new regimes are not sufficiently strong to be able to do that, and moreover being nationalistic, every attempt towards internationalization would soon backfire and end in a clash between two or several such autocratic or illiberal regimes. Nationalistic regimes, by their very 'constitution' or ideologies, cannot be effectively international or global. But they can rule parts of the globe, each individually – and together, as in an arithmetic summation – but nothing more.

The attempt to undermine global neoliberalism may ultimately fail. The elites created by the neoliberal policies over the past forty years are strongly entrenched and in many areas they enjoy intellectual and cultural hegemony. They cannot be removed easily. They will fight back. What seems most likely, and the rest of this chapter will discuss, is that the counter-revolution, as often in history, will be only partially successful. Global neoliberal hegemony may be terminally weakened, but the ideological hegemony of neoliberalism, especially in the economic sphere domestically, may be preserved. Its internationalism and global pretence will be gone, though. It will be transformed into national liberalism that at first sight, knowing that liberalism always was internationalist, may seem a contradiction in terms. But similar transformations happened with socialism; its international prefix was replaced by national, and such a system, national socialism or 'socialism in one country', gained widespread popular support in half-a-dozen of the most advanced and populous countries. The same may happen now: American and European global neoliberalism will be shorn of its international aspect, and become simply neoliberalism applied to the domestic market. It will be *national market liberalism* or, for short, *national liberalism*.

National market liberalism

The fall of the global neoliberal order and the birth of national market liberalism

The global neoliberal order has two components that can be analytically separated, but in any historical investigation must be looked at together. The first is the 'global' component best reflected in the 'rules-based global liberal order', which are the rules imposed by the political West. An inseparable part of these rules is a unipolar world that is hierarchically structured with the United States at the top, subimperial powers like the UK, France, Australia and Japan on the second rung, and all the way down to protectorates, vassals and small countries – a system that we'll explore later in this chapter. It is the current Western view of the world, as discussed in Chapter 2, as one of the four ideational divisions (column 1, Table 2.4). That part of the global neoliberal order was put under stress by the rise of China and other geopolitical changes that we have seen in Chapter 1. As argued there, the very rise of China and its inability to fit into that global order made it inevitable that the order, and thus the rules of globalization, would be changed.

The second part of the neoliberal order involves the domestic economic and political order. As Gary Gerstle writes in his excellent review of the rise and fall of the neoliberal order in the United States, an ideology becomes an 'economic order' only when it is acquiesced, or accepted by, large parts of the electorate and the most important parts of the political establishment. Even the

National Market Liberalism

parties and the groups that previously held different views come to accept this new thinking. Their acquiescence makes it an 'order'. In the case of the neoliberal order in America, this occurred, according to Gerstle, when Bill Clinton extended many of the neoliberal policies originally introduced by the Reagan administration.[4] It was, as Gerstle writes, an 'Eisenhower moment', referring to the time in the early 1950s when similarly Dwight Eisenhower, a Republican president, did not reverse the changes in capitalism introduced by Roosevelt's New Deal. There were thus two 'great' economic and political orders in the United States: the New Deal that lasted from 1932 to 1980, and the neoliberal order that lasted from 1980 to 2016.

The main features of the neoliberal order, which intellectually goes back to the Walter Lippmann Colloquium and the Mont Pèlerin Society (i.e., to the late 1930s and early 1950s), have been described extensively and need not detain us here.[5] In the shortest terms, they can be described, philosophically, as a striving for greater personal freedom clear of government interference, and economically, as a desire to increase the role of the markets even to the extent that they would infringe on the areas that were traditionally excluded from it (like family and personal relations). Common to both is a reduction of government regulation, government power and government interference. Logically, if such a power has to be diminished, taxes, which are the source of government influence, have to be minimized.

Such an order has not been characteristic of the United States only, but has spread and been sustained by all advanced economies, and was similarly and almost contemporaneously extended to developing nations. Its worldwide counterpart is best summarized under the moniker of the Washington Consensus, originally designed for policy reforms in Latin America in the early 1980s but later applied to Eastern Europe and Central Asia (after the fall of communism) and Asia (after the financial crisis in 1998). Its main components were fiscal stabilization (meaning absence of government deficit), deregulation and privatization. Neoliberal policies were adopted hook, line and sinker after the fall of communism in almost all 'transition' countries. They spread to India in 1991 with the ending of the 'Licence Raj' under Manmohan Singh's government. They have been advised or imposed by the IMF and World Bank Structural Adjustment Lending (SAL) in Latin America and Africa. The introduction of SALs in the mid-1980s by the World Bank is even more indicative of the ideological and political climate of the times than the more widely known IMF programmes. The objective of the latter was always to squeeze government domestic spending so that more money will be left to repay foreign creditors. The IMF acted, in the past as well as under neoliberalism, as a debt-collecting agency for rich countries and private lenders. So its role did not change. But SALs were a signal departure from the hitherto forty-year-old practice of the World Bank to lend only for individual projects, and to be ostensibly politically neutral. Here, however, the World Bank, for the first time, was lending while asking in return for a commitment to neoliberal structural reforms, including deregulation and privatization. This would have been unthinkable had not neoliberal precepts become accepted not only in the United States but almost everywhere in the world.

The inclusion of China in that project was gradual: from the early agricultural reforms in 1978, to privatization of state-owned enterprises in the early 1990s, to accession to the WTO in 2001. China, however, never altered its domestic set-up to entirely reflect the desiderata of neoliberalism, as it maintained a much stronger state than in advanced economies and allowed a much greater role for state-owned economic enterprises. Yet many of the effects associated with neoliberalism, including the creation of a new elite (as we have seen in Chapter 3), have not bypassed China.

The decline of neoliberalism in the United States began with the Global Financial Crisis of 2008. The crisis's most significant ideological and later political outcome was the realization, by significant groups of the US population, that income gains from the neoliberal project were very unevenly distributed, and that the costs of the crisis were even more inequitably shared. Both parts of that realization are important. The first part is easily documentable by looking at real income growth rates along different parts of the US income distribution. We have seen it in Chapter 2 (Figure 2.1). This rising inequality might have been less of a problem had the overall growth been higher; but with real income growth below 1 per cent per capita annually for two-thirds of the population and with top incomes rising at almost thrice that rate, high inequality was resented more. And it was felt with particular acuity when the ability to borrow ended with the financial crisis in 2008. The second inequity (unfair distributions of the costs of the crisis) simply reflected the difference in political power. It was not only that the rich did much better from neoliberal globalization, it was also – it dawned on many – that these original gains were made thanks to their control of the political process. This was very obviously revealed as the crisis unfolded and its costs (unemployment, foreclosures, asset losses) had to be paid: many were borne by the middle and lower-middle classes.

The decline in the longer term. The decline of neoliberalism can be seen in a longer-term context too. One way to view it is in a Polanyian framework. Market excesses reached their apogee, and that led to 'society' (which is not a very precise term even if often used by Polanyi) fighting against them and rejecting them. Indeed, it could be argued that during the peak of neoliberalism the greatest commodification ever in history, of the 'fictitious commodities' of labour, land and money, occurred. We can see marketization, as Polanyi describes it, allegorically as an alien excrescence that the body social rejects. The story of *The Great Transformation* follows this pattern. The story of the decline, and perhaps the fall, of neoliberalism follows it, in parts, too.

However, the difference between the contemporary United States and the situation that Polanyi takes as paradigmatic – that of early-nineteenth-century England – is very large. Not only is the level of overall income and wealth much greater in the United States, but so also is the support available to the poor. Certainly, one can see the record-breaking US incarceration rates as playing the same role that in-house poverty relief played during the Industrial Revolution: large groups of people who could not find their place in a fully marketized system were taken out of it, by being forced to work either in prisons or in prison-like workhouses. (One can push the analogy even further and see the Soviet Gulag as a similar way to force the recalcitrant population, rejecting industrialization, into camps of forced labour.) Yet the extensive system of unemployment benefits, Medicaid, retirement savings plans, etc. available to all in the United States above the lumpenproletariat held in jails did not exist in the much poorer environment of the Industrial Revolution. This is a significant difference despite the formal similarity between the early marketization and neoliberalism.

The reaction to neoliberalism may, probably more fruitfully, be seen in the context in which it is situated by a couple of recent books, most notably Krishnan Nayar's *Liberal Capitalist Democracy* and Thomas Piketty's *Capital in the Twenty-First Century*. Both argue, although they give different reasons why, that capitalism left to itself, unmoored from social norms or government intervention, will tend to produce social instability. Both Nayar and Piketty think that the period of labour–capital reconciliation and cooperation that had characterized the New Deal order was a temporary aberration brought about by the triumph of socialism in the Soviet Union and the strength of the leftist political parties and trade unions linked to communist and socialist parties in the West.[6] Under pressure, capitalists agreed to share more income with trade unions and accepted increased government oversight so long as their property rights were protected and secure.

For Nayar, the mechanism is social Darwinism. Unbridled capitalism is Darwinian: the strongest survive, the weak are destroyed. This leads to social instability and anomie, which in turn empower right-wing parties that offer commonality instead of atomization, protection instead of competition. Capitalism, in Nayar's telling, if not embedded in society and if not accepting limits on what can be commodified, necessarily goes through recurrent periods of slump and prosperity.[7] But these two cannot be seen just as a plus and a minus that cancel each other out. Their political effects are very different. This is where Nayar takes to task many economists who saw the 1929–32 Depression as a cleansing period of capitalism eventually bound to result in a boom; and by analogy those who saw the 2008 financial crisis as a temporary anomaly whose political effects would soon be erased by renewed economic growth. The point, however, is that in politics we deal with real people and not mere numbers: many people are unwilling or unable to wait until the boom comes. They may not even be around for its coming. They vote for radical solutions or go out in the street. This is something often forgotten by economists, who treat individuals' incomes over the longer term as a mathematical summation without realizing that the political effects of the minuses are very different from those of the pluses. One such example that Nayar uses is Hitler's rise to power, which was made possible, or was even caused, by the 1929–32 Depression. The analogy can again be carried over to 2008. Nayar's argument is more expansive than the assumption that austerity policies are either responsible (or synonymous) with the right-wing reaction. Austerity policies have indeed their class component, which is the disciplining of labour. But Nayar believes that focusing only on austerity is not sufficient.[8] Capitalism itself, if its Darwinian aspect (survival of the fittest, and poverty for those who cannot succeed in a market economy) is left unchecked, is bound to produce anomie and then societal reaction.

Piketty's view of the inherent instability of capitalism is more grounded in economics, namely in the possibility that the rate of profit will, despite large increases in the accumulated capital, remain at a high level, above the average rate of growth of the economy (this is the famous $r > g$ relation, which means that the rate of return to capital, r, an income received by rich capitalists, will exceed the rate of income growth for an average person, g, and thus lead to higher inequality). If that relation persists for a sufficiently long time, inequality must, almost by definition, increase. There is then only a question of at what point such inequality begins to be socially unsustainable. Piketty's advocacy of higher tax rates on capital and on the rich is, according to him, the only way to break, in peacetime conditions, the logical chain that goes from concentrated capital ownership, to high returns to capital, to an ever increasing accumulation of capital, and thus to ever higher inequality.[9]

It is often argued that the decadence of the neoliberal order in the United States has led to two reactions and to two possible ideological claimants for succession. The right-wing populist reaction that was given coherence (if one can say so) and political importance by Donald Trump, and the left-wing populist reaction exemplified by Elizabeth Warren's and Bernie Sanders's policies. The question then becomes: if the neoliberal order is domestically at its end run, what type of new order will succeed it?

If one focuses on Trump as a person whose policies defined that reaction, the question to ask is, which of Trump's supporters' ideologies are compatible with the neoliberal order and represent its continuation, and which are not, and represent the break? Perhaps one should not overdo the dialectics here, but there seems to be a synthesis between the components that are part of the 'old' (meaning neoliberal) order and components that are new (even if they can go back to the ideologies that pre-date the modern neoliberal order).

National market liberalism. When discussing Trump and interpreting what he might, or does, represent, we run into two problems. The first is that Trump's recombination of ideas is not conventional and cannot be easily put into one ideologically recognizable box. Trump's own volatility and knee-jerk reactions make classification even more difficult. The second problem derives from the interpreter's side. We do not know what shape the successor order to neoliberal capitalism will take – it could go from neoliberal reinforcement, say super neoliberalism, to its total repudiation, passing through the most likely combination of parts from different ideologies – so that what might appear odd and unclassifiable in Trump may be due more to our unfamiliarity with the components of the new order. This problem is intensified by the absence of ideological preparation for the Trumpist order such as happened before the neoliberal project became dominant: as mentioned, ideological preparations of the neoliberal order go back some forty years before Thatcher and Reagan applied neoliberalism in practice. We do not, at least for now, see similar preparations having gone into Trumpism; although that might change in the future as some of the intellectual antecedents to the ideas of the new order become more recognizable.[10]

It is wrong, in addition, to link the shape of this future project to Trump. His political future is uncertain, but the dissatisfaction as well as a peculiar ideological mélange that Trump defined is not going to go away regardless of what happens to the man himself. Individuals certainly matter in history, but deep economic and political currents and subcurrents matter at least as much. After four years of Trump's first presidency, policies that, in the beginning, appeared unusual have been adopted by the rest of the body politic. They remained, and were even developed, post-Trump I. Thus the new political and economic order is already here. Trump's second administration is continuing along the same path, and even accelerating the change.

When Trump waged a trade war with China in 2017, it was an unusual idea with very little prior support from the political class. It has since become more broadly defined, more elaborate in content, and accepted across the entire American, and increasingly European, political spectrum. It has an economic component (China is responsible for the decline of the American middle classes), military interest (US security in Asia is jeopardized by China's rise) and political or values-driven agenda (China is run by a dictatorial regime). The last two parts were 'developed' after Trump left office in 2021, a further confirmation of the near universal acceptance of this new thinking.

Recourse to trade wars or sanctions of individual entities or persons expanded under Trump – for instance, the reintroduction of a tough sanction regime against Cuba, increased sanctions against Iran and Venezuela – but that policy was not discontinued under President Biden. In fact, nothing changed either in policies with respect to Cuba, Iran and Venezuela, while a multitude of new sanctions were introduced against Russia, China, North Korea, Yemen and other nations. As of August 2024, the United States had thirty-eight different sanction regimes that affect some fifty countries, and probably thousands of individuals. Economic coercion is now considered a normal part of the international economic policy toolkit.

The mercantilist approach to foreign trade and the view of markets as solely the terrains of contestation and combat is something that we can define as a 'businessman' view of economics: it sees economic activity as a permanent struggle; and does not see the 'invisible hand' of the market that reconciles various interests. The businessman view is now much more widely shared than a decade ago. The influential *Financial Times* commentator and writer Rana Foroohar gave it a veneer of respectability in her 2022 book *Homecoming*; new mercantilism is promoted by influential circles in the United States and the European Union, often under the guise of the need for greater geopolitical or military security. Bradford DeLong, a former US undersecretary of the Treasury under Bill Clinton, has come out defending industrial policies on the basis of national security, even using, out of context, Adam Smith's statement that 'defence is much more important than opulence'.[11] 'Friend-shoring' favours investments in politically friendly countries and de facto divides the world into competing trade blocs, not different in any essential way from the division of the world into economic blocs that reached its peak in the inter-war period. 'Friend-shoring' is Commonwealth Imperial Preferences or Japan's Co-prosperity Zone that dares not speak its real name.

What people who are arguing for such policies forget is that the 180-degree turn in Western policies regarding protectionism, trade blocs, industrial policy and economic coercion has international consequences. The entire post-1945 system of Bretton Woods institutions was set around the principles of free trade. Until the massive trade liberalizations in 1980, it did not exclude the use of tariffs and other protective measures but this had to be done within an international framework (first GATT, then WTO). With the ascendancy of the Washington Consensus, economic policies became further liberalized. It will therefore be difficult, if not impossible, to explain to the rest of the world that the entire post-1945 system ought to be revised. Should, for example, the World Bank suggest to Nigeria that it should increase tariffs and join a trade bloc? Or differently, if a country does exactly that and the World Bank still argues for trade liberalization, how seriously can the World Bank argue for it while the US and Europe are raising tariffs and creating trade blocs? Given the pre-eminent importance of the political West in the design and running of international organizations, a change towards national market liberalism cannot be looked at solely from the domestic angle, as if the previous neoliberal policies can be continued in other countries as before. The change in trade policies among the most powerful countries will inevitably have repercussions for the rest of the world, not only economic but also ideological. One would need to define a new global paradigm for international organizations like the World Bank and the IMF. National market liberalism, by putting the accent on 'national', is ill-equipped to do so.

The idea, and execution, of limiting immigration and increasing deportation is not exclusive to Trump. By speaking about it ceaselessly he has made it enter the political lexicon. The wall against Mexico continued to be built after Trump left office the first time, while children were still held in cages. Now, 'walling oneself off' from the rest of the world has become a politically acceptable approach globally. EU boats patrol the Mediterranean where about 3,000 people die annually while trying to cross to Europe (the statistics are intentionally vague); walls against immigrants have been erected on the Turko-Greek and Hungaro-Serbian borders. The EU's approach is uniquely schizophrenic: it prides itself on being a multicultural and multinational union, but holds it acceptable to build walls and electric fences on its borders. Trump's anti-immigration stance has not differed from that of Theresa May when she was the Home Secretary and prime minister in the UK or Giorgia Meloni in Italy (who is building in Albania camps for immigrants imprisoned by Italian authorities similar to the prisons in El Salvador to which the Trump administration sends unwanted migrants).

Trump's ethno-nationalism that in the US context means anti-black and anti-Latino policies is shared (as against 'their' minorities) by numerous European political parties, from the Finns Party in

Finland to the Freedom Party in the Netherlands, Le Pen's Rassemblement National in France and Vox in Spain, among others. It is when we put these ideas together (tariff wars, sanctions as a way to conduct economic policy, trade blocs, halt to immigration, and ethno-nationalism) that we can better appreciate that the new ideological package 'proposed' by Trump is not just his own but is similar or the same as the 'packages' already applied by many in the political West. And these 'many' are not just the so-called populist parties: smaller or larger parts of the 'package' have been appropriated by the mainstream parties too.

A new set of political beliefs, unrelated to whether Trump is in power or not, has been created, and is likely to remain long after he is gone. One can see this clearly by listing four areas that are each in direct opposition to neoliberal ideas: (i) instead of globalization, there are tariff wars and economic exclusion zones; (ii) instead of economics being insulated from politics, there are politically motivated sanctions and state-led industrial policies;[12] (iii) instead of the aspiration to full mobility of people around the world, there are walls and fences; and (iv) instead of cosmopolitanism (as a desired ideology), there are openly nationalistic movements in positions of power.

There are also elements of neoliberalism that are likely to survive under this new ideological amalgam. It is, in Trump's case, as already mentioned, a businessman's approach to neoliberalism. It nevertheless has commonalities with standard neoliberalism: low taxation of high incomes and inheritance; tax preference given to incomes from capital vs incomes from labour; deregulation; limited state spending; no government interference in private matters (including rejection of the affirmative action, gender-related policies and other attempts to level the playing field between different groups).

The term that might be the most appropriate for this amalgam of ideas is *national market liberalism*. It includes parts of both classical liberal and neoliberal thinking when it comes to markets, but it rejects – or is at least sceptical about – other parts of the liberal project that include civil equality. Further, it rejects internationalism that was integral to both classical liberalism and neoliberalism. Of the four quadrants in Table 4.1 that in principle would hold for global neoliberalism, it retains only quadrant (1,1) and parts of quadrant (2,1), and rejects almost entirely quadrants (1,2) and (2,2). Hence, the prefix that I think indispensable is 'national'. It may be deemed inconsistent to append the term 'nationalist' to an ideology that was universalist, in favour of free global movement of goods, people, capital and technology. Quinn Slobodian in his excellent book *Globalists: The End of Empire and the Birth of Neoliberalism* traces the evolution of neoliberal thinking, and notes the distinction that its founders made – once they realized that the dream of a global neoliberal political federation is not achievable – between 'imperium' that deals with political, cultural and symbolic matters, and 'dominium', an internationally regulated economic system within which the symbolic 'imperium' is encased. The dominium ensured not only free movement of factors of production and goods and services, but also monetary stability and compatibility of legal norms. Liberals as well as neoliberals were always cosmopolitan or internationalist; their ambitions were not limited to one or two countries. The world as envisaged by fellow-Austrian political economists Ludwig von Mises and Friedrich Hayek was a borderless world. This is, as we have seen above, very far from the ideas that Trump and other challengers to neoliberalism have in mind.

	National level	International level
Economic	(1,1) Free market Profit-principle Strong property rights Low regulation Privatization	(1,2) Free movement of capital, goods and services Low tariffs Free and flexible exchange rates Aspirational free mobility of labour
Social	(2,1) Negative freedoms Positive (welfare state) freedoms Racial and gender equality Multiculturalism	(2,2) Aspirational social equality of all individuals

Table 4.1. Global neoliberalism and national market liberalism

The ideological amalgam that combines 'national' with an ideology that is fundamentally internationalist is not a novelty. National socialism put together, not only in words, but in deed, the two elements that were considered incompatible: socialism that was always internationalist, and nationalism. National socialism proved that such a combination was possible and enjoyed enormous political success. Stalin's 'socialism in one country' can also be placed in the same group of systems. There, however, a communist party jettisoned internationalism and adopted Russian, or probably more exactly Soviet, nationalism. Domestically, it remained socialist.

Socialism shorn of its internationalist component produced national socialism in its Hitlerite and Stalinist versions. Global neoliberalism shorn of its internationalist component gives us a vision of the new emerging consensus: *liberal policies limited to national markets and mercantilism abroad*. This also, I believe, convincingly proves that the critics of the new consensus are wrong to call it 'fascist'. Yes, it shares a nationalistic element with 'fascism', but not more so than mercantilist policies in general. But domestically, it eschews any socialistic element – nay, explicitly rejects them – and in that part it comes close to, or is indistinguishable from, neoliberalism.

Donald Trump and the nature of democratic politics

As Trump enters history, many pundits are reviewing the reasons that brought him to power, his two presidencies, and are trying to guess what his legacy may be. Many such assessments are trivial, turgid and tedious. He is being reviled for his callousness, racism, xenophobia, arrogance, inefficiency, ineffectiveness, ignorance. Many who will defend him will probably do so for the same reasons: because for them xenophobia, racism and arrogance may be considered virtues, not deep moral flaws.

My assessment is entirely different. First, where I think Trump was right, and second, what Trump allowed us to learn regarding both US politics and business.

Trump was right in the essential principles of foreign policy:

America First and mild isolationism. One ought to realize that there are only two possible foreign policies for the United States of America: American exceptionalism and America First. American exceptionalism is, as the name suggests, based on an ideology of American pre-eminence, held to be earned and deserved on account of the unique *virtu* of the new republic. Pre-eminence for the USA clearly implies a structured hierarchical system of countries where the USA is at the top and other countries play subsidiary and inferior roles. The ultimate unspoken objective of that policy is the mastery of the world.[13] The US is not the first country to have entertained such dreams: from Egypt, Rome, the Christian Empire of Byzantium, the Muslim Empire, Charlemagne, the Huns, Tamerlane, Napoleon, Hitler, the Communist Empire of the USSR, the list is long. While achieving such an empire is most unlikely, the road to that objective is paved with wars. This is why the ideology of the 'indispensable nation' almost by definition calls, in Gore Vidal's terms, for 'perpetual war for perpetual peace'. It is not by some accident that America has been at practically uninterrupted war for seventy years.

America First at least formally puts all countries on the same level. It argues that America will follow its own interests but it does not expect less from others. As Trump, not a scholar of international relations, stated in his 2019 United Nations speech, he would expect the same approach, as regards their own countries, to be followed by everybody from Algeria to Zimbabwe. In the generalized *My own country first* policy, the US will always, because of its size and importance, punch more than the rest, but it will have no desire to (or illusion that it has to) rule others or tell them how they should order their internal affairs. In terms of the ideal-typical view of the world from Chapter 2, America will not aim to 'convert' autocracies into democracies by using regime change, war or subversion. It might welcome it if countries become more democratic, but this will not be a stated objective of the government. (This may remain an objective of NGOs or individual organizations, but not of the US government.) The US will behave transactionally, which is indeed a policy that makes war much less likely. Interests can be negotiated, ideologies cannot.¹⁴ As Henry Kissinger wrote criticizing those who reject 'transactionalism' as a somehow callous or unworthy policy:

> a pejorative adjective has been entered into the debate, dismissing rational diplomacy as 'transactional'. In that view, a constructive long-term relationship with nondemocratic states is not sustainable almost by definition. The advocates of this course start from the premise that true and lasting peace presupposes a community of democratic states . . . If adopting American principles of governance is made the central condition for progress in all other areas of the relationship, the deadlock is inevitable.¹⁵

What did Trump allow us to learn? Trump has made two signal contributions to our knowledge of politics and business. To politics he has brought all the skills he had practised for almost half a century in business. He considers citizens as his employees whom he can push around and fire at will. He sees presidency as Jeff Bezos views his own position at Amazon: he can do anything, almost unconstrained by any rules and laws. He understands politics simply as an extension of the economy, as a new job akin to the management of his real-estate fiefdom.

Trump tore down the curtain that divides citizens, the spectators of the political game, from the rulers and displayed the wheeling and dealing, exchange of favours, the use of public office for private gain in an open, in-your-face manner, available to see to all who attend the show. While in past administrations such illegal and semi-legal actions as receiving money from foreign potentates, moving from one lucrative position to another, cheating on taxes, drafting non-disclosure agreements to hide sexual abuse, were done with discretion and some decorum, with the curtain lowered so that the spectators could not see and participate in the malfeasance, this is now done in the open. It was thus thanks to Trump that we could see the corruption lying at the heart of the American political process. He merely lifted the curtain.

But he did more. When he came to the presidency with these

corrupt manners they were the manners honed by fifty years of business dealings that also involved all sorts of semi-legal or illegal shenanigans. But this did not stop him in his business ascent. Rather, they made the ascent possible, letting him enjoy a brilliant career in the New York business world, become rich, and be a valued guest at many parties, including as an esteemed contributor to political campaigns like Hillary Clinton's for the US Senate. The very fact that his climb to business power was not seen in any way as exceptionable or unacceptable shows that everybody else around him used the same means to get to the top.

Thus from knowing more about Trump we know more about the means used to succeed in the rich business milieu of New York, and even of the world, as Trump and his companions made deals in Scotland, Russia, the Middle East, China and elsewhere. His close confidantes and family members who betrayed him in order to garner multi-million-dollar 'tell-all' book contracts exhibited a behaviour that Trump himself would have indulged in (and approved of) and that showed clearly what ethical standards are prevalent in that environment. There is no loyalty, only crude momentary material interest. Trump thus gave us another very valuable lesson: he showed us the rot, corruption and impunity that lay at the heart of many powerful businesses.

His persona revealed the depth of corruption at the centre of politics and at the centre of business. These are unpardonable sins. Sins enjoyed in secret are acceptable or overlooked; sins flaunted are not. Once his second term is over, those who replace Trump will do their best not to end corruption, because it has become a systemic feature, but to cover it up. But now that the 'spectators' have seen the truth it will be difficult to go back and pretend that nothing ever happened. Thus, Trump's legacy will be one of public cynicism towards all policies and politicians. In that too Trump differs from fascism that presented an ostentatious façade of incorruptibility (even if it was truly corrupt within), while Trump, Musk and their merry band of destroyers of conventions revel in the displays of power, graft and nepotism.

Statism

China: a very long New Economic Policy (NEP) or the return to capitalism?

Many political scientists, journalists and commentators see the recent policy changes in China as 'the return to communism'. They point in particular to a number of measures whose objective is to limit lending by internet companies, to ban for-profit tutoring, and to put a squeeze on companies producing internet games (the latter were, tellingly and ominously, likened by the authorities to 'the spreaders of the spiritual opium among the Chinese youth'). Western commentators are shocked by the Chinese government's apparent indifference to what such measures might do to the stock markets in Shanghai, Shenzhen and Hong Kong. This is in contrast with the government's concern, and even panic, when the Chinese stock market went through severe turbulence in the summer of 2015.

Political and financial commentators 'transfer' or impute to China their own ideological bias. That bias consists in an excessive focus on the stock market as almost the sole indicator of an economy's health. This, of course, is not surprising in a nation like the US where 92 per cent of financial assets are held by 10 per cent of the population.[16] The latter are also the richest people in the country and consequently what affects them is – given that they control the media either directly, as Michael Bloomberg does with the eponymous Bloomberg Network, Jeff Bezos with the *Washington Post* and Elon Musk with X, or indirectly (because they are the main buyers of the news) – much more extensively reported than whatever affects the other 90 per cent of the population. All of this makes the stock market acquire a hypertrophied importance compared to its real significance.

A memory of mine encapsulates the importance of the stock market for the world's rich. In August 1991, I was on vacation at Martha's Vineyard, the Massachusetts island rightly known as the abode of very rich Democrats. (A recent house owner there is Barack Obama.) The vacation coincided with the anti-Gorbachev coup in Moscow (19–22 August). Everybody in the small enclave where I was rushed in that morning to watch the news on TV (this was before the internet and smartphones). Absolutely dramatic events, with globally historic consequences, were occurring in Moscow: the coup leaders were giving a badly organized press conference, the army had occupied the main government buildings, demonstrators began to gather in the streets, Yeltsin seized the Russian parliament building, it was unclear if Gorbachev was arrested or not . . . One was watching history unfold. But after about half-an-hour of live coverage, the liberal elite decided that that was enough: they switched channels to the New York Stock Exchange, and most attentively watched developments there, as they mentally calculated how good (or bad) the events in Moscow were for their portfolios. Those who cared more about the fate of the Soviet Union, communism and the world than about stock quotations were in the minority, and had to divine the events in Moscow from the gyrations of the stocks in New York.

China under Xi Jinping wants to be different. In a society of political capitalism, the state maintains its autonomy. Under political capitalism the state must not allow itself to be co-opted or 'contaminated' by capitalist interest. In other words, capitalist interest is one of the interests to consider – but not the only one, or even perhaps not the chief one. 'Politics' and 'capitalism' are there together defining the system but each rules its own realm.

The Chinese political philosopher Gan Yang writes:

> In China, only by first upholding the socialist ideals and values can the ideals and values of freedom be truly established. If socialism is abandoned, freedom in China is likely to become the freedom of the minority. The freedom of the rich, the freedom of the boss, not the freedom of most workers. At the same time, freedom can truly take root in China only on the premise of adhering to the autonomy of Chinese civilization, otherwise the so-called freedom may be just another name for comprador-ism, semi-colonialism, and self-enslavement.[17]

A small incident that I witnessed in 2019 illustrates the relative power of the state and the private sector in China. It was a very pleasant day in Beijing and I went strolling in a residential part of the city, bought a cappuccino in a luxury European-owned hotel and walked outside to drink it. An interesting scene attracted my attention. In front of me was a wide four-lane avenue with trees planted in the middle. Brand new cars were circulating. Suddenly, a group of three very young soldiers stepped out onto the road: from their shy and confused gaze one could imagine they had come straight from the countryside only a few months or even days ago. They were led by a slightly older soldier, probably a non-commissioned officer, and they weren't paying any attention to the traffic, pedestrian crossings or red lights. When they walked out, the BMWs and Mercedes that were driving at a not inconsiderable speed suddenly stopped. No one honked, no one protested. The rich people sitting behind the wheels of expensive cars remained there, silently watching and waiting until the four soldiers, looking straight ahead as if the rest of the world did not exist, crossed to the middle of the road. The pattern repeated in the next two lanes, as the drivers saw the soldiers coming from some distance and stopped their cars even before the soldiers reached the road. I thought: such a scene would not happen if the people driving the BMWs were not only rich, but in possession of political power too.

This division between the state and the private sector is consistent with the long Chinese tradition of the state keeping merchant and capitalist interests at arm's length. The sociologist Ho-fung Hung describes how the Qing bureaucracy sided with workers in industrial disputes, and not with 'masters' as was commonly the case in Britain in the nineteenth century.[18] The same argument is made by numerous economic historians. Peer Vries writes:

> [In China], people acting as capitalists never even came close to having the kind of political clout that they had in Britain or in other mercantile states in Western Europe. There was no institutionalized collusion between them and the state. In contrast, the state as a rule

fiercely opposed the emergence of a merchant class that might become a threat to its power.[19]

Fernand Braudel in *Civilization and Capitalism* similarly argues that China lacked the top capitalist class because the state never allowed it to emerge. Jacques Gernet contrasts medieval China and Europe: during the thirteenth-century Southern Song period merchants were rich but, unlike in contemporary Europe, failed to transform themselves into a 'class for themselves'. A powerful central government was there from the start to check the influence of merchants or anybody else.[20] Kenneth Pomeranz writes in *The Great Divergence*: 'the state . . . *interfered* less with its merchant class than its European counterparts, but it also *created* fewer opportunities and privileged riches for them' (emphasis in the original).[21]

Furthermore, if one looks at the current Xi-led CPC from a Leninist perspective (which Xi may not be loath to do), the same conclusion is reinforced. Chinese capitalism may be seen as one 'long New Economic Policy' – which might last a century or even two[22] – wherein capitalists are given a free hand in practically all areas of economics, but politics and the commanding heights of the economy are preserved for the state. This means that they are under the Party's control and political power is not shared with anyone. The state maintains freedom of action vis-à-vis the socially most powerful group (capitalists) and can ignore their complaints when an overarching social interest is at stake.

The closest ideological antecedent of Chinese political capitalism is Lenin's New Economic Policy (NEP), introduced in 1921 and formally ended with collectivization and the First Five-Year Plan in 1928.[23] The NEP was, according to Lenin, a learning experience: once communist cadres have learned how to do business and run the economy, the NEP could be shut down ('state capitalism is capitalism that we shall be able to restrain, and the limits of which we shall be able to fix'[24]). The justification of the NEP was that while it was a retreat from the ideals of socialism, it was a temporary retreat and after its objectives had been achieved, future advances would be much more powerful because they would be better organized and sustainable. And the country would be richer. These are also the objectives that Deng Xiaoping clearly stated many times. It was repeated, in an unusually blunt way, by the reformist Prime Minister Zhu Rongji to a German journalist: 'We won't go down this road [of privatization] nor will we adopt a policy of privatization. We can allow state owned enterprises to sell shares to individuals, but the majority of shares must remain under state control.'[25] Capitalists will provide the engine and the fuel, but the Party will hold the steering wheel.

In his 1922 speech on the New Economic Policy to the Eleventh Party Congress, Lenin made a distinction between (a) state capitalism under capitalist conditions and (b) state capitalism under socialist conditions.[26] He rejected the view that the two were the same, and criticized Bukharin who wrote that the term 'state capitalism' under socialism is a logical absurdity. In Lenin's view, (a) is when the state, ruled by the capitalist class, takes over some of the private sector functions while the substantial part of the economy remains capitalist. And there is (b), state capitalism, where the state is controlled by the Party, and allows capitalists to function in order to boost productivity and to learn management skills from them. So, state capitalism under socialism, according to Lenin, is entirely different, in the political sense, from state capitalism under capitalism. The political power is held by the Party and this enables communist rulers, whenever they decide to do so, to curtail capitalists' involvement in the economy. The power remains solidly with the Party.

This last point is very relevant for the understanding of the Chinese approach to state capitalism today. Under that interpretation, we can see current Chinese state capitalism as a protracted NEP that began in 1978, and continues today and may last for another century. That 'Leninist' interpretation, however, seems to overlook the possibility that with a very long NEP the economic and political power will gradually seep from under the Party and the very nature of the state will change. Those who have money will dictate things, as in capitalist countries. The state may not be able to control them and the commanding heights of the economy may change hands. This happened under Jiang Zemin and Hu Jintao: the development of state capitalism under socialist conditions led to the increasing influence of rich people and owners of capital, including their inclusion in most of the Party organs, while 'The Three Represents' – the CPC's theory under Jiang Zemin – gave a pretence of ideological acceptability to such an evolution.[27] We have shown empirically in Chapter 3 how much the Chinese urban elite has changed since the 'reform and openness' policies were inaugurated in 1978 by Deng Xiaoping, and, most interestingly regarding the relationship between the political power and capitalist interests, how the very top of the new Chinese elite is composed of large-scale capitalists with CPC membership.

This long-term aspect of the NEP, overlooked by Lenin, was not overlooked by Xi. Indeed, Xi Jinping's policies are a purposeful change compared to the policies of his predecessors: it is an attempt to reassert the power of the state over the capitalist sector and the rich. Or, to use Lenin's distinction between the two: an attempt to move from state *capitalism* to *state* capitalism. It is a readjustment in the political power between the two sectors: the state, ruled by a bureaucratic stratum, and the rich. It represents the analogue of the populist reaction in Western democracies: the feeling that the business elite has become too powerful, has no discernible interest in the problems of ordinary people, and has to be reined in. We can see Xi Jinping as both heir to Lenin's New Economic Policy and, in more contemporary terms, as a populist responder to the excesses of the new rich.

Not looking at China's policies in the long term, but being obsessed by their short-term zig-zags, leads to the overestimation of temporary departures from the 'main policy line' – and a lack of appreciation for the flexibility with which 'the line' is applied. Thus, the head of Rockefeller International Ruchir Sharma extols, and shows his surprise at, Xi's discontinuation of zero-Covid restrictions, stronger support for globalization and a nod towards the private sector.[28] As the title of his article, 'The Xi nobody saw coming', reveals, for Sharma these policies are a sudden and unexpected volte-face. Instead of going down the Maoist path that the Western mainstream media and majority of academics have predicted during the past several years, Xi has decided to suddenly change course. Sharma's main hypothesis is wrong. There is no sudden turn-around or change. This is still the same Xi, and the policy is one of 'readjustment' or 'rectification'.

To understand how intelligent politicians operate in the countries of political capitalism, one needs to start with two cardinal principles of governance: tactical flexibility, and the 'bird in a cage'. The first term goes back to Lenin. Its meaning is clear. Policies ought to be flexible, in a tactical sense, while never losing sight of an ultimate vision. In Xi's case, this ultimate vision is 'socialism with Chinese characteristics', 'moderately prosperous society' and 'common prosperity'.[29] The second term ('bird in a cage') goes back to Chen Yun (the father of China's First Five-Year Plan). If the private sector is controlled too tightly, it will, like an imprisoned bird, suffocate. And the people will suffer. But if it is left entirely free, it will fly away, bringing (as it did in the second term of Hu Jintao's rule from 2002 to 2012) all the negative effects of capitalism: increased inequality, lack of social mobility, monopolies, rule of moneyed elites, corruption, etc. Thus, a smart politician needs permanently to maintain the middle line. But maintaining the middle line, in a strategic sense, is possible only by favouring alternatively pro-leftist and pro-rightist policies.

With the situation that Xi inherited in 2012, the only way forward was to move against pervasive corruption by arresting those engaged in grand embezzlement and sale of favours, and to try to lessen economic inequality through state transfers. More recently, Xi relaxed the *hukou* system of obligatory city registration (which discriminated against the rural population that worked quasi illegally in big cities and could not access urban health care or education for their children), and reduced inequality of opportunities by implementing an ambitious policy of investments in Western provinces and eliminating extreme rural poverty.[30] Then, after Covid slowed things down, he aimed to 'correct' the power of the very loosely regulated financial and non-financial giants (such as Alibaba), by limiting the types of financial products they could offer.

These corrective measures were, perhaps because they were also accompanied by Xi's cult of personality, interpreted as steps towards a new Maoism. But they were never that: they were tactical movements necessitated by the desire to keep the achievement of the strategic objective in mind.

This policy is not markedly different from the strategy of Deng Xiaoping. It is sometimes forgotten that Deng's policies were 'tactically flexible', both when he came back to having some measure of power in the last years of Mao's rule (before being 'purged' for the third time), and most obviously during and after the Tiananmen Square events. The Tiananmen crackdown – decided by Deng – led to the strong leftward lurch in economic policy. Thus it was not just a political, but also an economic policy, shock. Yet, after three years of 'leftist policies', Deng, through his Southern Tour, inaugurated the reintroduction of 'pro-rightist' policies. To an unsophisticated observer, these appear as sudden policy shifts; they seem like movements that presage further policy changes in the same direction. But they are not: they are tactical 'rectifications'. And such policies in one direction will, necessarily, be followed after several years by policies in the opposite direction.[31]

When Air France Flight 447 crashed into the Atlantic in 2009, the inquiry revealed that the main cause of the crash was the inability of the crew, when the plane was losing altitude, to perform a complicated manoeuvre, where in order to regain altitude, the plane needed first to dive down. The same holds for economic policy makers in state capitalist societies. To make the economy grow 'harmoniously' in the long term, they have to accept short-term slowdowns and policy changes. To simple observers, they look like zig-zags; to the perceptive eye, they look like a straight line.[32]

The Great Global Transformation
Xi Jinping against the rule of nihilists

Can Xi Jinping's policies fail, the autonomy of the state end and the bourgeoisie take over the Chinese state as it did in the West? It is quite possible. The modernization theory argues that. There are, I think, four ways in which it could happen.

First, there could be a middle-class or bourgeois revolution. It should be noted, however, that no revolution against a communist regime has ever succeeded. The one that came closest was the Hungarian Revolution in 1956, but it was crushed externally, by Soviet arms. So that possibility, so long as the Party-state is united, is extremely unlikely.

The second possibility is 'Gorbachevization'. This means that the top echelons of the Party move towards social-democracy. Ideologically this makes lots of sense given that communists were originally part of social-democracy. The ideological gap between the two is not very wide. The end of communist regimes in Eastern Europe and the Soviet Union came when several communist parties became social-democratic in fact, either at the top (like the Communist Party of the Soviet Union, principally through Gorbachev and his chief ideologue Alexander Yakovlev) or throughout its membership. The latter was the case, by 1988–89, for at least the Hungarian, Polish and Slovenian communist parties. They came close to the Italian Communist Party (PCI), ideologically and politically. They shared the ideals of Eurocommunism that was started by the Italian, Spanish and French communist parties in the mid-1970s and that became practically indistinguishable from social-democracy. Not surprisingly, the bulk of the PCI later dissolved into the newly formed Democratic Party that combined liberalism and social-democracy (one of the PCI's former leaders Giorgio Napolitano became the President of Italy), French communists deserted the Party and the Spanish Communist Party went through several transformations. In all such cases, the formerly communist parties became social-democratic parties accepting democracy, the multi-party system and private ownership of most productive assets.

The third possibility is 'Jiang Zeminism' whereby the Party increasingly accepts capitalists among its top members and reflects their interests. This is a distinct possibility, as seen in the change in the composition of the richest 5 per cent in urban China between 1988 and 2018 (Chapter 3). The 'insinuation' of the rich into the top Party ranks was rationalized by Jiang Zemin under the ideology of 'The Three Represents'.[33] One does not hear much about 'The Three Represents' nowadays (it seems to have been replaced by Xi Jinping Thought), so that path to change is currently politically blocked. Still, given the composition of the elite (including within the CPC), this seems a likely post-Xi scenario.

All these three ways ultimately lead to a multi-party system where the CPC has to obtain power through the ballot box, share that power with other parties, or is totally ousted from power. It also leads to capitalists, not only surreptitiously as they do today, but openly coming to political power. This alone – given China's history of keeping merchants and capitalists far from power, both in imperial courts and bureaucracies, and in the past seventy years under the communist state – would be a novelty for the country.

There is a fourth way in which the CPC could evolve after Xi, and it is different from the other three in several important respects. We can name it after Gennady Zyuganov, the founder and long-serving leader of the Communist Party of the Russian Federation. His party was never in government (it was founded in 1993), but remained close to power throughout Putin's years. What is interesting in the present context is that it ideologically abandoned both its commitment to socialist property relations and to internationalism. Zyuganov converted the party that in principle could be seen as the heir of the Soviet Communist Party into a national-socialist party that interprets the national interest often in purely chauvinistic or imperialistic ways – and is willing (and even happy) to collaborate with prominent capitalists that are sufficiently 'nationally conscious'. Thus in 2018 it had Pavel Grudinin, a minor oligarch, as its relatively successful presidential candidate. That evolution shows us another type of movement that is ideologically not too difficult for communist parties to effect: instead of a movement towards social-democracy (from which, as already mentioned, communists were indistinguishable at the inception of the workers' movement), they can move towards socialism under the nationalist flag (i.e., national socialism). Such a Chinese Communist Party would be strongly nationalistic, ready to go much further than 'The Three Represents' in its acceptance of capitalists and might begin to resemble Kuomintang, the nationalist party that lost the civil war and decamped to Taiwan. One can even argue that in the same way that the end of communism as a viable ideology pushed European communist parties back to their socio-democratic roots, the end of communism as a viable ideology may push the CPC towards its own ideological roots that lie in Kuomintang (from which it too was almost indistinguishable at the inception and with whom it collaborated until 1927). From an international relations point of view, that last evolution would be the most interesting, and challenging for the West, because a nationalistic China would be very unlikely to accept joining an international system that is hierarchically organized with the United States at the apex (discussed below). Geopolitically, it would not change current matters much; if anything, it might make them more difficult to deal with and more perilous.[34]

The future will tell us if the Chinese state gets taken over by the rich in one of these four ways or not – that is, whether it remains autonomous in its decision-making. To look more carefully at this question, we should go back to an important and programmatic speech entitled 'Regarding the Construction of Socialism with Chinese Characteristics' that Xi Jinping delivered in January 2013 (soon after his elevation to the highest position in the Party) to the members of the Central Committee of the CPC. The speech may have an even greater resonance now, more than ten years after it was delivered, because it sheds light, indirectly, on the very current problem of the Russian war on Ukraine too.

Two points are worth highlighting: Xi's interpretation of the end of the Soviet Union, and his emphasis on ideology.

In the speech, Xi says the break-up of the Soviet Union and the end

National Market Liberalism

of the Communist Party of the Soviet Union (CPSU) was the result of 'ideological nihilism': the ruling strata ceased to believe in the advantages and the value of the system, but lacking any other ideological coordinates within which to situate their thinking they plummeted into nihilism. This can be easily seen, for example, in the memoirs published by Andrei Kozyrev, Yeltsin's most pro-American minister of foreign affairs. The book is not only striking in its total absence of any ideology, but also shocking in showing the inability of the creators of foreign policy, including Kozyrev, to even define Russia's interests, how Russia views the international system and under what principles its foreign policy should be conducted.[35] It is revealing that throughout the book Kozyrev cites only newspaper articles, and not one theoretical or historical article or book on international relations. That kind of total ideological vacuum was not only Kozyrev's but was characteristic for most, or all, of the political elite of late Sovietism.[36] Xi is right that, ideologically, the elite did not come up with an alternative ideology, but came up with . . . nothing. (Unless we understand an assemblage of common-sensical trivialities and verities, unencumbered by any critical thinking, as not 'nothing'.)

Here is Xi:

> Why did the Soviet Union disintegrate? Why did the Communist Party of the Soviet Union fall to pieces? An important reason is that in the ideological domain, competition is fierce! To completely repudiate the historical experience of the Soviet Union, to repudiate the history of the CPSU, to repudiate Lenin, to repudiate Stalin was to wreak chaos in Soviet ideology and engage in historical nihilism. It caused Party organizations at all levels to have barely any function whatsoever. It robbed the Party of its leadership of the military. In the end the CPSU – as great a Party as it was – scattered like a flock of frightened beasts! The Soviet Union – as great a socialist state as it was – shattered into pieces.

The lack of belief in the system stemmed from the failure of the Soviet Union in the economic arena, and an inability to propose a system of participation in the decision-making that appealed to, or was accepted by, most of its population. The roots of the debacle were both economic and ideological. Once the party loses the control of its ideology, Xi argues, once it fails to provide a satisfactory explanation for its rule, objectives and purposes, it dissolves into a party of loosely connected individuals linked only by personal goals of enrichment and power.[37]

The party is then taken over by 'ideological nihilism'. While in some cases, this ideological void caused by the disappearance of communist ideology was filled by nationalism, almost nowhere was it filled by liberalism, as I have argued many years ago in 'Democracy of convenience, not of choice': namely, that the revolutions of 1989 were not revolutions of democracy but of national independence and self-determination.[38] This, however, was not – as we can see from Xi's speech – the worst outcome. The worst outcome, and perhaps what Xi fears for China, is that the country be taken over by people with no ideology whatsoever but with an entirely cynical and self-serving desire to rule. This is what happened in Russia where the country was hijacked by the ideological nihilists of the intelligence services.

The ideological nihilists of the KGB were often seen, in the West, as much more preferable rulers than communists. Thus for John Lewis Gaddis, perhaps the best-known US historian of the Cold War, the only praiseworthy Soviet leader (in *The Cold War: A New History*) before Gorbachev was Beria precisely because Beria was completely non-ideological and willing to have any system so long as he remained in charge. In the latter days of the Soviet Union, KGB people were seen as the only ones who could impose some order and get the economy growing again. Hence the election of Andropov to lead the CPSU – a total reversal of the traditional subservience of the intelligence apparatus to the Party. (It is not for nothing that Stalin never allowed the Cheka in its various appellations to decide on policies, but only to execute them, at times literally by shooting people.) The dependence on the intelligence service was repeated in the last years of Yeltsin's rule when four out of his last five prime ministers (a position from which the person would quasi-automatically succeed Yeltsin) were linked with the KGB (Primakov, Stepashin, Kiriyenko and finally Putin). This intellectual void enabled the rule of ideological nihilists – people who by the very nature of their jobs were pragmatists to the bone, without any concern with, or interest in, ideology.

The focus on the external or superficial aspects of one's rule, and disregard of the ideology that motivates those in power, leads many liberal commentators to speak of Xi's and Putin's 'autocracies' as if they belonged to the same species. But, as Xi's speech shows, they do not. What differentiates them is that in one case there is an attempt to preserve the hegemonic rule of the communist ideology, and *therefore* to control the organs of brute power (the army and the police) – in Mao's famous words, 'the Party controls the gun, and the gun must never be allowed to control the Party' – and in the other case, there is a complete replacement of the ideological and the political by the pragmatism of naked power and self-interest.

Unlike the ebullient commentators of the end of communism who liked to think that its end would bring forth the flowering of democracy, Xi puts the emphasis on something much more grim and perhaps realistic: 'ideological nihilism' that opens the way to adventuresome policies devoid of any ideological or even logical justification. They might have been, as in the case of Putin's Russia's attack on Ukraine, adopted either because of misjudgement or because of a desire to provide some superficial nationalist veneer to an otherwise ideologically empty regime. Whatever the case, they were unmoored from any ideology. Xi is right to argue that once belief in a better future society and hence the focus on the economic success that is supposed to bring about that future society are abandoned, the power is surrendered to the 'opportunistic cliques' who may plunge their countries into wars and destruction either because they believe in nothing or because they are in search of some justification for their nihilistic rule.

For now, 'The Party's leadership defines the fundamental nature of Chinese-style modernization. The Party's nature, purpose, original mission, beliefs and policy directions determine that Chinese-style modernization is socialist modernization and *nothing else*' (my emphasis).[39]

Xi may be, in his own view, the last rampart before the tide of cynical, purely pragmatic and self-interested politicians overwhelms the Party and the state. His anti-corruption campaign, the single-minded pursuit of elimination of rural poverty that remained rampant even when China's economy grew at two-digit rates,[40] control of the new oligarchs and the emphasis on SOEs' leading role in high-tech industries can all be seen as part of the same project. This is not a return to a fictitious Maoism, as the superficial resemblance in the cult of personality might indicate, nor is it a different Xi, but a consistent attempt to instil an ideology that should prevent the decomposition of the CPC and perhaps even of the state. As Xi explained in 2017, in a selection of his writings and speeches published under the title *Anecdotes and Sayings of Xi Jinping*, the ideological campaign's objective is to instil the 'rule of virtue' ('morality within, virtue without').[41] If Confucian-cum-communist ideology is disregarded and everything is simply esteemed in terms of money, there cannot be a moral and virtuous rule. To quote Confucius, as the editors of the book of Xi's sayings do, 'If one allows oneself to follow [only] profit in one's behavior, there will be many with cause for complaint.' There could be a fair procedural selection of rulers, say, by election, but not necessarily a virtuous rule. The latter can be assured only through the education of rulers.

The key question, unanswered in Xi's book, then becomes: is it possible to achieve an educational and moral 'rejuvenation' under the current 'normal' conditions of capitalism, where money-making is held by the majority of the population to be the highest objective, revealing also one's individual virtue? Can the examples dredged up from the revolutionary era, from the Yen'an forum[42] to early Mao, be relevant for a new generation raised in the world of relentless commercialization? One is allowed to doubt. This does not make the ideological campaign conducted by Xi less relevant – it makes it rather more so. Xi is fighting against the spirit of the times, and while his struggle may be driven by a genuine desire to create a morally superior China, or at least morally superior rulers, the odds of succeeding in this endeavour are not particularly high.

The danger is that forced or ritualistic ideologization that at times consists of mindless electronic clicks on the 'Study the Great Nation' app that follows Xi Jinping's every move or speech, may produce, in the medium term, the very opposite results of those that are being sought. An ideology that is imposed and not reaffirmed sincerely in daily life provides fertile ground for the vices that Xi tries to guard against: cynicism and nihilism. He finds himself in a difficult position where doing nothing but following the path of his two predecessors abuts necessarily into a Party controlled by the rich; or where doing something to prevent that course of events may, on the contrary, and paradoxically, make them inevitable.

Multipolarity: in an uncertain struggle

The Russia–Ukraine war as the catalyst of a new global system

Now, I will consider the geopolitical background to the Russia–Ukraine war and the likely geopolitical effects of the conflict. The first is important for our better understanding of the problems inherent in unipolarity and the second is relevant for the present time when a struggle for a multipolar world is being waged.

The geopolitical roots of the conflict are relatively unambiguous. They go back to the way that the Cold War ended, or rather to the way the end of the Cold War was perceived in the United States and in the Soviet Union, that is, in Russia.

In the US and in the West, the end of the Cold War was seen as an almost unconditional victory of one set of countries and of the system of liberal capitalism with which they were associated.

In Russia, it was, on the contrary, seen not as a defeat, but as Russia having voluntarily abandoned one system to join the countries of liberal capitalism. This huge misunderstanding is similar to the confusion that accompanied the end of World War I and the Versailles Peace Conference. According to the Western allies, the end of the war came as Germany was defeated. For Germans, however, the end of the Great War was an armistice where they still held troops on foreign soil rather than the Allies controlling their territory. That misunderstanding coloured the subsequent two decades and, in conjunction with the Great Depression, brought Hitler to power.

The difference in the way that the end of the Cold War was perceived in the USA and in Russia led to the difference in expectations about the new world order. For Russians, Russia was not a defeated power, but rather a power that had simply changed camps, from socialist to capitalist – while its size and significance entitled it to an important role within the new geopolitical structure. This explains the creation of the NATO-Russia Council that Russia liked to see as a significant move towards that role, and that the West saw as a largely meaningless exercise done to appease Russian great-power vanity.

In the opinion of Russian elites, the position that Russia should have in the new order, while not equal to that of the United States, would equate to that of the 'second circle' countries. It implied that the hegemon would agree to a Russian zone of influence in the same way that the United States tolerates the French zone of influence in West Africa and continued influence of the United Kingdom in many Commonwealth countries. But these expectations were disappointed. It is significant that the US never recognized as an international organization the Commonwealth of Independent States, a loose association built on the ruins of the USSR, precisely because it saw it as an attempt by Russia to maintain its own zone of influence. It became increasingly clear to the Russian elites that the US would not accept any special role for Russia in the region that belonged to the Russian Empire in the past or to the Soviet Union.[43]

Ukraine played a key role in the jockeying for influence over the Eurasian territories, because of its population and geographical size and because it was perceived by Russia as its closest 'brother nation'. It was, hence, a nation in which for cultural and historical reasons Russia expected to have significant influence. But it was precisely that closeness which bred enmity among a significant share of the Ukrainian political establishment who wanted to unambiguously reinforce their distinctiveness. The differences between Russia and Ukraine, although papered over at the time of the dissolution of the Soviet Union, were present from the very beginning. Only days after the signing of the Belovezha Accords that dissolved the USSR, Boris Yeltsin, who in ninety-nine out of a hundred cases supported Ukrainian independence, proclaimed in the Russian Duma that the accords did not imply Russian acceptance of 'Leninist' borders and more or less delineated the contested territory along the same lines as the currently annexed Ukrainian provinces and the Crimea.[44] On the other side, for the United States Ukraine was a particularly useful tool to undermine Russian influence in the former Soviet Union. It hewed closely to the ideas originally expressed by the former US National Security Advisor Zbigniew Brzezinski in *The Grand Chessboard: American Primacy and Its Geostrategic Imperatives*, which argued that Russia will cease to be an empire only if it is shorn of Ukraine (and for good measure also broken into several parts).

While the background to the war is relatively clear, the geopolitical effects of the war are very difficult to predict. They might range between the two extreme outcomes. One extreme would be a total defeat of Ukraine, where a rump Ukraine would continue to exist but would fall under NATO's full control with the latter being represented primarily by Poland. Ukraine could then be de facto divided between NATO (i.e., Poland) and Russia in the same way that Poland was divided between the Soviet Union and Nazi Germany in 1939. The other extreme outcome is the total defeat of Russia, which would probably bring about the break-up of the Russian Federation not only into the various Muslim-dominated parts and the rest of Russia but even into other parts of the far-flung federation.

Leaving aside these two extreme possibilities, neither of which looks very likely today, we should concentrate on what could be predicted with somewhat greater certainty. It seems to me that there are two such prospects.

The first is that Russia, by force of circumstances, will have to orient itself away from the West. This will be a historical change, because Russia from its very beginning as an empire under Peter the Great turned towards the West, culturally and technologically, to catch up with it through modernization and economic advancement. It was relatively successful in the late nineteenth century under Sergey Witte, and then under Stalin and his successors. But if future relations with the West remain politically tense and economically almost non-existent because the US and European sanctions will not be lifted (unless Russia accepts conditions that can be presented only to a defeated power), it is hard to see how Russia can fail to look South and East instead of West.

The economic estrangement, the cordon sanitaire like the one that existed against Soviet Russia in the 1920s, would remain. Western sanctions are quick to impose and very long to lift as the experiences of the Soviet Union, Cuba, Iran and Venezuela show. The Russian economy will have to orient itself much more towards China, India, Iran, the Gulf states and other countries not belonging to the political West. This would be hard to do because of Russia's technological dependence on the West: for example, as of November 2024, almost one-half of Russian company-owned Airbus A320s and A321s could no longer be flown because of maintenance issues.[45] According to Russian sources, more than 90 per cent of production that is automated in Russia is dependent on Western-made software. Such dependence is not impossible to overcome (e.g., Chinese cars have already become the most popular cars in Russia whereas their share before the war was close to zero), but it will take time, effort and, most importantly, resources. In addition, one must consider the huge geographical distance that exists between the largest Russian cities, all close to Europe, and the far eastern part of the Russian Federation as well as countries lying south and east from Russia. A train ride from Moscow to Vladivostok takes seven days, and flying time is nine hours. It would be very difficult for Russia to replicate the American bicoastal distribution of economic activity, because so much of its population is currently concentrated east of the Urals.

The second likely geopolitical change is global: the creation of a group of countries (BRICS) that are unwilling to be part of what is emerging as a global NATO or a global Western bloc led by the United States and promoting the so-called rules-based global liberal order. The Russia–Ukraine war plays there the role of a catalyst, similar to the role played by Covid in the spread of remote work. The BRICS, being a very diverse group, do not represent a bloc and should not be viewed as such. They should simply be seen as countries that believe that the Western rules, whether regarding interference in internal affairs, promotion of democracy, protection of intellectual property rights, patrolling of the seas, or global finance, are not neutral, but serve the West and were defined at the time when the West controlled international organizations and thus the rule-making.

While Russia is objectively contributing to the erosion of such Western rules and asks for a return to the rules proclaimed in the UN Charter, it is ironically doing so by violating that very same covenant. By invading Ukraine, Russia is ignoring Ukraine's status as an independent country, which, under UN rules, is guaranteed territorial integrity, with the right to make an appeal for collective security to enforce it. This is therefore the very unusual situation of a country arguing for the observance of the UN Charter while simultaneously violating it. (Of course, Russia is hardly a unique case – see the US and UK's war on Iraq, or Israel's annexation of the Golan Heights and East Jerusalem.) Putin, in a recent Valdai Discussion Club meeting (a premier political event in Russia) in Sochi, went to great lengths to explain away this contradiction by arguing that what Russia did was not in contravention of international law, because the invasion was motivated by the discrimination of the Russian minority and its right to self-determination.[46] Of course, Putin, like everybody else, is aware that there is an inherent tension between the stress on territorial integrity and the right to self-determination. However, in the correct interpretation of the UN rules, territorial integrity takes precedence simply because, by becoming members of the UN, countries automatically enjoy territorial protection within the borders with which they were accepted.

Transition to a multipolar homogeneous system. A multipolar world is emerging because of the logic of economic development. Very large countries with expected further increases in population and GDP are no longer willing to accept the tutelage of Western powers, many of which (not necessarily the United States but certainly countries in Europe) are in decline both in terms of their overall economic importance and in terms of population. While it is well known that in 2015 China overtook the US by the size of its GDP expressed in international dollars and now has a GDP one-quarter greater than America's, it is not sufficiently appreciated that similar developments are happening between other Asian and Western economies. Forty years ago, India and the UK had the same share of global GDP in international dollars (3 per cent each); nowadays, India's share is 8 per cent of the global output whereas the United Kingdom's share is 2 per cent; Indonesian and Dutch economies were of the same size around 1980, while Indonesia is now four times greater (see Chapter 1). Under such conditions it hardly makes sense to maintain the current voting and power structure of international organizations like the UN, the IMF and the World Bank, where European countries are heavily overrepresented compared to their population size and economic power. The reform of such institutions, however, is almost impossible because those who hold the veto are supposed to acquiesce to the loss of power. This is why the BRICS have turned towards the creation of new financial and economic institutions that would replicate the existing ones but be differently controlled.

The current transition to the multipolar world is a peculiar one, in that it is a transition away from what Raymond Aron called a bipolar heterogeneous world to a multipolar homogeneous world.[47] In the bipolar system of the Cold War, both blocs had their own supporters in the countries of the other bloc. Thus, for example, the Soviet Union used communist parties in Western countries to promote its own interests; likewise, the Western bloc used NGOs, the Helsinki process, which formally committed Communist countries to observe human rights, and dissident movements to promote its own interests and undermine the Soviet-bloc regimes. The emerging multipolar system, however, may be characterized by relative homogeneity in the sense that none of its individual countries (i.e., the poles of the new world system) is able to influence the internal domestic power structure of other countries. For sure, the US will try to use NGOs and think tanks to further its own interests within China; but Chinese ideological influence in Western countries, India or Brazil is almost nil. The same is true for India in China or Russia. Russian influence in the US is limited to disruptive clandestine activities but is otherwise non-existent. The new global system would thus be markedly different from what the world has experienced in the past century or more. We would have moved from a bipolar heterogeneous system through the unipolar 'moment' that existed between the end of communism and 2016, to a multipolar homogeneous system. The rules for such a system remain to be written. Hopefully, not only in blood.

Impossibility of absorbing China into the US-led global system

The principal reason why the geopolitical competition between the United States and China is so difficult, and most likely impossible to resolve, is the inability of the current US-led global system to absorb a country of the size of China. For many historical reasons the group of countries that composes the political West is hierarchically structured with the United States at its head. The historical reasons for this go back to the crucial role the US played in ending World War I and of course much more importantly in winning, together with other allies, World War II in Europe, winning it alone in Asia; and then also winning almost single-handedly the Cold War against the Soviet Union.

Combined with the economic power of the United States and its intellectual and military leadership, this has given rise to a hierarchically ordered system. The system is composed of several concentric circles of countries. Large or culturally close countries are in the first and second circle, a group of mid-size countries in the third, and thus all the way to the bottom circle composed of countries like

Albania, Montenegro, Cyprus and Malta whose only advantage that they bring to the political West is strategic positioning in the Mediterranean.[48] The same could be said of the small Pacific islands that are not formally in NATO, but maintain close military ties with the United States. The first circle is composed of English-speaking countries that are part of the so-called Five Eyes, a system of free exchange of secret or confidential information that includes only the US, UK, Canada, Australia and New Zealand, and from which even France and Germany are excluded. The second circle may be seen as being composed of important countries like France, Germany and Japan. In his excellent book *Subimperial Power* Clinton Fernandes describes the position of Australia as one such subimperial power: 'A subimperial power is both subimperial and powerful. It is not a client state. It subordinates important aspects of its sovereignty, defence and foreign policy in service of the imperial system while exerting significant power in its own area of influence.'[49] It exerts a kind of proconsular power in the area of the world in which it has interests. For Australia, as Fernandes describes, this is Indonesia, Papua New Guinea, Timor-Leste and the rest of the small Pacific islands – some of which (as Vanuatu recently) can be the object of mutual jealousy between the United States and China. The proconsular powers are allowed, in such areas, to follow their own interests so long as they are compatible with those of the United States. Most of the time they are. This division of labour is very efficient as it gives a role, and often the reality of power, to smaller members and saves the hegemon's resources for more important tasks. As previously mentioned, France was similarly allowed to exert a special role in West Africa, in the so-called *Françafrique*, the former French colonies that became politically independent in the 1960s but have remained economically and culturally closely linked with France. Similarly, the US does not object to the special role that the United Kingdom has in many of its former colonies now 'unified' in the British-led Commonwealth.

The problem arises with large countries that, if they join the political West, expect to be treated according to what they perceive to be their importance. I have already mentioned above that this created the 'absorption problem' of Russia after the end of the Cold War: Russia wanted to maintain its traditional zone of influence in the former Soviet republics (with the possible exception of the Baltic states), but the US objected to it. But an even graver problem would be the absorption of China into a US-led order. The reasons are rather obvious. China is a very big country whose GDP is already now one-quarter greater than that of the United States; it has four times more people than the United States; in some of the top technologies it rivals the United States, and if we project growth rates for the next twenty years, assuming not unreasonably that the gap would remain 2 percentage points per year in favour of China, by 2045 Chinese GDP would be more than twice the size of American GDP. At the same time China is significantly increasing military expenditure, and in some new technologies that also have military applications it is in the lead. It is then obvious that such a giant country cannot be easily placed in a system where it would have to play a subsidiary role to the leader. China would expect that it should have at least an equal, if not paramount, role in East Asia to that of the US, and possibly a significant, perhaps a co-hegemonic, role in the rest of the world.[50] In the words of the Indian American political scientist Ashley J. Tellis: '[China] aspires to build a unipolar system in Asia that subordinates its regional competitors [including India] to first achieve bipolarity with the United States before eventually replacing it as *the* global hegemon [emphasis in the original].'[51] It is unthinkable that the US would agree to either. Sharing its power in Asia would nullify the outcome of World War II for the United States; sharing its power in the rest of the world would relegate the US to leadership of only one part of the world, and openly renounce its claims on the rest. Such voluntarily accepted defeat would negate practically all that the US has achieved in the past century, commencing with the Versailles Peace Conference where the American delegation insisted, claiming highest moral principles, that the zones of influence were unacceptable while in reality saying that the US was free to have its own zone of influence wherever in the world it wished to have one, unconstrained by any other power.[52]

The British historian and diplomat E. H. Carr writes:

> Any international order must rest on some hegemony of power. But this hegemony, like supremacy of a ruling class within the state, is itself a challenge to those who do not share it; and it must, if it is to survive, contain an element of give-and-take, of self-sacrifice on the part of those who have, which will render it tolerable to the other members of the world community.[53]

America has certainly accepted many 'gives-and-takes', and even some 'self-sacrifice' when this was also a matter of national interest, as in the Marshall Plan and in the decision to open its market to Japan, South Korea and Taiwan, but asking a hegemon to include its own 'supremacy' among the give-and-take is pushing things too far. 'Self-sacrifice' of such proportion is never on the agenda.

Thus China is simply unabsorbable in the current US-led system. That in turn means that, by staying outside of the system, a giant country like China will attract towards itself other large and small countries that for whatever reason do not want to be part of the political West and global NATO. The organization of BRICS, which has recently doubled in membership, is not an oddity, nor a passing fad that might subside. Its existence is inescapable in the world organized as it is now: a single hierarchically ordered bloc, with the rest of the countries dispersed, to use Sun Yatsen's expression (the founding father of modern China), like 'pieces of sand on a sheet of paper'. As in celestial mechanics where a bigger body attracts smaller bodies around it, the exclusion of China from the political West would immediately create another political pole. If a big body cannot be integrated within the existing structure, an alternative structure will, almost by necessity, arise.

Some people naïvely, and others wrongly, believe that the problems would go away if China's domestic governance were to change and China became a liberal democracy. They are misled by looking at the political West through very special domestic lenses, and noticing that all countries that are a part of the system are (broadly speaking) democracies. They assume that each new country that would become a democracy would be eager to join the system regardless of the role the system assigns to it. For many countries that assumption was right; as we have seen, all East European former communist countries have joined the political West, and they were fairly easily integrated. But that assumption is not correct for all countries, and most patently not for China. Whether China is democratic or not has no bearing on the fact that China would ask to have at least a co-hegemonic role in East Asia and possibly in the world. That international role is entirely independent of Chinese domestic governance. It is a matter of international relations. And similarly, whether China is democratic or not, the US will not acquiesce to sharing its global power with China. Hence, the issue of absorption is orthogonal to its political system.

There is, however, one way that domestic politics and global power may become entwined. If the introduction of democracy in China makes China domestically weaker in some respects – for example, by leading to the break-up of China into smaller states such as Tibet, Xinjiang, Manchuria, etc. – such a diminished nation could not aspire to a globally powerful role. In that case, a rump China, or the largest component out of what might become independent nations, could be integrated into the current world order, by giving it a significant but not preponderant or co-hegemonic role. Of course, this begs the question not only whether such an outcome is likely or feasible, but whether it is sustainable – since there would always be forces in China, due to the depth of its historical tradition, that would push for reunification. In effect, alternate periods of consolidations and splits have characterized China for the past three millennia: from the Spring and Autumn period to the end of the Qing dynasty and the foundation of the Republic, China was united for 935 of its 2,686 years, or just over one-third of the time.[54]

The point that I argue is simply that if we take as a given the relative weight of China in terms of its overall economic and military power, it is immaterial whether it is democratic or non-democratic: its absorption into a US-led international order is impossible either way. Only if one believes that the democratization of China would lead to its break-up into smaller states, or to its diminished power, say, because of political and economic turmoil, might such a China accept a subsidiary role within the US-led system. For this to happen, seismic change would have to occur in China to diminish its domestic power and size; but if it were to become a democracy that, through chance, remained unified and as strong as ever, it would be a great mistake to assume that it would simply bend the knee to the current world order.

Great men and deterministic forces

It has been a tacit or implicit premise of this book that historical forces determine political outcomes, and the role of individuals is limited within the realms that history allows. The exercise of free will within the constraints of deterministic forces was well captured in the phrase 'libertas in imperio' ('freedom under constraint') coined by the Indian writer and philosopher Nirad Chaudhuri: '[It] allow[s] for the play of free will within its limits in [a] very deterministic view of human life.'[55] At critical junctures in history, it is very difficult to establish the right proportions between the historical or deterministic forces and the ability of extraordinary individuals to produce change. This is quite obvious when we look at the present moment. There are dramatic changes in the relative economic power between Asia and Europe, the abandonment of global neoliberalism by the main powers that championed it, political polarization in Western countries itself brought about by the effects of global neoliberalism and the rise of Asia, three or four simultaneous wars, and, at the same time, the emergence of powerful leaders who seem, at least to a less than careful observer, to hold the keys of the future, of war and peace. But when we try to see a hypothetical future that would exist if Donald Trump, Xi Jinping and Vladimir Putin suddenly left the scene, it does not seem that the coming times would look very different.

When we look at past historical developments, we can distinguish between those that are more easily explained by endogenous forces,

National Market Liberalism

or are culminating from moving tides of history, and those where an individual caused change. However, the power of the individual may often be an optical illusion. It is frequently said (including here in Chapter 2) that an endogenous explanation of World War I is readily available: the competition of the major powers for new markets, which itself was caused by maldistribution of income domestically. Even if not all elements of the hypothesis are accepted, the imperialist competition that preceded the war and then exploded in August 1914 – merely weeks after the trigger in Sarajevo was literally and metaphorically pulled – is thought to be a sufficient explanation for the conflict's beginnings. But similar endogenization is more difficult to prove for World War II unless one holds that it was simply a sequel, a continuation, of the preceding war, and that the period 1919–39 was merely a long armistice.[56] Or perhaps one can treat the war, or more precisely the advent of Adolf Hitler to power in Germany, as due to the inherent instability of the capitalist system that regularly produces crises such as the Great Depression that empower right-wing forces and demagogues.

Certain features of World War II are perhaps with some good reason attributed to the decisive role of individuals. Could it not be argued that the way Germany conducted the war, especially in regard to the Holocaust, was the 'contribution' of Hitler's personal view of the world, and that it is very unlikely that other nationalist right-wing leaders of Germany would have implemented a policy of total annihilation of the Jews? This seems to lend some credence to the view that the role of the individual in history can be fairly significant. Yet we may claim for individuals more than can be justified. Let us stay within the same example of Hitler's role, which seems, due to the strength of his inner convictions and the immense power he held, a particularly propitious case to stress the role of the individual, or of free will. But did not Hitler, we can ask, also deeply despise and dislike Christianity, seeing it as an outgrowth of Judaism and a religion of meekness, both attributes that made it, in his eyes, defective and undesirable for German youth? Was not the celebration of a Jewish dissident, who preached almost entirely to Jews and was uninterested in other races, in such a manifest contradiction with Hitler's own and the Nazi regime's implacable opposition to all Jews, even to those who distinguished themselves by bravery in the previous German wars and held high positions in the Wehrmacht? Was not German Paganism with its martial convictions a much more attractive religion? SS induction ceremonies and endless productions of Wagner give an insight into what was truly liked. Yet Hitler was unable to go against Catholic and Protestant churches and fight the clergy, even when the clergy issued proclamations that openly disagreed with some of his policies. Instead of going head-on against the recalcitrant clergy and destroying their followers, Hitler, during large parts of his rule, ignored such disagreements.[57] Even for a dictator endowed with seemingly unbounded power, the field of permissible action was limited by what the longer-term social forces permitted him to do. A full-scale attack on Christian churches would not have been suffered quietly by society and the Great Dictator had to restrain himself. In one case there was no force that could prevent him from engaging in the Holocaust; in the other case he clearly was unable to control Christian churches and their clergy, much less destroy them.

The problem is addressed in the famous Second Epilogue of Tolstoy's *War and Peace*. Tolstoy rejects both extreme theories of history: the one that claims that history is the result of the free will of actors, and the other that sees history as predetermined by economic and ideological forces and philosophers' claims to have discovered immutable historical laws. Regarding the first, the great men are not the creators of history, and it is a conceit on their part to see themselves as such. As for the second, it is a conceit of philosophers and academics to believe that they have discovered immutable laws of motion of history. As Isaiah Berlin writes in 'The Hedgehog and the Fox', 'Tolstoy turns with ever greater savagery upon scientific sociology, which claims to have discovered laws of history, but cannot possibly have found any because the number of causes upon which events turn is too great for human knowledge or calculation.'[58] Historical events are, according to Tolstoy, explained by the intermingling or co-dependency of a myriad of individual actions. Each of them is indeed a product of cause and effect, but there are millions of such small causes and effects. These 'infinitesimal' actions need to be 'integrated' in order for the event to be comprehended. If we were omniscient, we could, by 'integrating' all these small individual causes and effects, come to understand historical events. But such 'integration' of information on each and every individual case, numbering thousands if not millions of people, is not accessible to humans. 'So in history what is known to us we call laws of inevitability, what is not known [to us], we call free will. Free will is for history only an expression for the unknown remainder of what we know of laws of human life.'[59]

There is also an epistemic issue. The way that our thoughts are formed is dependent on how the actual historical events have unfolded. The further an event is from us, the more unshakeable it seems, and the more difficult it is to imagine counterfactuals since we are fully enmeshed with the consequences of the event and are living in a reality created by the event. Even in imaginary thinking, it is difficult to emancipate oneself from the hold that the act, the fait accompli in the most literal sense, has on us.[60] As Isaiah Berlin says:

> Our imagination and ability to calculate, our power of conceiving . . . what might have been if the past had, in this or that particular, been otherwise, soon reaches its natural limits – limits created both by the weakness of our capacity for calculating alternatives – 'might have beens' – and (we may add by a logical extension of Tolstoy's argument) even more by the fact that our thoughts, the terms in which they occur, the symbols themselves, are . . . determined by the actual structure of our world.[61]

Or as E. H. Carr writes: 'It is significant that our historical judgments, except those relating to a past which we can ourselves remember as the present, always appear to start from the presupposition that things could not have turned out otherwise than they did.'[62]

Going back to the question posed, whether the world would evolve differently if the three leaders of the 'counter-revolution' were to leave the scene, I think that the answer would be that, except for some modest readjustments, the historical processes described here would not change.

5.
Nationalism, Greed and Property

Nationalism, greed and property define the era of neoliberalism and will continue to define the period of what I have called here 'national market liberalism', probably even more so because all three, but especially the nationalistic factor, are globally becoming stronger.

The three factors, genealogically, have to be analysed in exactly the opposite order in which they appear to us. This means that we ought to begin with property.

Security of private property has become paramount thanks to two developments: increased production, and increased commodification of such new products.

The increase in the production of goods and services has been, as we have seen in Chapter 1, tremendous: the world's GDP has doubled in the past twenty years. This simply means that there are many more 'things' that can be owned. (Throughout this chapter, 'things' are understood not only as physical objects, but as all services – itself a capacious term because it covers practically everything – that are, or can be, commodified. In fact, even the definition of what is a 'service' is fluid. In reality, it becomes a service only when it is commodified.)

More goods and services as such do not directly translate into a greater need for the protection of private property. But here is the second element: an increasing share of things produced or 'born' (i.e., that previously did not exist) is commodified. It is precisely because many of the new commodities are not physical products (i.e., they are the 'weightless economy') that a greater effort has to be deployed to commodify them compared to the old-fashioned physical commodities and thus to protect one's property in them. Private property protection must be reinforced, and at the same time it is more difficult to do so. When we produce a table, the ownership and the possession of the table are relatively clear. The possession may diverge from ownership but both can be established rather unambiguously. Thus the property rights – if legally defined – can be enforced easily. But with many of the newly invented commodities (software programs, access to internet platforms, internet advertisements, electronic books, artificial intelligence, etc.), the very possession, the ability to access the good and benefit from it are not easy to establish. New rules have to be devised to protect one's property. Property is established even upon something that a person is allowed, or not allowed, to say through so-called non-disclosure agreements. Thus, even past events, history as it were (since non-disclosure agreements mostly relate to past events that the parties agree not to discuss openly), become private property. Such new immaterial products require much greater effort to fence in. But fencing in new goods overflows to other areas, thus leading to assigning property rights to everything. It is only paradoxical at first sight that the greater difficulty of protecting intangible property has led to increased protection of all property. But in reality, it is exactly so: greater ingenuity has to be deployed to protect private property of new products, and make sure that such rights are enforced, and that greater ingenuity spills over to the rest. Greater cost of enforcement over these new immaterial things ultimately pays off by fencing in one's property ever more tightly throughout the entire world of things, including over the ones that existed before.

Capitalism develops horizontally and vertically. Horizontal development is the expansion of capitalism and of commodification to the new geographical areas where other modes of production (traditional, semi-feudal or socialist) used to exist. By including new territories within its domain, capitalism fights against the tendency of the rate of profit to fall, and widens its field of action, thus commodifying things that were previously commonly held or public. In the nineteenth century, this was at its most obvious, in Europe in the movement of enclosures in England, or in the private appropriation of forests, right to hunt, collect wood, etc. in Central Europe:

the rights that, prior to the development of capitalism, were vested in a community. The same happened in Africa where communal land was commodified and people who alienated it to foreigners, by ostensibly signing pieces of paper brought by the Europeans, were never aware of what they were doing (the assumption of common property of land having been so strong). Similarly, more recently, the wave of privatization in formerly communist economies, as well as in select sectors in capitalist countries, widened the field of applicability of capitalism and of private property.

The vertical spread of capitalism's field of action occurs through technological change and the creation of new commodities, and thus of new wants. As mentioned, many of the new commodities are difficult to 'fence in'; they require new rules about what constitutes their private consumption, how it can be ascertained, measured and controlled, and how money can be made from it. The movement in many industries away from the sale as a one-off event to the sales of services that are quasi-automatically extended on a monthly basis represents an example of these new commodities. Instead of a software program being sold once, the users are forced to rent it on a monthly basis. It enables companies to have a steady and guaranteed stream of income. The day may not be far away when garments will no longer be sold, but the payment will be extracted upon their use: a chip built into a shoe would convey information on how much the shoe is used and the customer would be billed accordingly. But it is clear that in this case, like with the use of software, it is hard to monitor things and the need to control and protect property becomes ever greater. In other words, it is precisely because enforcement is difficult that new and clever ways to protect property rights, especially intellectual property, have to be invented. New technological developments have made the protection of private property and the definition of what exactly *is* private property much more central than they used to be. It is one of the defining features of national market liberalism.

The existence of more things that have owners (i.e., that enjoy exclusiveness of use and exclusion of others) naturally leads individuals to want more of such things. If property extends far and wide, then the only way to have access to a valuable thing is to have one for oneself. The realm of property expands; its corollary is that each individual owner wants to expand their share in that increasing domain. The value of owners' control over things goes beyond direct utility provided by things. Things possess an indirect utility because they convey to the others the image of wealth and power of the owner. Since the image of wealth and power is not bounded from above – that is, does not have any physical limits (unlike, for example, food or clothing one can consume over a given period of time) – it becomes what is commonly called greed, the *pleonexia* of Plato and the Greeks, the all-consuming and never assuageable greed.[1] Greed is extrinsic. It cannot be ascertained or judged from within, in the sense that one cannot objectively claim that the increase in the number of commodities owned above a certain limit does not bring additional utility. The utility it brings comes from an external spectator who, by being made aware or acknowledging our ownership of things, validates it, confirms that they are useful to us, and makes us want to have more so that the validation may be even stronger. Ubiquitous use of smartphones to take photos of the most trivial activities or events in one's life fulfils that function: it commodifies time, and that new commodity acquires its value only extrinsically, when it is shown to others. Taking pictures of our own lunches or walks in the woods and keeping them for ourselves is wasteful. It brings nothing, or almost nothing, in addition to the potential pleasure one gets from the activity itself. But sharing it with others brings the recognition of either one's wealth or, perhaps more importantly, of one's happiness.[2] Having one's happiness confirmed by others is one of the features of greed. Pleasure is no longer contained in the activity or good itself, but in the appreciation by others of the happiness that the activity or the good are supposed to have brought to us. Matters can go even further: activities that bring no utility, or that are even chores, but can be presented as happiness, obtain their value precisely from that presentation, and not from any intrinsic quality. I may dread or be extremely bored by listening to classical music, but if I can send a picture that shows me attending an important or expensive performance (and ostensibly being happy even when feeling miserable), the utility that comes from the conviction that others see me as happy will be sufficiently strong to overwhelm my boredom during the performance itself.

Greed thus spreads to all activities. Greed is the 'motor' that drives our obsession with property since its acquisition is seen to be the ultimate objective – not only because of the hedonistic pleasure it gives, but because it shows the worth of an individual. Greed is, as Marx defined it, 'abstract hedonism'. The increased production of things would soon reach its limits if there were no greed. But greed knows no limit. Consequently, there is no limit to production, even in the areas where we might believe that wants are limited and thus capable of satiation. Without greed there is no endless production. Endless production is needed to permanently 'feed' the greed and never satisfy it. Greed satisfied ceases to be greed.

Where does nationalism come from? From greed. It is born from the fear that our goods, if not sufficiently well protected, may be taken by others; perhaps they might trick us and steal them. But more likely, these 'others' might prove more apt in producing more, and since ownership of things often depends on being a member of a community or of a nation (rich countries are composed of rich people), the possibility of another country overtaking our country and producing more things means that people from that other country might ultimately have more things than us. The nation-state is a tool that is used to prevent such an outcome. We need to protect ourselves against the 'other'. The 'other' becomes a problem: he or she may be simply better at producing things; or may come in the form of a migrant who tries to 'steal' our job, and thus deprive us of things; or in the form of a foreign good that is produced more cheaply and makes us lose our customers; or in the form of a long-distance worker who does the same job as we do for less money; or in the form of a nation that, we believe, does not observe fully the property that is being 'fenced in' but tries to circumvent it and 'steal' things that we have produced. Or the 'other' may simply be somebody whom we cannot easily charge for the use of immaterial things as we can do domestically; the writ of our law not fully covering the surface of the globe. Thus, nationalism grows on the terrain of never-satiated mass plenty and greed; and the desire that plenty – which because of greed always remains a relative plenty (i.e., plenty in comparison to the plenty of others) – may be preserved, for ever. Wars are our way to try to reach for that 'for ever'.

Bibliography

Abramovitz, Moses (1986), 'Catching up, forging ahead, and falling behind', *Journal of Economic History*, vol. 46, pp. 385–406.

Achcar, Gilbert, *The New Cold War: The United States, Russia and China from Kosovo to Ukraine*, Haymarket Books, 2023.

Albuquerque Sant'Anna, André, 'A spectre has haunted the west: did socialism discipline income inequality?', Munich Personal RePEc Archive (MPRA) Paper No. 64756, 20 April 2015.

Alvaredo, Facundo, Atkinson, Anthony and Morelli, Salvatore (2017), 'Top Wealth Shares in the UK Over More than a Century', draft. Available at https://papers.ssrn.com/sol3/papers.cfm?abstract_id=2903853##

Aron, Raymond, *18 Lectures on Industrial Society*, Weidenfeld & Nicolson, 1967.

Aron, Raymond, *Peace and War: A Theory of International Relations*, Transaction Publishers, 2003. Original English translation in 1966; originally published in French in 1960.

Arrighi, Giovanni (1996), 'The Rise of East Asia: World Systemic and Regional Aspects', *International Journal of Sociology and Social Policy*, 1 July 1996.

Arrighi, Giovanni (2002), 'The African Crisis: World Systemic and Regional Aspects', *New Left Review*, May–June 2002.

Atkinson, Anthony, Piketty, Thomas and Saez, Emmanuel (2011), 'Top Incomes in the Long Run of History, *Journal of Economic Literature*, vol. 49, no. 1, pp. 3–71.

Autor, David H., Dorn, David and Hanson, Gordon H. (2016), 'The China Shock: Learning from Labor-Market Adjustment to Large Changes in Trade', *Annual Review of Economics*, vol. 8, pp. 205–40.

Bairoch, Paul, *Economics and World History: Myths and Paradoxes*, University of Chicago, 1993.

Bibliography

Bairoch, Paul, *Victoires et déboires: histoire économique et sociale du monde du XVIe siècle à nos jours*, Gallimard, 1997.

Bartel, Fritz, *The Triumph of Broken Promises: The End of the Cold War and the Rise of Neoliberalism*, Harvard University Press, 2022.

Bartels, Charlotte (2017), 'Top incomes in Germany, 1871–2013', draft. Available at http://wid.world/wp-content/uploads/2017/12/066-Bartels-2017-slides.pdf

Baumol, William (1986), 'Productivity growth, convergence, and welfare: what the long-run data show', *American Economic Review*, vol. 76, no. 5, pp. 1072–85.

Bell, Daniel, *The Coming of Post Industrial Society: A Venture in Social Forecasting*, Basic Books, 1976.

Benda, Julien, *The Treason of the Intellectuals*, Norton, 1982.

Berlin, Isaiah, 'The Hedgehog and the Fox' in *Russian Thinkers*, edited by Henry Hardy and Aileen Kelly, Penguin Books, 1979.

Berman, Yonatan and Milanovic, Branko (2024), 'Homoploutia: Top Labor and Capital Incomes in the United States, 1950–2020', *Review of Income and Wealth*, vol. 70, no. 3, pp. 766–84.

Bickers, Robert, *Out of China: How the Chinese Ended the Era of Western Domination*, Harvard University Press, 2017.

Blyth, Mark, *Austerity: History of a Dangerous Idea*, Oxford University Press, 2013.

Bourguignon, François and Morrisson, Christian (2002), 'Inequality among world citizens: 1820–1992', *American Economic Review*, vol. 92, no. 4, pp. 727–44.

Braudel, Fernand, *Civilization and Capitalism*, 3 volumes, University of California Press, 1992; originally published between 1967 and 1979.

Brooks, Stephen G. and Vagle, Ben A. (2025), 'The Real China Trump Card: The Hawk's Case Against Decoupling', *Foreign Affairs*, March–April 2025.

Brzezinski, Zbigniew, *The Grand Chessboard: American Primacy and Its Geostrategic Imperatives*, Basic Books, 1997.

Burnham, James, *The Managerial Revolution: What Is Happening in the World*, Lume Books, 2021; first published in 1941.

Carr, E. H., *The Twenty Years' Crisis, 1919–1939: An Introduction to the Study of International Relations*, Perennial, 2001; first published in 1939.

Bibliography

Case, Anne and Deaton, Angus, *Deaths of Despair and the Future of Capitalism*, Princeton University Press, 2020.

Chaudhuri, Nirad, *Thy Hand, Great Anarch! India 1921–1952*, Addison-Wesley Publishing Company, 1987.

Chun, Lin, *Revolution and Counterrevolution in China: The Paradoxes of China's Struggle*, Verso, 2021.

Corak, Miles (2013), 'Income Inequality, Equality of Opportunity, and Intergenerational Mobility', *Journal of Economic Perspectives*, vol. 27, no. 3, pp. 79–102.

Debord, Guy, *The Society of the Spectacle*, translated by Fredy Perlman, Black and Red, 2000; originally published in French in 1969.

DeLong, Bradford, 'America Has No Alternative to Industrial Policy', *Project Syndicate*, 5 September 2024.

Dunfort, Michael (2022), 'The Chinese path to common prosperity', *International Critical Thought*, vol. 12, no.1, pp. 35–54.

Edelstein, M., *Overseas Investment in the Age of High Imperialism: The United Kingdom, 1850–1914*, Columbia University Press, 1982.

Fernandes, Clinton, *Subimperial Power: Australia in the International Arena*, Melbourne University Publishing, 2022.

Foroohar, Rana, *Homecoming: The Path to Prosperity in a Post-Global World*, Crown, 2022.

Friedberg, Aaron L. (2024), 'Stopping the Next China Shock: A Collective Strategy for Countering Beijing's Mercantilism', *Foreign Affairs*, September/October 2024.

Gaddis, John Lewis, *The Cold War: A New History*, Penguin Books, 2006.

Galbraith, John Kenneth, *The New Industrial State*, Penguin Books, 1967.

Gernet, Jacques, *Daily Life in China on the Eve of the Mongol Invasion 1250–76*, Stanford University Press, 1962.

Gerstle, Gary, *The Rise and Fall of the Neoliberal Order*, Oxford University Press, 2022.

Gewirtz, Julian, *Unlikely Partners: Chinese Reformers, Western Economists, and the Making of Global China*, Harvard University Press, 2017.

Gibbs, David N., *The Revolt of the Rich: How the Politics of the 1970s Widened America's Class Divide*, Columbia University Press, 2024.

Bibliography

Gill, Graeme, *The Collapse of a Single-Party System: The Disintegration of the Communist Party of the Soviet Union*, Cambridge University Press, 1994.

Goldin, Claudia and Margo, Robert A. (1992), 'The Great Compression: The Wage Structure in the United States at Mid-Century', *Quarterly Journal of Economics*, vol. 107, pp. 1–34.

Hauner, Thomas, Milanovic, Branko and Naidu, Suresh, 'Inequality, foreign investment and imperialism', Munich Personal RePEc Archive (MPRA) Working Paper No. 83068, November 2017. Available at https://mpra.ub.uni-muenchen.de/83068/1/MPRA_paper_83068.pdf

Hayek, Friedrich A., *The Road to Serfdom*, University of Chicago Press, 1972; first published in 1944.

Hirschman, Albert, *The Passions and the Interests: Political Arguments for Capitalism Before Its Triumph*, Princeton University Press, 1977.

Hobson, John A., *Imperialism: A Study*, James Pott & Co., 1902.

Hsin, Chi, *Teng Hsiao-ping: A Political Biography*, Cosmos Books, 1978.

Huang, Yasheng, *The Rise and Fall of the EAST*, Yale University Press, 2023.

Hung, Ho-fung, *The China Boom: Why China Will Not Rule the World*, Columbia University Press, 2015.

Jacques, Martin, *When China Rules the World*, Allen Lane, 2009.

Keynes, John Maynard, *The General Theory of Employment, Interest and Money*, Harcourt, Brace, 1935.

Kissinger, Henry, *On China*, Penguin Press, 2011.

Kissinger, Henry, *Leadership: Six Studies in World Strategy*, Penguin Books, 2022.

Klein, Matthew and Pettis, Michael, *Trade Wars Are Class Wars: How Rising Inequality Distorts the Global Economy and Threatens International Peace*, Yale University Press, 2020.

Kozyrev, Andrei, *The Firebird: The Elusive Fate of Russian Democracy*, University of Pittsburgh Press, 2019.

Lakner, Christoph and Milanovic, Branko (2016), 'Global income distribution: from the fall of the Berlin Wall to the Great Recession', *World Bank Economic Review*, vol. 30, no. 2, pp. 203–32.

Legutko, Ryszard, *The Demon in Democracy: Totalitarian Temptations in Free Societies*, Encounter Books, 2016.

Lenin, Vladimir Ilych, *Lenin's Final Fight: Speeches and Writings, 1922–23*, Pathfinder Press, 2010.

Li, Bozhong and van Zanden, Jan Luiten (2012), 'Before the Great Divergence? Comparing the Yangtze Delta and the Netherlands at the beginning of the Nineteenth Century', *Journal of Economic History*, vol. 72, no. 2, pp. 956–89.

Li, H., Liu, P., Zhang, J. and Ma, N. (2007), 'Economic returns to Communist Party membership: Evidence from urban Chinese twins', *Economic Journal*, vol. 117, pp. 1504–20.

Lindert, Peter (1986), 'Unequal British wealth since 1867', *Journal of Political Economy*, vol. 94, no. 6, pp. 1127–62.

Lofgren, Mike, *The Deep State: The Fall of the Constitution and the Rise of a Shadow Government*, Viking, 2016.

Lovell, Julia, *Maoism: A Global History*, Knopf, 2019.

Lyons, N. S., 'The China Convergence: Yes, the West is becoming more like China. Here is the real reason why', The Upheaval Substack, 3 August 2023. Available at https://theupheaval.substack.com/p/the-china-convergence

Lyons, N. S., 'The Total State and the Twilight of American Democracy', 9 September 2024. Available at https://theupheaval.substack.com/p/the-total-state-and-the-twilight

Markovits, Daniel, *The Meritocracy Trap: How America's Foundational Myth Feeds Inequality, Dismantles the Middle Class, and Devours the Elite*, Penguin Press, 2019.

Mattei, Clara, *The Capital Order: How Economists Invented Austerity and Paved the Way to Fascism*, University of Chicago Press, 2025.

Matveev, Ilya, 'We Live in a World of Growing Imperialist Rivalries', *Jacobin*, 28 May 2024.

Mazower, Mark, *Governing the World: The History of an Idea, 1815 to the Present*, Penguin Books, 2012.

McGregor, Richard, *Asia's Reckoning: The Struggle for Global Dominance*, Allen Lane, 2017.

Mian, Atif, Straub, Ludwig and Sufi, Amir, 'The saving glut of the rich', National Bureau of Economic Research Working Paper No. 26941, April 2020.

Milanovic, Branko, Lindert, Peter and Williamson, Jeffrey (2011), 'Measuring ancient inequality', *Economic Journal*, vol. 121, no. 1, pp. 255–72.

Milanovic, Branko, *Global Inequality: A New Approach for the Age of Globalization*, Harvard University Press, 2016.

Milanovic, Branko, 'Inequality, imperialism, and the outbreak of World War I' in Steve Broadberry and Mark Harrison (eds), *The Economics of the Great War: A Centennial Perspective*, VoxEU Ebook, November 2018.

Milanovic, Branko, *Capitalism, Alone: The Future of the System That Rules the World*, Harvard University Press, 2019.

Milanovic, Branko (2022), 'After the crisis: the evolution of the global income distribution between 2008 and 2013', *Review of Income and Wealth*, vol. 68, no. 1, pp. 43–73.

Milanovic, Branko (2023), 'The Great Convergence: Global Equality and Its Discontents', *Foreign Affairs*, July–August 2023, pp. 78–91.

Milanovic, Branko, *Visions of Inequality*, Harvard University Press, 2023.

Milanovic, Branko (2024), 'The three eras of global inequality, 1820–2020 with the focus on the past thirty years', *World Development*, vol. 177.

Milanovic, Branko, *The World Under Capitalism*, Polity Press, 2025.

Moyn, Samuel, *Not Enough: Human Rights in an Unequal World*, Harvard University Press, 2018.

Myrdal, Gunnar, *Asian Drama: An Inquiry into the Poverty of Nations*, 3 volumes, Allen Lane, 1968.

Nayar, Krishnan, *Liberal Capitalist Democracy: The God that Failed*, Hurst, 2023.

Nicolson, Harold, *Peace Making 1919*, Harcourt, Brace and Company, 1939; first published in 1933.

O'Rourke, Kevin H. and Williamson, Jeffrey G., *Globalization and History: The Evolution of a Nineteenth-Century Atlantic Economy*, MIT Press, 1999.

Orain, Arnaud, *Le monde confisqué: Essai sur le capitalisme de la finitude (XVIIe–XXIe siècle)*, Flammarion, 2024.

Peyrefitte, Alain, *Quand la Chine s'éveillera . . . le monde tremblera*, Fayard, 1973.

Philippon, Thomas and Reshef, Ariell (2012), 'Wages and Human Capital in the US Finance Industry: 1909–2006', *Quarterly Journal of Economics*, vol. 127, no. 4, pp. 1551–609.

Piketty, Thomas and Saez, Emmanuel (2006), 'The Evolution of Top Incomes: A Historical and International Perspective', *American Economic Review*, vol. 96, no. 2, pp. 200–205.

Piketty, Thomas, *Le capital au XXIe siècle*, Editions du Seuil, 2013.

Piketty, Thomas, *Capital in the Twenty-First Century*, Harvard University Press, 2014.

Piketty, Thomas and Zucman, Gabriel (2014), 'Capital is Back: Wealth-Income Ratios in Rich Countries, 1700–2010', *Quarterly Journal of Economics*, vol. 129, no. 3, pp. 1255–310.

Polanyi, Karl, *The Great Transformation*, Foreword by Robert M. MacIver, Beacon Press, 1957; first published in 1944.

Pomeranz, Kenneth, *The Great Divergence: China, Europe and the Making of the Modern World Economy*, Princeton University Press, 2000.

Ranaldi, Marco and Milanovic, Branko (2022), 'Capitalist systems and income inequality', *Journal of Comparative Economics*, vol. 50, no. 1, pp. 20–32.

Rančić, Dragoslav, *Kina posle Mao Ce Tunga*, Politika, 1978.

Rawls, John, *A Theory of Justice*, Harvard University Press, 1971.

Rawls, John (1993), 'The Law of Peoples – A Summary', *Critical Enquiry*, vol. 20, no. 1, pp. 36–68. Available at http://www.jstor.org/stable/1343947

Rawls, John, *The Law of Peoples*, Harvard University Press, 1999.

Rostow, W. W., *The Stages of Economic Growth: The Non-Communist Manifesto*, Cambridge University Press, 1960.

Schell, Orville and Delury, John, *Wealth and Power: China's Long March to the Twenty-First Century*, Random House, 2014.

Schumpeter, Joseph, 'The Sociology of Imperialisms' in Richard Swedberg (ed.), *Joseph Schumpeter: The Economics and Sociology of Capitalism*, Princeton University Press, 1991; first published in 1918.

Schumpeter, Joseph, *Capitalism, Socialism and Democracy*, Harper Perennial Modern Classics, 2008; first published in 1942.

Sharma, Ruchir, 'The Xi nobody saw coming', *Financial Times*, 14 January 2023. Available at https://www.ft.com/content/f6c47c54-b928-46ee-aa63-fb903e74b2e6

Slobodian, Quinn, *Globalists: The End of Empire and the Birth of Neoliberalism*, Harvard University Press, 2018.

Smith, M., Yagan, D., Zidar, O. and Zwick, E. (2019), 'Capitalists in the twenty-first century', *Quarterly Journal of Economics*, vol. 134, no. 4, pp. 1675–745.

Smolensky, Eugene and Plotnick, Robert (1993), 'Inequality and poverty in the United States, 1900 to 1990', Institute for Research on Poverty, University of Wisconsin-Madison, Discussion Paper No. 998-93.

Stevenson, David, *1917: War, Peace and Revolution*, Oxford University Press, 2019.

Tellis, Ashley J., 'Great Expectations: India amid US–China Competition' in Hal Brands (ed.), *Lessons from the New Cold War: America Confronts the China Challenge*, Johns Hopkins University Press, 2025.

Vries, Peer, *Escaping Poverty: The Origins of Modern Economic Growth*, Vienna University Press, 2013.

Wang, Hui, *China's New Order: Society, Politics, and Economy in Transition*, Harvard University Press, 2003.

Weber, Isabella, *How China Escaped Shock Therapy: The Market Reform Debate*, Routledge, 2021.

Weitzman, Martin L. and Xu, Chenggang (1994), 'Chinese Township-Village Enterprises as Vaguely Defined Cooperatives', *Journal of Comparative Economics*, vol. 18, pp. 11–142.

Wenar, Leif and Milanovic, Branko (2009), 'Are Liberal Peoples Peaceful?', *Journal of Political Philosophy*, vol. 17, no. 4, pp. 462–86.

Wesseling, H. L., *Divide and Rule: The Partition of Africa, 1880–1914*, translated by Arnold J. Pomerans, Praeger, 1996.

Wiles, Peter, 'Power without Influence: the Economic Impact' in Arnold Toynbee (ed.), *The Impact of the Russian Revolution, 1917–1967: The Influence of Bolshevism on the World Outside Russia*, The Royal Institute of International Affairs, Oxford University Press, 1967.

Williams, David Lay, *The Greatest of All Plagues: How Economic Inequality Shaped Political Thought from Plato to Marx*, Princeton University Press, 2024.

Wolff, Edward, *A Century of Wealth in America*, Harvard University Press, 2018.

Xi, Jinping, 'Regarding the Construction of Socialism with Chinese Characteristics', RedSails.org, 2013. Available at https://redsails.org/regarding-swcc-construction/

Bibliography

Xi, Jinping, *Anecdotes and Sayings*, China Daily, September 2017.

Xi, Jinping, 'Comprehensively Promoting the Construction of a Strong Nation and the Great Rejuvenation of the Chinese Nation through Chinese-style Modernization', February 2023, published in *Qiushi*, January 2025.

Yang, Li, Novokmet, Filip and Milanovic, Branko (2021), 'From workers to capitalists in less than two generations: A study of Chinese urban elite transformation between 1988 and 2013', *British Journal of Sociology*, vol. 72, no. 3, pp. 478–513.

Yang, Li, Milanovic, Branko and Lin, Yaoqi (2024), 'Anti-corruption campaign in China: An empirical investigation', *European Journal of Political Economy*, vol. 85.

Zubok, Vladislav, *Collapse: The Fall of the Soviet Union*, Yale University Press, 2021.

Acknowledgements

The book has its origin in a series of phone conversations I had with Casiana Ionita during the long days of Covid lockdowns. Casiana came up with the idea, and asked me if I was interested, of reworking, updating and presenting in a new, and better, framework some of my writings that dealt with globalization, neoliberalism and inequality. It seemed a tempting proposal but I did not do much then, busy with other projects. The international scene, already gloomy and stormy, took a dramatic turn for the worse in 2022. The issues on which I wrote and that Casiana wanted me to think about again became even more important, their significance illuminated, as it were, by the fire of the tanks and explosion of the drones. It became clear to me that there was an invisible thread, both in intellectual history and in the observable facts, going from the early 1990s to today (2025). I was a witness to some of these events, not only through my writings, but through direct and indirect involvement.

Thus, I went back to the project. I then met Hana Teraie-Wood, with whom I further discussed and elaborated the idea, and who, through several stages of edits and re-edits, influenced the book's structure. I am very grateful to her for excellent, and super friendly, comments and uncommon patience with my counter-arguments. Chad Zimmerman, the editor of the US version of the book, contributed with his comments too, as did several anonymous reviewers. The final copy-editing was done by Tamsin Shelton and Rebecca Lee, who went carefully through the text, corrected missing, or in some cases, deleted superfluous, definite articles, caught other mistakes, fixed citations and provided excellent comments. I am grateful to them all.

And indeed, I have to register my gratitude to many co-authors with whom I have written papers whose results I use in this book: Yonatan Berman, Thomas Hauner, Christoph Lakner, Yaoqi Lin,

Acknowledgements

Suresh Naidu, Filip Novokmet, Marco Ranaldi, Roy van der Weide, Leif Wenar and Li Yang. I am also grateful to Tongdong Bai, Bob Cheng, Zhexun Mo and Li Yang, who helped me with numerous Chinese articles and books and discussion of China. Obviously, in all these cases, the final interpretation and the opinions, and thus responsibility for possible errors, are mine.

The book was written while I was working and teaching at the Graduate Center, City University of New York.

Notes

1. The Rise of Asia

1 Perhaps the New International Economic Order should be seen as the second challenge to the West, the first being the communist challenge of the Soviet Union, early Maoist China, and Soviet-affiliated countries. To some extent that challenge carried over in the calls for the NIEO and non-aligned movement, but it was still distinct.
2 The term 'Third World' was first used by the French demographer Alfred Sauvy. It was supposed to convey the idea of an underrepresented majority, taken from the French *Tiers État*, that included before the French Revolution everybody but the clergy and nobility.
3 Calculated from World Bank, World Development Indicators. GDP expressed in international dollars of equal purchasing power parity ($PPP).
4 See Gunnar Myrdal, *Asian Drama*; published in three volumes in 1968.
5 I witnessed myself the suddenness of the economic shock. I spent December 1973 in London. It was just two months after the Yom Kippur war and after the oil embargo was declared. The UK had not by then begun to exploit the North Sea oil; it was a big importer of energy. The shops in London stayed open only three days a week; the heating in the midst of winter was reduced to a minimum; kerosene lamps replaced, in many instances, electric light. And quite memorably the escalators in the Underground were shut down to save energy. I did not particularly care because I was then with my girlfriend; we had a very good time regardless. But I was impressed by the stoic and even slightly amused attitude of the Londoners. Nobody complained. Everybody took the new hardship in their stride. Even – I had the impression – slightly enjoying it, believing that it would be temporary. Perhaps people still remembered the Blitz . . .

6 Claudia Goldin and Robert A. Margo, 'The Great Compression: The Wage Structure in the United States at Mid-Century', *Quarterly Journal of Economics*, vol. 107, pp. 1–34.

7 When did I know that the socialist system as existed then was unsustainable? In the summer of 1978, I had to go to a hospital in Belgrade due to some post-appendectomy complications. I stayed in a large room, shared by about ten other patients. My bed was next to a window. On a rainy day, I got up from my bed, looked out of the window, and there on the grounds, in the courtyard, I saw several unopened large cardboard boxes labelled 'Siemens' and containing probably newly purchased medical equipment. The machines arrived but there was no one to unload the packages, move the equipment indoors, and install it. The rain kept on falling, soaking the boxes and the equipment. Thousands of dollars' worth of things that were supposed to help patients and perhaps save lives were simply left outdoors, to the vagaries of the elements. Nobody cared.

8 Peter Wiles, 'Power without Influence: the Economic Impact', in Arnold Toynbee (ed.), *The Impact of the Russian Revolution, 1917–1967: The Influence of Bolshevism on the World Outside Russia*, The Royal Institute of International Affairs, Oxford University Press, 1967.

9 'Even once the Soviet Union started providing aid through the UN after Stalin's death, the sums involved were tiny, compared with the American contributions – a mere $2 million pledged in the late 1950s, for instance, against around $38 million by the United States'. Mark Mazower, *Governing the World: The History of an Idea, 1815 to the Present*, p. 277; quoting data from Alexander Dallin, *The Soviet View of the United Nations*, MIT Press, 1959, p. 65.

10 China made a momentous decision not to go that route (borrowing), but rather to become more open to foreign (principally American) foreign investment. For the debate on China's reforms, see the excellent book by Isabella Weber, *How China Escaped Shock Therapy*, and Julian Gewirtz, *Unlikely Partners: Chinese Reformers, Western Economists, and the Making of Global China*. China's strategy will be discussed further in Chapter 2.

11 See Fritz Bartel, *The Triumph of Broken Promises*, especially Chapter 5,

Notes

and Vladislav Zubok, *Collapse*, Chapter 9, dealing with the failed Soviet attempts to get Western financing of reforms.

12 Fritz Bartel, *The Triumph of Broken Promises*, p. 136.
13 Source: calculated from micro data available in the Luxembourg Income Survey based on US Current Population Survey.
14 See Clinton Fernandes's excellent *Subimperial Power*, discussing Australia alone but easily applicable to several other countries.
15 In addition to Oceania, which was always considered a part of the political West.
16 Source: calculated from World Bank, World Development Indicators. GDP expressed in international dollars of equal purchasing power parity ($PPP).
17 This is of course speculative because military potential depends on many things that are difficult, or impossible, to measure *a priori*. It could be thus argued that a population that is ten times greater must also provide more of a military 'punch'; furthermore, it is doubtful whether a much greater number of nuclear weapons possessed by Russia compared to China makes a difference since only a limited number of such weapons may be sufficient to completely annihilate an enemy. Killing somebody ten times does not make much sense.
18 See an excellent book on the events and ideology of the period: Samuel Moyn's *Not Enough: Human Rights in an Unequal World*.
19 Including all countries in Asia, inclusive of Western Asia, but excluding China, India, and Japan and South Korea; the latter two are classified as political West.
20 Source: own calculation based on World Bank, World Development Indicators.
21 Source: own calculation based on World Bank, World Development Indicators. All expressed in international dollars.
22 Strictly speaking, it need not always be so. A country might have been relatively rich in the past, then gone through a period of depression, and currently growing fast but with its relative peak GDP still below the one achieved in the past. An example is Russia whose GDP per capita in relation to the world peaked in 1985 (as a republic of the USSR), then declined precipitously in the 1990s and increased again in

the first decade of the twenty-first century without coming close to its erstwhile maximum.

23 Source: own calculation based on World Bank, World Development Indicators.

24 The Gini coefficient is a measure of inequality whose lowest value is 0 when everybody's income is the same and the maximum value is 1 when just one unit (person, household or country, depending on what is being studied) takes the entire income.

25 Regarding the latter case, it is important to point out that in this calculation I keep the country sample of the West unchanged throughout (i.e., I do not add to the West the post-communist countries that have joined it after 1990). Therefore, the absence of convergence in the West over the past half-century is all the more intriguing since the original literature on economic convergence (e.g., Abramovitz 1986; Baumol 1986) used precisely the empirical finding of income convergence among the rich countries to argue either for club convergence (which no longer takes place) or for the general case of convergence, namely that it should hold globally, with poorer countries tending to grow faster than richer countries. Contradicting these claims, global between-country convergence has not happened during the past seventy years and the club convergence of Western countries has stopped. Given the original claims for convergence as a 'law' of economics, it is a subject that might require further attention from economists.

26 Source: own calculation based on World Bank, World Development Indicators. GDPs per capita expressed in international dollars of equal purchasing power parity ($PPP).

27 Source: own calculation based on World Bank, World Development Indicators. GDPs per capita expressed in international dollars of equal purchasing power parity ($PPP).

28 That number is also somewhat exaggerated until the mid-1960s because of the lack of data for the USSR. Around the mid-1960s, USSR share of global output was 7 per cent, and adding it to the world output would slightly reduce US share.

29 Source: calculated from World Bank, World Development Indicators.

30 Source: calculated from World Bank, World Development Indicators.
31 Most of the discussion in this chapter is based on Milanovic, 'The three eras of global inequality, 1820–2020 with the focus on the past thirty years', *World Development*, vol. 177, May 2024, and Milanovic, 'The Great Convergence: Global Equality and Its Discontents', *Foreign Affairs*, July–August 2023, pp. 78–91.
32 And surely that would be the case in 2023 or 2024, if the data were available.
33 Source: Milanovic, 'The three eras of global inequality . . .', *World Development*, vol. 177, May 2024.
34 Note that $PPP 18,000 is not, as is sometimes interpreted, annual salary. It is after-tax household per capita income. To explain better what it means, imagine a four-member household. Its total income from all sources would, under this scenario, be $PPP 18,000 $\times$ 4 = $PPP 72,000. Add to that a direct tax of about 25 per cent, and we get a gross household income of almost $PPP 100,000. It is this last form (household gross income) that many people use to assess and compare incomes.
35 We take here as the middle class all those whose incomes are in the range of 20 per cent below to 20 per cent above the global median income. The global median per capita after-tax income in 2018 was just under $PPP 3,300.
36 Source: Milanovic, 'The three eras of global inequality . . .', *World Development*, vol. 177, May 2024.
37 This ratio is higher than the ratio of US vs China GDPs per capita, because the share of personal income and personal consumption is lower in Chinese GDP than in US GDP.
38 Income gaps calculated in dollars at the market exchange rate are even greater.
39 Assessing the relative costs of the trade war, the *Wall Street Journal* writes: 'Overall, the damage to China's gross domestic product from the trade war was three times as high as the hit to the U.S., according to some Chinese economists' ('Beijing Braces for a Rematch of Trump vs. China', *Wall Street Journal*, 2 May 2024, p. 8). Available at https://www.wsj.com/world/china/trump-china-rematch-beijing-0b0a9c6e. Union Bank of Switzerland (UBS) estimates the effects of the proposed

60 per cent tariff on Chinese imports to 'cost' 1.5 per cent of Chinese GDP ('Trade War Would Hit China Hard', *Wall Street Journal*, 15 November 2024, p. A8). Similarly, Yasheng Huang in *The Rise and the Fall of the EAST* (p. 310) cites the estimates of Beijing think tank the Institute for International and Strategic Studies that show that, while decoupling is a lose-lose proposition, the economic costs are greater for China. Finally, Stephen Brooks and Ben Vagle explore a number of scenarios of trade disruptions in the case of a US–China economic war. In all scenarios they find disproportionately larger losses for China, ranging from five times as great as those of the US to twelve times (Stephen G. Brooks and Ben A. Vagle, 'The Real China Trump Card: The Hawk's Case Against Decoupling', *Foreign Affairs*, March–April 2025).

40 Since the catch-up is defined in terms of the number of affluent people, higher population growth rate of the Asian countries does, all things being equal, make the catch-up point come earlier.

41 Source: GDP data are from World Bank, World Development Indicators. GDP per capita are expressed in real PPP terms.

42 For the illustration of the Chinese advance into the middle ranges of global income distribution, the Chinese urban population (more than 800 million people) is more relevant than the Chinese rural population.

43 Source: Milanovic, 'The three eras of global inequality . . .', *World Development*, vol. 177, May 2024. The data for Germany are for 1993 and 2018.

44 To get a more precise definition of who is in the top group, we divide populations of China, India and Indonesia into their urban and rural parts.

45 Source: Milanovic, 'The three eras of global inequality . . .', *World Development*, vol. 177, May 2024.

46 If we consider as a 'unit' each year within the episodes of African countries' growing at 5 per cent per capita, there were only 64 such 'units' between 1960 and 2020. Given that during these sixty years there were about fifty-five countries in Africa, and thus potentially 3,300 units, one can appreciate how rare such events were (64 out of 3,300 is less than 2 per cent).

Notes

2. Convergence and Conflict

1 This is an opinion that to an observer of the current world situation (2024–25) may not be totally alien.
2 Friedrich Hayek, *The Road to Serfdom*, p. 14; first published in 1944.
3 Montesquieu's most important work *The Spirit of Laws* was published in 1748; Quesnay and Mirabeau's *La Philosophie Rurale* was published in 1763.
4 A contemporary reader of Trump's various pronouncements cannot fail to observe how much the state power is put in service of individual capitalist interests. And similarly, how the monopolies of today (Microsoft, Amazon, Tesla, Google, etc.) do not shy away from appealing to the state to protect their interests.
5 I attended a couple of Francophone economic associations' meetings. At first, the conferences were entirely in French, but subsequent conferences were conducted in French and English. It was striking to me how little mutual interest there was to engage in discussion, including on ordinary matters, between the French and African economists speaking French. The former wanted to speak with Americans, the latter were left to converse among themselves. That was in strong contrast to what happens in Hispanic conferences where Spanish and Latin American economists have a lot of common topics. The reason is simply a difference in development levels. An ordinary French macro economist has little to say, and little knowledge, of Burkina Faso's economic problems. The same is not true for a Spanish and an Argentine economist.
6 Ivan Bloch, *The Future of War*, a multi-volume *plaidoyer* on destructiveness of wars among commercially integrated countries, originally published in Russian in 1898; Norman Angell, *The Great Illusion*, William Heinemann, 1910, a huge international bestseller at the time.
7 According to Albert Hirschman, Montesquieu was one of the originators, or perhaps the founder, of this view: 'the general opinion on the effects of commerce on international discord or harmony changed

substantially from the 17th to the 18th century. Whether because of mercantilist doctrine or because of the fact that markets were in fact so limited that an expansion of the commerce of one nation could only be secured by displacing that of another, commerce was characterized as "perpetual combat" by Colbert and as "a kind of warfare" by Sir Josiah Child.' (*The Passions and the Interests*, p. 79.) That, according to Hirschman, changed in the eighteenth century and accordingly influenced philosophers to view trade much more favourably.

8 *The Great Transformation*, p. 189.
9 And even this is an exaggeration of the attention that Montesquieu gives to trade since most of the discussion (in effect the entire Book XXI) is devoted to the description of historical conquests, trade routes used by the Egyptians, Greeks, Romans, Tatars, Chinese, etc., geographic knowledge of the ancient peoples, their writings, etc.
10 Book XX, Chapter 23.
11 This was the so-called Second Serfdom in Eastern Europe.
12 'those who are most in want . . . will find an advantage in putting a stop to all commercial intercourse'. (Book XX, Chapter 23.)
13 Book XX, Chapter 2.
14 Montesquieu's *doux commerce* can also be seen as 'commercial internationalism', and such internationalism, according to Julien Benda, 'is a protest against national egotism, not on behalf of a spiritual passion, but on behalf of another egotism, another earthly passion. It is the impulse of a certain category of men – laborers, bankers, industrialists – who unite across frontiers in the name of private and practical interests, and who only oppose the national spirit because it thwarts them in satisfying those interests.' (Julien Benda, *The Treason of the Intellectuals*, p. 82.)
15 As in the famous quote of nobody ever having seen a dog deliberately exchange bones with another dog.
16 *The Wealth of Nations*, Book IV, Chapter 2, p. 583.
17 It shifted the natural flow of commerce and increased prices of imports for the British customers. 'Since the establishment of the Act of Navigation . . . the colony trade has been continually increasing, while many other branches of foreign trade, particularly of that to other parts of Europe, have been continually decaying. Our manufactures for foreign

sale, instead of being suited, as before the Act of Navigation, to the neighbouring market of Europe, or to the more distant one of the countries which lie round the Mediterranean sea, have the greater part of them, been accommodated to the still more distant one of the colonies; to the market in which they have the monopoly, rather than to that in which they have many competitors. The causes of decay in other branches of foreign trade, which . . . have been sought for in the excess and improper mode of taxation, in the high price of labour, in the increase of luxury, etc., may all be found in the overgrowth of the colony trade.' (*The Wealth of Nations*, Book IV, Chapter 7, pp. 757–8.)

18 *The Wealth of Nations*, Book IV, Chapter 7, pp. 813–14.
19 *The Wealth of Nations*, Book IV, Chapter 3, p. 513.
20 *The Wealth of Nations*, Book IV, Chapter 3, p. 621. Book IV deals with the systems of political economy, and it is there that Smith proposes his views on trade and the connection between trade and peace, and criticizes mercantilists.
21 *The Wealth of Nations*, Book IV, Chapter 7, p. 795.
22 The relationship has been the subject of many disagreements among economists, not just theoretically, but even in terms of empirical results. Paul Bairoch, for example, in a three-volume long-run historical study *Victoires et déboires* (and in a shorter book available in English, *Economics and World History: Myths and Paradoxes*) finds that periods of relative closeness to trade were associated with higher growth rates; the opposite result is emphatically stated by Kevin O'Rourke and Jeffrey Williamson who write in *Globalization and History: The Evolution of a Nineteenth-Century Atlantic Economy* (p. 167): 'the history of the Atlantic economy offers an unambiguous positive correlation between globalization on the one hand and [income] convergence on the other. This book [O'Rourke and Williamson's] argues that the correlation is *causal*' (my emphasis).
23 *The Theory of Moral Sentiments*, Part VI, II. 46, p. 206.
24 *The Theory of Moral Sentiments*, Part VI, II. 29, p. 200.
25 See John Hobson in *Imperialism: A Study* (1902), Rosa Luxemburg in *Accumulation of Capital* (1913), Vladimir Ilych Lenin in *Imperialism: The Highest Stage of Capitalism* (1917).

26 According to Ernest Mandel (*Traité d'économie marxiste*, vol. 3, Juillard, 1962), the economic motivations for colonization were the following: (1) guarantee safety of capital invested in a country, (2) get rid of other European competitors, (3) control the sources of raw materials, and (4) get access to a cheap labour force. A story of conflicting national economic interests is beautifully told in Barry Unsworth's 1979 novel *Pascali's Island*, set on an Ottoman-ruled Greek island around the turn of the twentieth century where rumours abound of the discovery of valuable minerals. This leads to a competition between German and English capitalists.

27 Hundreds, if not thousands, of books have been written on the subject. However, it may be worth highlighting three, each dealing with a different part of the world: H. L. Wesseling's *Divide and Rule: The Partition of Africa, 1880–1914*; Robert Bickers's *Out of China*; and David Stevenson's *1917: War, Peace and Revolution* (especially the last two chapters dealing with the Middle East and India).

28 See *The Great Transformation*, Chapter 1.

29 'It is not industrial progress that demands the opening up of new markets and areas of investment, but maldistribution of consuming power which prevents the absorption of commodities and capital within the country.' (*Imperialism*, p. 85.)

30 Hobson's was an under-consumptionist theory to which Keynes in *The General Theory* paid explicit homage. Keynes, however, was reluctant to get fully engaged along that road, even if his frequent use of diminished marginal propensity to consume coming with higher income made his analysis of lack of effective demand similar to Hobson's. He did so probably because of 'political' reasons related to the acceptance of *The General Theory*: he thought that the mainstream economists treated under-consumptionists as, in his own words, the 'underworld of economics' and Keynes wanted to stay away from it. The 'underworld' to which Karl Marx, Silvio Gesell and Major C. H. Douglas are consigned is mentioned in *The General Theory of Employment, Interest and Money*, Chapter 3, p. 32. A more reasonable, and at times laudatory, discussion of under-consumptionists is made in Chapter 23.

31 *The Great Transformation*, p. 217.

32 Thomas Hauner, Suresh Naidu and I have done the first empirical test of the Hobson-Lenin-Luxemburg hypothesis using the historical pre-World War I data. We find the results are fully consistent with the hypothesis: income and wealth inequalities in key belligerent countries (UK, France and Germany) were at their historical peak around 1910–14, returns on foreign assets outperformed returns on domestic assets, and the rich held a disproportionate amount of foreign assets. The only thing that remains to be shown (and which is not easy) is that the rich exerted a disproportionate influence on countries' foreign policies (see Thomas Hauner, Branko Milanovic and Suresh Naidu, 'Inequality, foreign investment and imperialism', Munich Personal RePEc Archive (MPRA) Working Paper No. 83068, November 2017, and Branko Milanovic, 'Inequality, imperialism, and the outbreak of World War I' in Steve Broadberry and Mark Harrison (eds), *The Economics of the Great War: A Centennial Perspective*, VoxEU Ebook, November 2018).

33 Atif Mian, Ludwig Straub and Amir Sufi, 'The saving glut of the rich', National Bureau of Economic Research Working Paper No. 26941, April 2020.

34 Ilya Matveev, 'We Live in a World of Growing Imperialist Rivalries', *Jacobin*, 28 May 2024. Available at https://jacobin.com/2024/05/us-china-rivalry-imperialism-brics-periphery/

35 In the early 2020s, Chinese consumption as a share of GDP was only 38 per cent while on average in the rest of the world the ratio exceeds 60 per cent. In the United States, it is almost 70 per cent.

36 Matthew Klein and Michael Pettis, *Trade Wars Are Class Wars*.

37 However, it may also be thought that this difference is more apparent than real: capitalist systems of the early twentieth century also used non-economic means, especially through suppression of trade unions, to depress wages and consumption.

38 'A will for broad conquest, without tangible limits, for the capture of positions that were manifestly untenable – this was typical imperialism.' ('The Sociology of Imperialisms', p. 157.)

39 'The Sociology of Imperialisms', p. 193–4.

40 'The Sociology of Imperialisms', p. 194.

41 'The Sociology of Imperialisms', p. 200.

42 Schumpeter was among the few economists who had experience working and living in a Third World country. He spent two years (1907–08) working as a financial adviser to a local potentate in Egypt.
43 'The Sociology of Imperialisms', pp. 201–2.
44 *Capitalism, Socialism and Democracy*, Chapter VIII, p. 105.
45 Schumpeter mentions favourably the possibility of domestic economic sources of imperialism: '[neo-Marxism] views imperialism simply as the reflex of the interests of the capitalist upper stratum at a given stage of capitalist development. Beyond doubt this is by far the most serious contribution toward a solution of our problem.' ('The Sociology of Imperialisms', p. 144.) Likewise, he thought that this was characteristic of the Roman Empire: 'The ruling class [in Rome] was always inclined to declare that the country was in danger when it was really only class interests that were threatened . . . History offers no better example of imperialism rooted in the domestic political situation and derived from class structure.' ('The Sociology of Imperialisms', p. 179.)
46 Arnaud Orain, *Le monde confisqué: Essai sur le capitalisme de la finitude (XVIIe–XXIe siècle)*.
47 So much so that China allowed the United States to establish listening stations in western China to monitor Soviet military. As Richard McGregor (*Asia's Reckoning: The Struggle for Global Dominance*, p. 106) writes: 'In an episode largely forgotten in the strategic suspicion that typifies current U.S.-China relations, the CIA top officials had travelled in secret to Beijing in 1980, negotiating for an entire week an agreement to place surveillance equipment on Chinese soil.'
48 The first reaction, though, was not to look abroad but to go back to China's own period of reform (1957) before the Great Leap Forward (see Isabella Weber, *How China Escaped Shock Therapy*, and Yasheng Huang, *The Rise and Fall of the EAST*).
49 According to the Washington Consensus opinion at that time, such a strange property combination could never prove efficient. Martin L. Weitzman and Chenggang Xu ('Chinese Township-Village Enterprises as Vaguely Defined Cooperatives', *Journal of Comparative Economics*, vol. 18, pp. 11–142, 1994) argued the opposite, and studied the success of

Township and Village Enterprises that 'presents a severe challenge for traditional property rights theory'.

50 The argument was, of course, made many times, but perhaps the best explanation of the geopolitical bases of the East Asian economic miracle was made by Giovanni Arrighi ('The African Crisis: World Systemic and Regional Aspects', *New Left Review*, May–June 2002, and 'The Rise of East Asia: World Systemic and Regional Aspects', *International Journal of Sociology and Social Policy*, July 1996) who insisted on the double crucial role of the United States: provision of technology through direct investment, and openness of its market to Asian exports. As Arrighi showed, Africa never had the strategic importance for the United States compared to that of East Asia and thus could never count on such an accommodating policy. One could add that Latin America was always considered a US backyard, and there was no need for the United States to be very accommodating to Latin American countries as they were already part of the US sphere of influence. It is thus entirely ahistorical to argue, as Martin Ravallion does in 'Poverty in China since 1950: A Counterfactual Perspective' (National Bureau of Economic Research Working Paper No. 28370, January 2021), that China could have followed East Asian economic strategy without accommodation with the United States that was certainly not forthcoming in the 1950s and 1960s when the US and China had no diplomatic relations, US recognized Taiwan as the only government of China and maintained an embargo on trade with 'Red China'.

51 'Building cooperation with China to counter the Soviet Union was an overriding American interest during the Cold War.' (Henry Kissinger, *Leadership*, p. 176.)

52 Henry Kissinger, *On China*, p. 274. But it is notable that, like in a highly choreographed dance *à trois*, Kissinger notices that early signs of Soviet weakness during the Reagan era were immediately followed by a more distant policy by China vis-à-vis the United States (pp. 392–4).

53 It is often argued that globalization, exemplified by China's entry into the WTO in 2001, was structurally biased in China's favour. But this is hard to reconcile with the fact that Charlene Barshefsky, US Trade

Representative at the time, said that no country had made as many trade concessions as China, and that the Chinese authorities did not publish some of China's later trade concessions in Chinese but only in English (see Lin Chun, *Revolution and Counterrevolution in China*). The Opium Wars cast a long shadow.

54 The summary of what happened in the US after 2007–08 can be taken straight from Polanyi's *Great Transformation*: 'the strain sprang from the zone of the market; from there it spread to the political sphere, thus comprising the whole of society' (p. 219).

55 Source: calculated from US micro data available at the Luxembourg Income Study, based on US annual Current Population Survey.

56 See Christoph Lakner and Branko Milanovic, 'Global income distribution: from the fall of the Berlin Wall to the Great Recession', *World Bank Economic Review*, vol. 30, no. 2, July 2016, pp. 203–32.

57 Schumpeter saw it clearly too: 'Secular improvement that is taken for granted and coupled with individual insecurity that is acutely resented is . . . the best recipe for breeding social unrest' (*Capitalism, Socialism and Democracy*, p. 145).

58 Daniel Markovits, *The Meritocracy Trap*, Chapter 2.

59 This section is based on my paper 'The three eras of global inequality, 1820–2020 with the focus on the past thirty years' published in *World Development*, vol. 177, May 2024, and two more descriptive papers published in *Foreign Affairs* ('The Great Convergence: Global Equality and Its Discontents', July–August 2023) and *Le Monde Diplomatique*, German edition, October 2017.

60 Or perhaps did not differ at all, as argued by Kenneth Pomeranz (*The Great Divergence*), who holds that Western Europe, China and even India had similar levels of development in many respects (technology, protection of property, competition, institutions in general, demography) around 1750–1800. Bozhong Li and Jan Luiten van Zanden ('Before the Great Divergence? Comparing the Yangtze Delta and the Netherlands at the beginning of the Nineteenth Century', *Journal of Economic History*, vol. 72, no. 2, 2012, pp. 956–89) reject Pomeranz's claim by showing that the real wage difference between the most developed parts of Europe and China (the Netherlands and the

Yangtze Delta) was 2 to 1 around 1820. Maddison's data (version 2020) estimate that in 1820 Chinese GDP per capita was $PPP 882, British $PPP 3,306 and Dutch $PPP 3,006. Thus, the estimates seem to range from no gap at all to about 3 to 1.

61 Source: 1820–1980 from Bourguignon and Morrisson 'Inequality among world citizens: 1820–1992', *American Economic Review*, vol. 92, no. 4, 2002, 1988–2008 from Lakner and Milanovic 'Global income distribution: from the fall of the Berlin Wall to the Great Recession', *World Bank Economic Review*, vol. 30, no. 2, 2016, and 2013 and 2018 from Milanovic 'After the crisis: the evolution of the global income distribution between 2008 and 2013', *Review of Income and Wealth*, vol. 68, no. 1, 2022.

62 Both 0 and 100 are obviously only theoretical possibilities. The higher the Gini the greater the inequality.

63 For Britain, see Peter Lindert, 'Unequal British wealth since 1867', *Journal of Political Economy*, vol. 94, no. 6, December 1986, pp. 1127–62, and Branko Milanovic, Peter Lindert and Jeffrey Williamson, 'Measuring ancient inequality', *Economic Journal*, vol. 121, no. 1, 2011, pp. 255–72. For the US, Eugene Smolensky and Robert Plotnick, 'Inequality and poverty in the United States, 1900 to 1990', Institute for Research on Poverty, University of Wisconsin-Madison, Discussion Paper No. 998-93, March 1993.

64 David H. Autor, David Dorn and Gordon H. Hanson, 'The China Shock: Learning from Labor-Market Adjustment to Large Changes in Trade', *Annual Review of Economics*, vol. 8, 2016, pp. 205–40. Available at https://www.annualreviews.org/content/journals/10.1146/annurev-economics-080315-015041

65 See Milanovic, *Global Inequality*, Chapter 3.

66 Recent riots in England, accompanied by what has by now become a routine looting of stores, confirm the positional character of such goods. As in many similar riots in rich countries, the stores that are looted are not food stores, but those selling expensive brands of clothing or footwear or smartphones and tablets. So, it is not real physiological deprivation that is reflected in the looting, but the 'hunger' for the display of one's wealth position.

67 Source: Milanovic, 'The three eras of global inequality ...', *World Development*, vol. 177, May 2024.

68 We can drop the last category because it never plays a role in *The Law of Peoples* and it is not even clear why it is introduced at all. Nor is it clear who are the benevolent absolutist societies in real life. Perhaps China?

69 'The liberal law of peoples does not justify economic sanctions or military pressure on well-ordered hierarchical societies to change their ways, provided they respect the rules of peace and their political institutions satisfy the essential conditions we have reviewed. If however these conditions are violated, external pressure of one kind or another may be justified depending on the severity and the circumstances of the case.' ('The Law of Peoples – A Summary', *Critical Enquiry*, vol. 20, no. 1, 1993, p. 67.)

70 'It is a mistake to believe that a just and good society must wait upon a high material standard of life. What men want is meaningful work in free associations with others, these associations regulating their relations to one another within a framework of just basic institutions. To achieve this state of things great wealth is not necessary. In fact, beyond some point it is more likely to be a positive hindrance, a meaningless distraction at best if not a temptation to indulgence and emptiness.' (*A Theory of Justice*, Chapter V, §44, pp. 257–8.) Also, 'Great wealth is not necessary to establish just (or decent) institutions ... Thus the levels of wealth among well-ordered societies will not, in general, be the same.' (*The Law of Peoples*, p. 107.)

71 'The thought that real savings and economic growth are to go on indefinitely, upwards and onwards, with no specified goal in sight, is the idea of the business class of a capitalist society.' (*The Law of Peoples*, p. 107fn.)

72 'If it [society] is not satisfied [with its wealth], it can continue to increase savings, or, if that is not feasible, borrow from other members of the Society of Peoples.' (*The Law of Peoples*, p. 114.)

73 Making a Rawlsian point, Joshua Cohen writes: 'once we accept the value of collective self-government, there is no reason to hope for convergence in living standards – the absence of convergence is not a

defect awaiting correction' ('Comments on Rodrik', at the conference Alternatives to Neoliberalism, 23–24 May, 2002).

74 All things just mentioned must explicitly not happen in liberal societies à la Rawls.

75 *A Theory of Justice*, p. 225. In reality, though, chances to influence political decisions are more likely proportional to one's income. For example, total spending during the 2020 US presidential campaign amounted to almost $6 billion, and the largest contributors to Super PACs such as Sheldon and Miriam Adelson and Michael Bloomberg contributed respectively $220 million and almost $100 million each. (Bloomberg's total contribution to his own campaign exceeded $1 billion.) Data from Molly E. Reynolds and John C. Green (eds), *Financing the 2020 Election*, Brookings Institution, 2023, pp. 58 and 170.

76 Leif Wenar and I question at times the explicit contention by Rawls that liberal peoples are 'satisfied peoples' who do not covet other peoples' goods and territories and are hence peaceful; see 'Are Liberal Peoples Peaceful?', *Journal of Political Philosophy*, vol. 17, no. 4, July 2009, pp. 462–86.

77 The notional consultative hierarchy in *The Law of Peoples* is, perhaps somewhat bizarrely, called Kazanstan.

78 The graph is based on the data presented by V. I. Lenin in 'Report On The International Situation And The Fundamental Tasks Of The Communist International', 19 July 1920. Available at https://www.marxists.org/archive/lenin/works/1920/jul/x03.htm

79 Lenin's view of the world can be made identical to the official Soviet view during the Cold War by simply moving West Germany into the Western or winners' camp, and Austria into the middle (neutral) camp.

80 According to Google's Ngram, there is a remarkable increase in the use of the term from the early 1990s.

81 '. . . the world today actually consists of three parts, or three worlds, that are both interconnected and in contradiction with one another. The United States and the Soviet Union make up the First World. The developing countries in Asia, Africa, Latin America and other regions

make up the Third World. The developed countries between the two make up the Second World.' Deng Xiaoping's speech at the Special Session of the UN General Assembly, 10 April 1974, cited in Chi Hsin, *Teng Hsiao-ping: A Political Biography*, Cosmos Books, 1978, p. 165.
82 Dragoslav Rančić, *Kina posle Mao Ce Tunga*, p. 45.
83 *Peace and War*, Chapter V.
84 China did participate at the 1955 Bandung conference, and the Third World provided substantial support to the People's Republic to get its place at the UN and to eject the Republic of China (Taiwan) from that position. However, most of the time China remained in 'splendid isolation', which reached its paroxysm during the Cultural Revolution when it withdrew all bar one of its ambassadors.
85 The full title of Fukuyama's book was *The End of History and the Last Man*. The first part of the title referred to Hegel, the second part to Nietzsche. The book was the extension of the immensely influential article 'The End of History?' (note the question mark) published in *National Interest* in the summer of 1989, around the same time as when I ran into Jeffrey Sachs and David Lipton in a Washington bookstore, the story that opens this book.
86 The text by the Russian expert in international relations Sergei Karaganov reported and discussed in *Le Grand Continent*, 'Dés-occidentaliser le monde: La doctrine Karaganov', 20 April 2024, presents that point of view very clearly. The term 'world majority' was interestingly used by both Lenin (in 'Better Fewer, but Better' written in 1923) and Stalin (in *The Foundations of Leninism*, Chapter VI), although of course in different historical contexts.

3. The Elites

1 Burnham was an American Marxist-Trotskyist, a strong critic of the Stalinist Soviet Union, who later in his life became ideologically associated with US neoconservativism.
2 The last two points are Burnham's general definition of the ruling class, applying to capitalism as well.

3 'Mass unemployment means that the given type of social organization has broken down, that it cannot any longer provide its members with socially useful functions.' (*The Managerial Revolution*, p. 28.)
4 *The Managerial Revolution*, p. 136.
5 *The Managerial Revolution*, p. 188.
6 Hayek, however, goes so far as to acknowledge the importance that new technologies might have on perfect competition and freedom of choice: 'But it must be admitted that it is possible that, by compulsory standardization or the prohibition of variety beyond a certain degree, abundance might be increased in some fields more than sufficiently to compensate for the restriction of the choice of the consumer.' (*The Road to Serfdom*, p. 51).
7 See Gary Gerstle's *The Rise and Fall of the Neoliberal Order* in which he dates the beginning of American neoliberal order to Reagan's presidency.
8 The same view was held by Schumpeter in *Capitalism, Socialism and Democracy*. He thought that ideologically there would be nobody willing to defend capitalism and private property (see Chapter XII entitled 'Growing Hostility' [of the intellectual class towards capitalism]) and that that attitude would be a reflection of things happening in the 'infrastructure', namely greater efficiency of large monopolies owned or managed by the state.
9 It was first defined and discussed in my *Capitalism, Alone* (Chapter 1) and has since generated several papers (Ranaldi and Milanovic 2022; Berman and Milanovic 2024; Ranaldi 2024).
10 *Capital in the Twenty-First Century*, pp. 435ff.
11 Note that technically one can be in both the top decile by labour income and the top decile by capital income and not be in the top decile by total income. The number of such people is, however, negligible. In our definition, to be part of the new homoploutic ruling class, one must be in the top decile by all three criteria.
12 The graph shown here is based on Luxembourg Income Study data that are, in turn, based on annual US household income surveys, Current Population Survey. For the sake of completeness Yonatan Berman and Branko Milanovic ('Homoploutia: Top Labor and Capital Incomes in the United States, 1950–2020', *Review of Income and Wealth*, vol. 70,

no. 3, September 2024, pp. 766–84) have used two additional US data sources: Distributional National Accounts (DINA) and Survey of Consumer Finances. Both show the same upward movement since the early 1980s (see Figure 1 in their paper).

13 Source: calculated from the household-level data available in the Luxembourg Income Study database.

14 Branko Milanovic, *Visions of Inequality*, p. 158.

15 See the work of Marco Ranaldi, e.g., 'Compositional Inequality: Measurement, Stylized Facts, and Normative Aspects', Stone Center on Socio-Economic Inequality Working Paper No. 87, May 2024. Ranaldi has developed an entire methodology (very similar to the Gini framework) to study compositional inequality, i.e., how much income *shares* of capital and labour differ along a given income distribution.

16 Psychic or imputed income derived from lived-in housing property (from which the owners obviously do not receive any financial income) is not included. Housing property is in many countries the main source of wealth for the middle classes, going all the way to the top decile or top ventile of income distribution. Only after that point does financial (property) income become important.

17 At the conventional 5 per cent real rate of return, this implies financial assets worth $8 million.

18 Source: calculated from the household-level data available in the Luxembourg Income Study database.

19 One becomes homoploutic through one's own effort by generating high labour, and later, capital income.

20 Yonatan Berman and Branko Milanovic (2024), 'Homoploutia: Top Labor and Capital Incomes in the United States, 1950–2020', *Review of Income and Wealth*, vol. 70, no. 3, pp. 766–84.

21 The same topic is addressed in Michael Sandel's *The Tyranny of Merit*, Penguin Books, 2020. His critique is more ethical and less sociological and thus, in my opinion, less incisive.

22 '. . . the excess investment in human capital made in a typical rich household – over and above the educational investments made not just in poor but also in middle-class households – today are equivalent to a

traditional inheritance in the neighborhood of $10 million per child.' (*The Meritocracy Trap*, p. 146.)
23 *The Meritocracy Trap*, p. 268.
24 'Meritocracy sustains dynasties [and the ruling class] by reconstructing the family on the model of a firm, the household on the model of a workplace, and the child on the model of a product.' (*The Meritocracy Trap*, p. 116.)
25 Members of the 'meritocracy' are hard-working ('today's Stakhanovites are the one-percenters', p. 81) and combine 'progressive virtues' of inclusion and privacy, with 'conservative virtues' of hard work, saving, and contempt for the poor.
26 See Anne Case and Angus Deaton, 'Accounting for the widening mortality gap between American adults with and without a BA', Brookings Papers on Economic Activity, Fall 2023, based on the path-breaking book by Anne Case and Angus Deaton, *Deaths of Despair and the Future of Capitalism*.
27 *The New Industrial State*. Galbraith termed it 'technostructure'.
28 *The Coming of Post-Industrial Society: A Venture in Social Forecasting*.
29 *La lutte de classes: Nouvelles leçons sur les sociétés industrielles*, Gallimard, 1964; and his earlier book *Dix-huit leçons sur la société industrielle*, Gallimard, 1962.
30 The professional-managerial class in Aron is composed of 'techniciens', which we may also translate as technocrats. The conflict between, on the one hand, bureaucrats and party-men, and on the other hand, technocrats is, according to Aron, the most salient class cleavage in the Soviet-type societies. (*La lutte de classes*, pp. 178, 331). More generally, 'Soviet and capitalist societies are only two species of the same genus, or two versions of the same social type, progressive industrial society.' (*18 Lectures on Industrial Society*, p. 42; lectures given in 1956.)
31 'The imperatives of organization, technology and planning operate similarly, and we have seen to broadly similar results, on all societies. Given the decision to have a modern industry, much of what happens is inevitable and the same.' (Galbraith, *The New Industrial State*, p. 388.)
32 Mike Lofgren's definition in his very successful book *The Deep State* is very pragmatic: the deep state is 'a hybrid association of key

elements of government and parts of top-level finance and industry that ... effectively govern the United States with only limited reference to the concerns of the governed as ... expressed through elections.' (*The Deep State*, p. 5.)

33 *The Managerial Revolution*, p. 93.
34 See *The Demon in Democracy: Totalitarian Temptations in Free Societies*.
35 There is some similarity between this view of a deep state that rules societies based on craftily imposed ideological uniformity and Ralf Dahrendorf's view that 'the ruling political class of post-capitalist society consists of the administrative staff of the state, the government elite at its head and those interested parties which are represented by the government elite' (Dahrendorf, *Class and Class Conflict in an Industrial Society*, cited in Daniel Bell, *The Coming of Post-Industrial Society*, p. 52).
36 N. S. Lyons, 'The China Convergence: Yes, the West is becoming more like China. Here is the real reason why', The Upheaval Substack, 3 August 2023. Available at https://theupheaval.substack.com/p/the-china-convergence. See also N. S. Lyons, 'The Total State and the Twilight of American Democracy', 9 September 2024. Available at https://theupheaval.substack.com/p/the-total-state-and-the-twilight
37 It is nevertheless true that one of the anthological definitions of classes (by Raymond Aron) accepts, as its third possibility, that class is 'a group of individuals having a similar way of thinking and living, knowing of that similarity and especially wanting to achieve their community' (*La Lutte de classes*, p. 78; my translation). It thus accepts that a class is not defined within the process of production but leaves quite open the question of the locus where that class emerges. Obviously, 'having a similar way of thinking' begs the question of how that similar way of thinking came to be and what maintains it.
38 According to the Maddison Project data (version 2020), British GDP per capita in 1800 was $PPP 3,351, which was almost exactly double Chinese GDP per capita in 1978 (the latter is estimated at $PPP 1,744). The UK reached an income 7.5 times greater than the one at the (putative) date of the beginning of the Industrial Revolution only around the late 1980s, thus almost two centuries later.

39 Source: calculated from Chinese Household Income Project (CHIP) surveys.
40 To do this, Allen used standardized social tables, which are the lists of salient social classes with their estimated mean incomes and population shares, for England and Wales.
41 Robert C. Allen, 'Class structure and inequality during the industrial revolution: lessons from England's social tables, 1688–1867', *Economic History Review*, vol. 72, no. 1, 2019, pp. 88–125; originally published as 'Revising England's Social Tables Once Again', Oxford Economic and Social History Working Papers No. 146, University of Oxford, Department of Economics, 2016.
42 Li Yang, Filip Novokmet and Branko Milanovic, 'From workers to capitalists in less than two generations: A study of Chinese urban elite transformation between 1988 and 2013', *British Journal of Sociology*, vol. 72, no. 3, 2021, pp. 478–513. The data in the paper are updated using the results of the newly released 2018 CHIP survey. Some of the results of this empirical investigation were also published in my *Capitalism, Alone*.
43 It is noticeable that the data on class composition of the population or the elite are much more easily available in Chinese than American data.
44 The cut-off point of eight hired workers is what, according to the Chinese official classification, separates large capitalist owners from small capitalist companies and self-employed businesses.
45 Source: Li, Novokmet and Milanovic, 'From workers to capitalists . . .', *British Journal of Sociology*, vol. 72, no. 3, 2021, pp. 478–513.' Calculated from the individual data available in the CHIP Survey, including the most recent 2018 CHIP (all obtained through the Luxembourg Income Study).
46 Source: Li, Novokmet and Milanovic, 'From workers to capitalists . . .', *British Journal of Sociology*, vol. 72, no. 3, 2021, pp. 478–513. Calculated from the individual data available in the CHIP survey including the most recent 2018 CHIP (all obtained through the Luxembourg Income Study).
47 I use the term 'de facto single-party system' because there are formally eight political parties in China that have deputies in the People's

Congress. This might seem a trivial legal detail except that a similar detail has made the transition to a real multi-party system much easier in Poland. When the semi-free elections took place in Poland in June 1989, the ruling Polish United Workers' Party would have still kept the majority in the Sejm despite being trounced at the polls were it not for the fact that its two satellite parties that had predetermined numbers of seats in the Sejm had suddenly changed sides and decided to support the Solidarity-led opposition.

48 The educational level of the elite has dramatically increased over the considered period: from 12 per cent with university education to more than half.

49 We do not have similar data for 2018.

50 The six classes shown in Figure 3.4.

51 Source: calculated from micro data from CHIP.

52 '. . . members of the political elite or their families directly participate in economic activity and have become agents for large corporations and industries . . . In China, political and economic elites have completely conflated.' (Wang Hui, *China's New Order: Society, Politics, and Economy in Transition*, Harvard University Press, 2003, p. 177.) 'In most capitalist countries, the exercise of state power and capital accumulation are taken by the two distinctive social groups, namely the bureaucrats and the capitalists. Chinese bureaucrats combine these two functions and are simultaneously entitled to salary (plus benefits) and a share of the surplus value.' (Au Loong-Yu, *China's Rise: Strength and Fragility*, quoted in Gilbert Achcar, *The New Cold War: The United States, Russia and China from Kosovo to Ukraine*, pp. 249–50.)

53 It should be mentioned, however, that CPC membership might also be a proxy for greater ability and ambition – not necessarily only for better political connections (Li et al. 2007). But without further study, it is difficult to disentangle the two.

54 Source: Li, Novokmet and Milanovic, 'From workers to capitalists in less than two generations . . .', *British Journal of Sociology*, vol. 72, no. 3, 2021, pp. 478–513.

55 See Charles Hucker, *The Censorial System of Ming China*, Stanford University Press, 1966.

56 https://finance.sina.com.cn/tech/2021-06-28/doc-ikqcfnca3716443.shtml
57 The database is the companion to the article by Li Yang, Branko Milanovic and Yaoqi Lin, 'Anti-corruption campaign in China: An empirical investigation', published in the *European Journal of Political Economy*, vol. 85, 2024 and on which most of the discussion here is based.
58 Li Yang, Branko Milanovic and Yaoqi Lin, 'Anti-corruption campaign in China: An empirical investigation', *European Journal of Political Economy*, vol. 85, 2024.
59 The graph is reproduced with permission from Roy van der Weide and Ambar Narayan, 'China and the United States: Different economic models but similarly low levels of socioeconomic mobility', in Carlos Gradín, Murray Leibbrandt and Finn Tarp (eds), *Inequality in the Developing World*, Oxford University Press, 2021.
60 Homoploutia in China, defined the same way as in the United States (percentage of people belonging to the richest income decile who are also among the richest capitalists and richest workers), was 21 per cent in 2018, against about 30 per cent at the same time in the United States.

4. National Market Liberalism

1 Between April and August 2024, investigations led to the arrest of seven Russian generals, including two deputy ministers of defence for large-scale bribery. *Kommersant*, 29 August 2024. Available at https://www.kommersant.ru/doc/6921370
2 Xi Jinping's father (Xi Zhongxun) was purged during the Cultural Revolution (Xi Jinping's education was interrupted and he was sent to work in the countryside). Zhongxun was rehabilitated in 1978. He later became Governor and CPC Secretary in the very important Guandong province where he was instrumental in the creation of the Shenzhen Special Economic Zone. He was also the only high-level official who raised the issue of legality of Hu Yaobang's removal as CPC General Secretary in 1987 (Yasheng Huang, *The Rise and Fall of the EAST*, p. 198). Hence his reputation for 'liberalism'. A recent biography of Xi Zhongxun was published by Joseph Torigian, *The Party Interests Come First*, Stanford University

Press, 2025. For an excellent review see Jonathon P. Sine, 'Xi Zhongxun: China Book of the Year', China Talk. Available at https://www.china-talk.media/p/life-and-times-of-xi-zhongxun

3 'Counter-revolution' and 'counter-revolutionary' are used here in a neutral sense to distinguish those who challenge the global neoliberal order as defined by the Thatcher/Reagan 'revolutions' that in turn can be seen as 'counter-revolutions' against the national welfare state. In other words, the terms 'revolution' and 'counter-revolution' as used here do not carry any normative meaning, nor have teleological implications.

4 Although some elements were introduced already by Jimmy Carter as argued by David N. Gibbs in *The Revolt of the Rich*.

5 See two excellent recent books: Samuel Moyn's *Not Enough: Human Rights in an Unequal World* and Quinn Slobodian's *Globalists: The End of Empire and the Birth of Neoliberalism*.

6 This hypothesis is also made by Gary Gerstle in *The Rise and Fall of the Neoliberal Order* and is empirically investigated, in a very important paper, by André Albuquerque Sant'Anna ('A spectre has haunted the west: did socialism discipline income inequality?', Munich Personal RePEc Archive No. 64756, 20 April 2015). Albuquerque Sant'Anna documents that the welfare policies that lowered income inequality were more developed in countries where either socialist or communist parties were strong or the military threat of the Soviet Union was greater.

7 'The free market is like Communism: perfect in theory, but it can't work in practice because it goes against human nature. The unemployed doctor will not agree to become a garbage collector. Unions will not allow wages to fall instantly with lower profits. Managers will not report the revenue position truthfully to workers. The successful rich man will not agree to make his son compete in the educational system on the same terms as everyone else's children. Countries will subsidize industries to prevent social devastation. Free market economists like the genial Schumpeter will assure us such devastation is only temporary, but the life of actual human beings is itself temporary. This is the largest political problem for free-market economies: it does not operate

on a human scale. It bases itself on a long-term logic that is faultless but inhuman.' (*Liberal Capitalist Democracy*, p. 351.)

8. The role of austerity policies in bringing to power right-wing movements is studied by Mark Blyth in *Austerity: History of a Dangerous Idea* and Clara Mattei in *The Capital Order: How Economists Invented Austerity and Paved the Way to Fascism*.

9. Under wartime conditions, according to Piketty, such a chain of accumulation and inequality is broken by destruction of capital. In other words, accumulation of capital can be interrupted either by its physical destruction or by taxation.

10. *Mandate for Leadership 2025*, known as *The Heritage Foundation Project 2025*, is indeed a set of actionable policies that distinguish Trump's second administration from the first. But it cannot compare with the thick ideological background of neoliberalism that was built over forty years until it had a chance to impact policies.

11. 'America Has No Alternative to Industrial Policy', *Project Syndicate*, 5 September 2024.

12. Somewhat bizarrely, industrial policies are at times justified by the need to do the same thing as China, thereby giving an indirect compliment to Chinese policies while arguing at the same time that the Chinese economic model is unsustainable (see, e.g., Aaron L. Friedberg, 'Stopping the Next China Shock: A Collective Strategy for Countering Beijing's Mercantilism', *Foreign Affairs*, September/October 2024).

13. 'Rather do I believe that our Great Maker is preparing the world, in His own good time, to become one nation, speaking one language, and when armies and navies will be no longer required.' (Ulysses Grant's Inaugural Address, 4 March 1873.) Available at https://www.contextus.org/Ulysses_S_Grant%2C_March_4%2C_1873_Second_Inaugural_Address.14?lang=en&with=all&lang2=en. For contemporary claims see Niall Ferguson, *Colossus: The Rise and Fall of the American Empire*, Penguin Books, 2005; Giovanni Arrighi, *The Long Twentieth Century: Money, Power and the Origins of Our Times*, Verso, 2010; and Andrew Bacevich, *After the Apocalypse: America's Role in a World Transformed*, Metropolitan Books, 2021.

14 In only two international areas does Trump share the views of more traditional US politicians: hatred of Iran, which is a generational issue among those old enough to remember the humiliation of the American diplomatic hostages in 1979; and an unconditional support for Israel, which, in Trump's case, is compounded by semitophilia whose origins are difficult to gauge. These two aspects (hate and love) came together in Trump's bombing of Iran's nuclear facilities in June 2025.
15 *On China*, p. 452.
16 The richest 10 per cent hold 91 per cent of stocks and mutual funds, 95 per cent of financial securities, 84 per cent of trusts, and 94 per cent of business equity. See Edward Wolff, *A Century of Wealth in America*, p. 104.
17 The website of the China Confucius Association (19 March 2021). The reference was kindly provided by Bob Cheng.
18 Ho-fung Hung, *The China Boom: Why China Will Not Rule the World*, pp. 27ff.
19 Peer Vries, *Escaping Poverty: The Origins of Modern Economic Growth*, p. 342.
20 Jacques Gernet, *Daily Life in China on the Eve of the Mongol Invasion 1250–76*, p. 61.
21 *The Great Divergence*, p. 173.
22 'Our policy of reform and openness will not change for one hundred years,' Deng said in October 1993 (quoted in Orville Schell and John Delury, *Wealth and Power*, p. 321).
23 'It appears that the number of transitional stages were necessary – state capitalism and socialism – in order to prepare by many years of effort for the transition to communism.' Lenin in *Pravda*, 18 October 1921 (quoted in Leszek Kolakowski, *Main Currents of Marxism*, vol. 2, Oxford University Press, 1978, p. 484).
24 *Lenin's Final Fight: Speeches and Writings, 1922–23*, p. 40.
25 *Zhu Rongji Meets the Press*, 6 March 1993; cited in Orville Schell and John Delury, *Wealth and Power*, p. 343.
26 'Communist tasks in the second year of the New Economic Policy', Political Report to the 11th Party Congress, 27 March 1922 in *Lenin's Final Fight: Speeches and Writings*, pp. 23–76. See also 'Five years of the

Russian revolutions and the prospect of the world revolution' in the same volume.

27 'The Three Represents' is supposed to mean that an advanced Communist Party represents the most (i) productive and (ii) culturally developed layers of society as well as (iii) the great majority of the Chinese population. The 'great majority' is undefined; implicitly, there must then be some people who are not represented by the Party. Linguistically and ideologically, the slogan was to replace the one that the Party stands for three revolutionary classes: workers, peasants and soldiers.

28 'The Xi nobody saw coming', *Financial Times*, 14 January 2023. Available at https://www.ft.com/content/f6c47c54-b928-46ee-aa63-fb903e74b2e6

29 'Common prosperity' was defined by Deng as the highest stage in the long-term economic development of China. The term itself was, however, first used by Mao in 1953 (see Michael Dunfort, 'The Chinese path to common prosperity', *International Critical Thought*, vol. 12, no.1, 2022, pp. 35–54).

30 It is important to realize what the 'elimination of rural poverty' means. It means bringing all the rural population to a still very low level more or less equal to subsistence. The Chinese rural poverty line is just under $2 per person per day at international prices (or about 2,500 yuan per capita annually), which is even lower than the World Bank absolute poverty line of $PPP 2.15.

31 'Strategic planning and tactical flexibility are crucial tools for navigating modernization.' Xi Jinping in his speech 'Comprehensively Promoting the Construction of a Strong Nation and the Great Rejuvenation of the Chinese Nation through Chinese-style Modernization', published in *Qiushi*, January 2025. The speech was delivered in February 2023. The Chinese text is available at https://archive.is/eTGeK

32 The same mistake but from the opposite (radical left-wing) political position is made by Lin Chun in *Revolution and Counterrevolution in China*. She argues that the entire post-1978 period was a counter-revolution and finds almost nothing positive to say regarding the entire period, except at the very end where, in an almost last-minute appended part, she entertains some hope that the CPC could return to a more revolutionary road both in foreign affairs and domestically.

Lin Chun's preferred approach is nevertheless to keep on working within the CPC whose potential, despite having strayed from the right path, is not yet, she believes, exhausted. She does not seem to have high hopes for the success of that project, however, and rejects the idea that Xi Jinping and Mao have much (or anything) in common.

33 Although Jiang Zemin is generally credited with the policy, it began under Hu Yaobang in the 1980s. In the ultra-conservative political climate after the Tiananmen massacre, Jiang, who then became CPC General Secretary, fiercely opposed it. He nevertheless adopted it later (see Yasheng Huang, *The Rise and Fall of the EAST*, p. 127).

34 'Nor is it clear that the emergence of a multiparty system would significantly alter Chinese foreign policy.' (Henry Kissinger, *On China*, p. 539.)

35 Andrei Kozyrev, *The Firebird: The Elusive Fate of Russian Democracy*.

36 Vladislav Zubok in his brilliant *Collapse* thus describes Gorbachev's entourage on foreign trips: 'One would expect that the General Secretary, bent on reforming the Soviet economy, would take with him on western trips economists, planners, directors of military industries, bankers and other technocrats. Instead, Gorbachev's huge entourage consisted mostly of journalists, social scientists, writers, theater directors, film makers and other cultural figures. Most of them shared his fascination, admiration, and envy for things Western.' (p. 46.)

37 In his narrowly focused study on the collapse of the Soviet Communist Party, Graeme Gill concludes: 'the party could adjust neither its organisational structures nor its culture to cope with its changed environment . . . it meandered into a dead end of indecision, ultimately becoming irrelevant to the course of political development. This suggests that the inflexibility of the administrative party system severely limited its capacity to cope with a changing environment, and was thereby the crucial factor in the collapse of communism.' (*The Collapse of a Single-Party System*, p. 184.)

38 See *The World Under Capitalism* (Chapter 10). The original article was published in June 2021.

Notes

39 Xi Jinping speech, 'Comprehensively Promoting the Construction of a Strong Nation and the Great Rejuvenation of the Chinese Nation through Chinese-style Modernization', published in *Qiushi*, January 2025. The speech was delivered in February 2023.

40 *China Rural Survey*, a book of rural remonstrances detailing rural poverty, was issued (and banned) in 2000, in the midst of supercharged economic growth but also recentralization of taxes away from provinces under Prime Minister Zhu Rongji (see Orville Schell and John Delury, *Wealth and Power*, p. 347).

41 *Anecdotes and Sayings* is available at www.china.org.cn/m/english/china_key_words/2017-06/19/content_41055520.html

42 The forum on literature and art held in the liberated Yen'an in 1942, and at which Mao gave several speeches on socialist art.

43 The slide of the Russia–US relationship from Russia being de facto a client state after the end of the Cold War to cold friendship, to competition and the famous Hillary Clinton–Lavrov reset, to enmity, the new Cold War, and finally a proxy war in Ukraine is masterfully chronicled in Gilbert Achcar's *The New Cold War: The United States, Russia and China from Kosovo to Ukraine*.

44 And the Russian parliament duly passed the resolution that 'RSFSR [Russia] reserves the right to raise the question of the revision of boundaries'. See Vladislav Zubok, *Collapse*, p. 324.

45 *Kommersant*, 'Двигатели выводят из оборота', 21 November 2024. Available at https://www.kommersant.ru/doc/7312839

46 Andrei Kolesnikov, 'Игра на поддержание', *Kommersant*, 8 November 2024. Available at https://www.kommersant.ru/doc/7284661?from=doc_vref

47 Raymond Aron, *Peace and War: A Theory of International Relations*.

48 Cyprus and Malta are not NATO members, but the UK maintains military bases in both.

49 'Q & A with Clinton Fernandes – Author of *Subimperial Power*'. Available at https://www.mup.com.au/blog/q-a-with-clinton-fernandes-author-of-subimperial-power. A slightly different definition is presented by Fernandes in his book: '[subimperial power] is subordinate to the imperial center, defends the imperial order known as a rules-based international

order, and projects considerable power and influence in its own region'. (*Subimperial Power: Australia in the International Arena*, p. 21).

50 In her recently published memoir *Freedom* (St Martin's Press, 2024, p. 563), Angela Merkel describes her conversations with Xi Jinping where the Chinese leader frequently goes back to the topic of China having been the most important country in the world in the past eighteen out of twenty centuries (of the conventionally calculated era), and his statements that the 'rejuvenation of the Chinese nation' implies a return to such a normal role. The past two centuries are an anomaly from the Chinese perspective while many Westerners see them as 'normal'. We find there a similar historical misunderstanding that I mentioned above regarding the end of the Cold War.

51 Ashley J. Tellis, 'Great Expectations: India amid US-China Competition' in Hal Brands (ed.), *Lessons from the New Cold War: America Confronts the China Challenge*.

52 'It was this divergence of habit, this gap between reason and emotion, which induced the Latins [the French and the Italians] to examine the Revelation of Woodrow Wilson in a manner more scientific, and therefore more critical, than we [the English] did ourselves . . . They [the Latins] observed, for instance, that the United States in the course of their short but highly imperialistic history, had constantly proclaimed the highest virtue while as constantly violating their professions and resorting to the grossest materialism. They observed that all Americans liked to feel in terms of Thomas Jefferson but to act in terms of Alexander Hamilton. They observed that such principles as the equality of man were not applied either to the yellow man or to the black. They observed that the doctrine of self-determination had not been extended either to the Red Indians or even to the Southern States. They were apt to examine "American principles and American tendencies" not in terms of the Philadelphia declaration but in terms of the Mexican war, of Louisiana, of these innumerable treaties with the Indian tribes which had been violated shamelessly before the ink was dry. They observed that, almost within living memory, the great American Empire had been won by ruthless force.' (Harold Nicolson, *Peace Making 1919*, p. 192.)

53 E. H. Carr, *The Twenty Years' Crisis, 1919–1939: An Introduction to the Study of International Relations*, p. 168.
54 Calculated from Debin Ma, 'Rock, Scissors, Paper: the Problem of Incentives and Information in Traditional Chinese State and the Origin of Great Divergence', LSE Department of Economic History Working Paper No. 152/11, March 2011, Appendix Table, p. 35.
55 Nirad Chaudhuri, *Thy Hand, Great Anarch! India 1921–1952*, p. xxviii.
56 An influential book with such a title was published in 1938 by William Orton (*The Twenty Years' Armistice, 1919–1938*, Farrar & Rinehart).
57 He sent several clergymen to Dachau, though, as a warning to others.
58 Isaiah Berlin, 'The Hedgehog and the Fox' in *Russian Thinkers*, p. 41.
59 Leon Tolstoy, *War and Peace*, Second Epilogue, Chapter X.
60 It is also, I think, true that if we are honest with ourselves, we often have a problem of – when placing ourselves at a moment in the past – imagining how the observed present could ever have happened. To put it in concrete terms: almost nobody could in good faith say today that in 1978 they were able to imagine that the China of 2025 would be such a powerful country. If we try to bring ourselves to the state of thinking of 1978, we simply cannot fathom how reality could have taken such a path. The lived reality seems, from the vantage point of the past, almost unreal.
61 Isaiah Berlin, 'The Hedgehog and the Fox' in *Russian Thinkers*, p. 75.
62 E. H. Carr, *The Twenty Years' Crisis, 1919–1939*, p. 67.

5. Nationalism, Greed and Property

1 For an excellent discussion of pleonexia in Plato, Rousseau and Marx, see the recent book by David Lay Williams, *The Greatest of All Plagues: How Economic Inequality Shaped Political Thought from Plato to Marx*.
2 'The spectacle is not a collection of images. It is a social relation between people that is mediated by image.' (Guy Debord, *The Society of the Spectacle*, Thesis 4.)

Index

Page references in *italics* indicate images.

absorption problems
   China absorption into US-led global system 183–8
   Russia post-Cold War 177–8, 183–8
Africa 2, 7, 22, 27, 42
   BRICS nations and 100, 102
   capitalism development within 195
   economic migrants from 93
   French zone of influence in West Africa 178, 184
   GDP per capita growth rates 17, 19, 20, 44–5, 83, 84, 85, 86
   global income distribution and 43
   population growth in 44
   relative income peak and 22, *22*
   strategic importance of 223n
   Structural Adjustment Lending (SAL) in 148
   Third (non-aligned) World and 94n, 97
   US–China rivalry and 65, 75, 78
   See also individual nation name
Airbus 180
Air France Flight 447, crash of (2009) 169
Algeria 14, 97, 159
Allen, Bob 125
Andropov, Yuri 174
Angell, Norman: *The Great Illusion* 54, 62, 217n

Aron, Raymond 119, 120, 182, 231n, 232n; *Peace and War* 96, 241n
artificial intelligence 114, 194
Asia
   convergence of real incomes between West and 82
   convergence within 23–4, *24*
   elites in *see* elites
   GDP growth rates 19–25, *20*, *21*, *24*, *25*, 37, *37*, 38, 182
   global income distribution and 2, 30, 32, 35, 38, *39*, 40, 43, 44, 86, 87, 188
   growth gap between populous Asian countries and OECD (1960–2022) 32, 37, *37*, 38
   Industrial Revolution and 79–80
   inequality in 23–6, *24*, *25*, 84–5
   migration and 84–5, 93
   'Other Asia' 19, *20*, 20
   relative income peak 21–3, *22*
   rise of vii, xiii, xiv, 1, 2, 3, 5, 19–26, *20*, *21*, 45, 46, 103, 188
   unipolar system in, Chinese ambition to build 185, 187
   US pivot to 73
   Washington Consensus and 147
   See also individual nation name
austerity ix, 151, 236n
autarky 55
autocracy 100, 101, 103, 145, 159, 175
Azerbaijan 93

Index

Bandung Conference (1955) 8–9, 228n
Bartel, Fritz 11
basic needs (reduction of absolute poverty globally) xii
Bell, Daniel 120
Belovezha Accords (1991) 179
benevolent absolutisms 89, 226n
Berezovsky, Boris 143
Beria, Lavrentiy 174
Berlin, Isaiah: 'The Hedgehog and the Fox' 190–91
Berman, Yonatan 115–16
Bezos, Jeff 160, 162
'bird in a cage' 168
Bloch, Ivan: *The Future of War* 54, 62, 217n
Bloomberg, Michael 162, 227n
Bloomberg Network 162
Bo Xilai 138, *138*
borders, 'just' 93
borrowing 9, 11, 71, 90, 149, 212n
Braudel, Fernand: *Civilization and Capitalism* 165
Bretton Woods Conference (1954) 154
BRICS nations 100, *100*, 102, 180–82, 186
Britain
    convergence and 51, 53
    Corn Laws 51
    cosmopolitanism and 60–61
    GDP per capita 20, 34, 124
    industrial disputes 164
    inequalities in 82
    naval protection 51
    population growth 21
    recession (1981) 11
    relative income peak 22, *22*
    Thatcher and ix, xi, 111, 152–3, 235n
    trade unions in 11
Brzezinski, Zbigniew: *The Grand Chessboard: American Primacy and Its Geostrategic Imperatives* 179
Burnham, James 228n; *Managerial Revolution* 105–111, 119, 120, 121, 122–3
Bush, George H. W. xi, *138*
'businessman' view of economics 154, 156
Byzantine Empire 47

capital
    elites and 104, 108, 111–16, *113*, *115*, 118, 119, 123, 125, 129, 139, 167
    free movement of 157
    homoploutia and 111–16, *113*, *115*
    managerialism and 105
    New Deal order and 150
    taxes on xi, 92, 151–2, 156
capitalism x
    capitalist core 6, *6*, 8, 9, 10, 13, 14, 15
    China and xi–xii, 125, 126, 127, 129, 130, 131, 139, 142, 144, 163–72, 176
    classical capitalism 104, 107, 111, 112, 118
    Cold War view of the world and 94, *94*, 95, 96
    credentialism and *see* credentialism
    current view of the world and 100, *100*
    End of History view of the world and 98, *98*, 99
    First World and 6, *6*
    free-market capitalism x, 46–7, 50, 67, 68, 236n
    Great Compression and 8
    Great Depression and x
    Hobson-Lenin-Luxemburg hypothesis and 49–50, 61, 62, 64, 65, 66
    horizontal and vertical development of 194–5
    instability of 151
    managerialism and 105–116, *113*

Index

people's capitalism 114
Schumpeter and 66–9
social Darwinism and 150–51
socialist economies and x, 18
state capitalism 70, 131, 165–7
term 96
Cárdenas, Lázaro 10
Carr, E. H. 186, 191
Case, Anne: *Deaths of Despair and the Future of Capitalism* 77
Chaudhuri, Nirad 188
Cheka 174
Chen Yun 168
Chile 23
China
 absorbing into US-led global system, impossibility of 183–8
 apartness/aloofness 7
 Belt and Road Initiative 65, 78
 'bird in a cage' term and 168
 capital ownership and 123–4
 Central Committee's Directorate of Inspection (CCDI) 131–6, 134
 challenge to West 17–19
 'China effect' 32–3, 38
 Chinese Household Surveys 104–105, 136
 communism and 2, 7, 70, 143, 162, 172, 174, 175, 176
 convergence and 32–8, 33, 37, 51, 53, 60, 64–5, 69–80, 76, 78, 82–3, 86, 87, 93, 94, 95, 96, 97, 99, 100, 102
 corruption in, elite 131–6, 134, 142, 143, 160–61, 168, 176
 CPC *see* Communist Party of China (CPC)
 Cultural Revolution 136, 137, 228n, 235n
 current view of the world and 100
 democratization of 47, 70, 187–8
 Deng's policies *see* Deng Xiaoping
doux commerce between United States and 69–70
dual system in 71–2
educational mobility in 136–7, 137
elites in xiv–xv, 78, 104–105, 123–40, 124, 126, 127, 128, 130, 134, 137, 138, 141, 142, 143, 144, 148, 167, 170–73, 233n, 234n
End of History view of the world and 98, 99
exports, expansion of 72
GDP per capita growth rates 15, 16, 17, 19, 20, 20, 27–9, 28, 30, 32–8, 33, 37, 123–4, 185
global hegemon ambition 185
Gorbachevization in 170
green technologies and electric cars, moves ahead of West in 53
growth gap between US, populous Asian countries, OECD and (1960–2022) 36–7, 37
hubristic mentality within xiii
imperialist competition theory and 63–5, 69–70
income distribution, global and 32–5, 33, 39, 39, 87, 87, 124, 124, 127
income gains among urban and rural populations (1988–2018) 124, 124
income sources of the elite, by sector of ownership (1988–2018) 127
inequality and 24–5, 80, 82, 83, 86, 87, 87
Japan's rise and 16
Jiang Zeminism 171
largest economy in world (in purchasing power parity terms, or PPP), overtakes United States as (2015) 20
Mao/Maoism *see* Mao Zedong *and* Maoism

China – *cont'd*
  middle classes, rise of global and vii, xiii, 30, 32–40, *33, 37, 39,* 42, 77, 170
  military expenditure 185
  modernization theory and 170
  multipolarity and 183–92
  nationalism in 143
  neoliberalism spread and 148
  New Economic Policy (NEP) and 165–7, 238n
  non-aligned movement and 6, 7, 10, 14
  political capitalism 163–9
  political elite interrelationships in 136–9, *138*
  population numbers/growth 6, 7, 15, 17, 18, 30, 32, *33,* 34, 35, 36, 37, 38, *39, 128,* 185
  privatization of state enterprises (1990s) 148
  relative peak income and 22
  'Regarding the Construction of Socialism with Chinese Characteristics' 172–7
  Revolution (1949) 7
  rural poverty, elimination of 168–9, 176, 239n, 240–41n
  state and private sector, division between 164–5
  state-owned enterprises (SOEs) 65, *128, 132, 133, 134,* 176
  socialist bloc and 96
  Soviet Union, conflict with 7
  tactical flexibility 168
  Taiwan and *see* Taiwan
  The Three Represents 167, 171, 172, 238–9n
  Third World and 14, 97
  Tiananmen Square crackdown (1989) xi
  Township and Village Enterprises 71
  underconsumption 65
  United Nations, People's Republic of China reintegrated into (1974) 94, 94n
  urban/rural income distribution 39, *39,* 124, *124*
  US government debt holdings and 64
  US/OECD, convergence with 32–3, *33*
  US, normalization of political relations with 72
  US presidential election (2016) and 72–3, 77
  US, relations with vii, 43, 47, 51, 60, 63, 64–5, 69–79, 76, 78, 153, 161
  World Trade Organization (WTO), accession into (2001) xii, 35, 148
  Xi Jinping and *see* Xi Jinping
  Zyuganov and future of 171–2
classical capitalism 104, 107, 111, 112, 118
Clinton, Bill xi, 137, *138,* 147, 154
Clinton, Hillary xiii, 74, 136, 137, 138–9, *138,* 161
club convergence 8, 214n
Cold War (1946–91) vii, 27, 29, 63, 88, 103, 110, 144, 174, 177, 178, 182, 183, 185
  Cold War view of the world 94–8, *94, 95*
Comintern (1920) 95
commodification, product 149, 150, 193–6
Commonwealth of Independent States 178
communism ix, xi
  China and 2, 7, 70, 143, 162, 172, 174, 175, 176
  Cold War view of the world and 94–5, *94,* 97
  East European former communist countries join political West 187

Index

End of History view of the world and 98–9, 98
fall of regimes xi, 9, 10, 13, 147–8, 172–5, 183
formerly communist political parties became social-democratic parties 170
nationalism and 174
New Deal order and 150
political parties *see individual party name*
Portuguese Revolution and 18
privatization in formerly communist economies 195
revolutions against communist regimes, failure of 170
Communist Party of China (CPC) 65, 105, 122, 123, 125, 131, 144, 165, 167, 171, 172
credentialism and 127–39, *128, 130, 138,* 143
Communist Party of the Soviet Union (CPSU) 170, 173, 174
comparative advantage, theory of 50
complexity, world 88–103
ideational political divisions 94–103, *94, 95, 98, 100*
Rawls and 88–94
conflict, economic convergence and 46–103
complexity and 52, 88–103, *94, 95, 98, 100*
fear of convergence and 79–88, *81, 87*
Hobson-Lenin-Luxemburg hypothesis 49, 61–6, 78, 220n, 221n
ideational political divisions 94–103, *94, 95, 98, 100*
international trade leading to peace or war 52–7

'liberty' or 'agency', trade and domestic 46–7
Montesquieu and *le doux commerce* 47–8, 53, 54–6
Quesnay and first sustained arguments in favour of free trade 47–8
Rawls and 88–94
Schumpeter and 49–50, 66–9
Sino-American relations and 51–2, 69–79, *76, 78*
Smith and 48–9, 53, 56–61
trade and peace: a synopsis 46–51
Confucius 176
consultative hierarchical societies 89–92, 100
convergence, economic x, 17, 214n, 219n, 226n
Asia, convergence of real incomes between West and 82
Asia, convergence within 23–6, *24, 25*
China and *see* China
club convergence 8, 214n
conflict and 46–103; *see also* conflict
cultural convergence and 53
end of 43
fear of 79–88, *81, 87*
inequalities and 55, 61, 63, 64, 65, 78, 80–85, *81, 87,* 91, 93
migration and 84–6
military power and 49, 59, 60
reshuffling of global income distribution and 86–8, *87*
system convergence 120
term 8, 17
US and *see* United States of America (USA)
Corn Laws 51
corruption, elite 131–6, *134,* 142, 143, 160–61, 168, 176

cosmopolitanism xiii, 56, 60, 156
counter-revolution
   China and 239n
   defined 235–6n
   elites, counter-revolutionary
     reaction against accumulated
     power/wealth of 2, 3, 73–4,
     141–92, 157
Covid-19 pandemic 12n, 35, 37, 43, 45,
   75, 100, 167, 168–9, 181, 209
credentialism
   CPC and 122, 127–39, 128, 130, 134,
     137, 138, 143
   homoploutia, combining
     credentialism and 118–20
Crusades 57–8
Cuba 10, 153, 180

Deaton, Angus: *Deaths of Despair and
   the Future of Capitalism* 77
decolonization 94, 95, 96
deep state 121, 231n
DeLong, Bradford 154
democracy
   China and 70
   deep state and 121
   faute de mieux 99
   Gorbachevization and 170
   illiberal 93, 100, 101, 103, 145
   liberal 88, 89, 91–3, 94, 96, 97, 98, 98,
     100, 100, 101, 103, 144, 186
   national market liberalism and
     158–61, 167
   neoliberalism and xii
   sovereign 101
Deng Xiaoping xi–xii, 72, 82, 94n, 96,
   137, 166, 167, 169, 227n
'deplorables' xiii, 74, 118
dictatorship 18, 92, 97, 98, 99, 100,
   101, 103

dissident movements 182
doux commerce 48, 54, 55, 69–70, 72, 77,
   218n

East Germany ix
East India Company 56, 57
Eastern Europe ix, 11, 35, 42, 71, 147,
   170; *see also individual nation name*
education 92, 97, 168, 176
   elites and xiii, 1, 104, 114, 115, 117, 119,
     121, 127–8, 128, 131, 133, 136–7, 137,
     139, 230n, 233–4n, 236n
   mobility 136–7, 137
Eisenhower, Dwight 147
'elephant chart', period of High
   Globalization (1988–2008) 75–6,
   76
elites 3, 10, 45, 62–3, 65, 104–40
   capital ownership and 104–105, 111–
     24, 113, 115, 139, 150–52, 156
   China and xv, 78, 104–105, 123–40,
     124, 126, 127, 128, 130, 134, 137, 138,
     141, 142, 143, 144, 148, 167, 171, 173,
     233n, 234n
   corruption and 131–6, 134, 142, 143,
     160–61, 168, 176
   counter-revolutionary reaction to
     accumulated power and wealth
     of 2, 3, 73–4, 141–92, 157
   creation and characteristics of new
     104–40
   credentialism and 116–40, 128, 128n,
     130, 134, 137, 138
   education and xiii, 1, 104, 114, 115,
     117, 119, 121, 127–8, 128, 131, 133,
     136–7, 137, 139, 230n, 233–4n, 236n
   features characteristic of new 119–21
   folksy nature of 139–40
   homoploutia and 104, 111–23, 113,
     139, 235n

Index

importance of 136–7, 137
income sources of the elite, by sector of ownership (1988–2018) 127
managerial class and 105–11
meritocrats and 117–19
national market liberalism and *see* national market liberalism
neoliberal capitalism and xii, xiii, xiv, xv, 1, 2, 110, 141
political elite interrelationships in United States and China 136–9, 138
private property and 106, 108–10, 112, 114, 115, 118–21, 123,
Russia and 141, 142, 144, 178
US and xv, 73–4, 78, 86, 104, 105–23, 113, 115, 233n
End of History era 13, 52, 91, 94, 228n
End of History view of the world 98–103, 98
ENI 121
Eritrea 10, 44, 89
Ethiopia 10, 14, 44, 93, 102
European Coal and Steel Community (ECSC) 79
European Union (EU) 13, 84, 154
euro xii, 79
migration and 85–6, 155
monetary union (1999) 79
exogenous shocks 42–5
exports 5, 34, 36, 44, 47, 55, 63, 64, 65, 71, 72, 79, 223n
extensive margin 125

fascism 18, 107, 158, 161
Fashoda Incident (1898) 62
Fernandes, Clinton: *Subimperial Power* 184

Finns Party 155–6
First World 6, 7, 8, 13, 14, 15, 51, 94, 96, 227n
Five Eyes 184
Ford Motor Company 121
foreign policy 73, 92, 158–9, 173, 184
Foroohar, Rana: *Homecoming* 154
Fourastié, Jean 8
France 7, 8, 13, 20, 40, 53, 60–62, 69, 146, 156, 169, 170, 178, 217n
Africa and 184
division of the world in 1920 as a result of World War I and 95
global GDP share 21
managerialism and 108, 109
relative peak income 22, 22
Revolution (1798) 47–8, 211n
free-market capitalism x, 46–7, 50, 67, 68, 236n
free trade 46–103
Bretton Woods institutions and 154
complexity and 52, 88–103, 94, 95, 98, 100
conflict and 46–103; *see also* conflict, economic convergence and
fear of convergence and 79–88, 81, 87
Hobson-Lenin-Luxemburg hypothesis and 49, 61–6, 78, 220n, 221n
ideational political divisions and 94–103, 94, 95, 98, 100
'liberty' or 'agency', trade and domestic 46–7
Montesquieu and *le doux commerce* 47–8, 52–3, 54–6
Quesnay and first sustained arguments in favour of 47–8
Rawls and 88–94
Schumpeter and 49–50, 66–9

Index

free trade – *cont'd*
   Sino-American relations and 51–2,
     69–79, 76, 78
   Smith and 48–9, 53, 56–61
free will 188, 189, 190, 191
Freedom Party 156
friend-shoring xiv, 154
Fukuyama, Francis: *The End of History and the Last Man* 99, 228n

Gaddis, John Lewis: *The Cold War: A New History* 174
Galbraith, John Kenneth 119, 120
Gan Yang 163
Gaza 43, 93
Gdansk, Poland 11
G8 101
General Agreement on Tariffs and Trade (GATT) 9, 154
Germany 28, 41, 42, 47, 62, 85, 179
   convergence and 53
   Five Eyes and 184
   homoploutia and 112
   managerialism and 107, 108, 109, 110
   positions of country deciles in global income distributions (1988 and 2018) 39, *39*, 40
   relative income peak 22, *22*
   World War I and 95, 178
   World War II and 189, 190
Gernet, Jacques 165
Gerstle, Gary: *The Rise and Fall of the Neoliberal Order* 146–7, 236n
Gini coefficient of inequality 23–5, *24*, *25*, 81, 81n, 82, 114, 139, 214n, 225n, 230n
Glass-Steagall Act, repeal of (1999) xii
Global Financial Crisis (2008) xiii, 10, 13, 35, 37, *37*, 47, 63, 64, 72, 75, 100, 144, 148
globalization xv, 72, 149
   American anti-globalization policies 36
   China and xiii, 167, 223–4n
   conflict and 62
   elites and 139, 141, 143
   free trade and 51
   High Globalization period (1988–2008) 75
   income convergence and 46, 53, 219n
   migration and 85, 93
   Rawls and 88, 91, 93
   refashioning of 77, 78, 79, 146
   success of xii
   tariffs and xiv, 156
   those left out of benefits of 2, 72–4, 76, 77, 78, 142
Global South 11, 15, 16–17, 100, 102
Gorbachev, Mikhail 163, 170, 174, 240n
Gorbachevization 170
Great Compression 8
Great Depression (1929–32) x, 82, 178, 189
great men and deterministic forces 188–92
greed 57, 193, 196–8
Gross Domestic Product (GDP) x
   Asian GDP per capita 20, 21, 23, 37, 211
   BRICS nations and 102
   Britain GDP per capita 124, 182, 232n
   capital, rising share of income from in 111
   capitalist core GDP per capita 6, 8, 15
   China GDP per capita 6, 15, 17, 19, 20, 21, 24–5, 27–9, 28,30, 34, 35, 37, 40, 43, 64, 123–4, 137, 182, 185, 186, 215n, 221n, 225n, 232n
   Concept 1 inequality and 23–4, *24*
   Concept 2 inequality and 24–5, *25*
   Covid-19 pandemic and 43

Index

First World GDP per capita 6–7, *6*, 8
GDPs per capita expressed in international dollars of equal purchasing power parity ($PPP) 20, 214n
  Gini coefficient of inequality and 23–4
  global distribution of 6–7, *6*, *15*, 20, *21*, *23*, 193, 214n
  Global South GDP per capita *15*, 16
  government spending as share of 110
  growth gap between China and US, and populous Asian countries and OECD (1960–2022) 36–7, *37*
  India GDP per capita 20, *20*, *21*, 29–30
  Italy GDP per capita 8
  Japan GDP per capita 30
  largest economies in world, share of GDP (1964–2022) *30*
  percentage shares of world GDP and world population (2022) *15*
  public sector x
  region, average growth rate of GDP per capita by *20*, *21*, *23*
  relative income peak and 21–2, *22*
  Russia GDP per capita *15*, 20, 213–14n
  Second World GDP per capita 6–7, *6*
  socialist countries *6*, 19
  Soviet Union GDP per capita 29
  state sector and x
  Third World GDP per capita 6–7, *6*
  United States GDP per capita 26–9, *28*, *30*, 35, *37*, 43, *137*, 186, 215n
  unweighted inequality of GDPs per capita 24–5, *24*, *25*
Group of 77 (G77), the non-aligned countries ('Third World') 5, 7, 94, 95, 96, 97; *see also* Third World
Grudinin, Pavel 171

Haiti 23
happiness 87–8, 93, 196
Hayek, Friedrich 46–7, 157, 228–9n; *Road to Serfdom* 109
Helsinki process 182
Hitler, Adolf 151, 159, 178, 189–90
Hobson, John 49, 61–3, 65–6, 78, 220n, 221n; *Imperialism* 62–3
Hobson-Lenin-Luxemburg hypothesis 61–2, 65–6, 78, 220n, 221n
Ho-fung Hung 164
Holocaust 189–90
homoploutia 104, 111–19, *113*, *123*, 139, 235n
  homoploutic ruling class and technocratic professional class, difference between 120–21
  homoploutic ruling class, managerial class and 'wokist' professional-managerial class, difference between 121–3
Hu Jintao 167, 168
human rights xii, 89
Hungary ix, 11, 62, 70, 71, 95, 155
  illiberal democracy 101
  Revolution (1956) 170

ideational political divisions 94–103
  Cold War view of the world 94–8, *94*, 94n, *95*
  division of the world in 1920 as a result of World War I (according to Lenin) 95, *95*
  End of History view of the world 98–100, *98*, *101*
  stadial or Whiggish theory of history 98
  unipolar or multipolar world 100–103, *100*
illiberal democracy 93, *100*, *101*, *103*, 145

immigration xiv, 84–6, 91, 93, 143, 155, 156, 197
imperialism 49–50, 62–3, 66–9, 75, 222n
  atavistic 66–9
  imperialist competition 61–6, 73, 75, 77, 78, 189
income distribution 3, 12, 15, 31, 33, 35, 36, 38, 39
  China and Asia catching up with United States/OECD 32–8, 33, 37
  China and United States (2018) 32–3, 33
  China's role in shaping global xiii, 1, 2, 3, 16, 32, 38, 40, 44
  Chinese rural and urban 124, 135, 136
  defined 30–31
  global income distribution (1988, 2008 and 2018) 30–31, 31
  global income positions of a person with US median income and a person at urban China's 9th decile (1988–2018) 87, 87
  Great Compression and 8
  High Globalization (1988–2008) and 75–6, 76
  homoploutia and 104, 111–16, 113
  Industrial Revolution and 79–80
  inequality and 82, 83, 84
  positions of country deciles in global (1988 and 2018) 39, 39
  relative peak income 21–2, 22
  reshuffling of global vii, xiii, 1–2, 3, 11, 12, 12, 12n, 13, 16, 38, 86
  top 5 per cent, composition of global (2008 and 2018) 41–2, 41
  top of, relative constancy at 41
  upward movement (improvement in the position) of urban deciles 39, 39
  US growth of real per capita disposable income across (1986–2016) 76
  US income gains by decile/growth incidence curves (1964–79)/(1979–2019) 12, 12, 12n, 13
  US income growth rates along different parts of 149
India 224n
  BRICS and 100n, 102
  Chinese ideological influence in 183
  colonial 27
  convergence and 43, 44
  Covid-19 pandemic and 43
  East India Company and 57
  economic liberalization (1991) 83
  First Five-Year Plan 10
  GDP growth rates/global income distribution and 2, 17, 19, 20, 21, 21, 22, 22, 29–30, 43, 44, 86, 182
  Industrial Revolution and 79, 80, 83
  inequality in 25, 82–3
  International Monetary Fund (IMF) bailout xi
  'Licence Raj' xi, 148
  Modi's economic reforms 83
  neoliberalism, enters xi
  population growth 21, 30
  relative peak income 22, 22
  urban population 42
Indonesia 2, 10, 20, 21, 22, 36, 42, 102, 182, 184
industrial policies 154, 156, 237n
Industrial Revolution vii, 1, 5, 38, 79–80, 83, 86, 124, 125, 149, 150, 232n
inequality
  artificial intelligence and 114
  Asia between-country inequality 24, 24
  autocratic governments and 55

Index

between countries (component B)
  24, *24*, 80–83, *81*, 84–5
China and 32, 44, 126, 135, 136, 168
Concept 1 23–5, *24*
Concept 2 24–5, *25*
convergence and national
  inequalities, interdependence
  between 83–4
Covid-19 pandemic and 43
elites and 139
Gini coefficient of 23–6, *24*, *81*, 139, 214n
Great Compression and 8
Hobson-Lenin-Luxemburg
  hypothesis and 61, 64, 65, 78
homoploutia and 112, *113*, 114, 115–16
migration and 84–5, 93
Rawls on 91
within individual countries
  (component A) 80–83, *81*, 84–5
inflation 8, 11, 12, 12n, 76, 124n
inheritance, capital through 114, 115, 118, 156
intensive margin 125
interest rates 11, 65, 67
international community 6, 92, 102
International Monetary Fund (IMF)
  xi, 5, 6, 9, 148, 155, 182
investment 9, 11, 36, 61–7, 71, 72, 74, 77, 78, 117, 154, 168, 220n, 223n, 230n
'invisible hand', market 154
Iran 10, 14, 99–100, 102, 153, 180, 237n, 238n
Iraq war (2003–11) 92, 181
ISIS 92, 100
Islamic Movement 100
Islamic regimes 92, 100
Italy 8, 22, *22*, 23, 40, 47, 85, 107, 108, 109, 110, 112, 155, 170
  Italian Communist Party (PCI) 170

positions of country deciles in
  global income distributions (1988
  and 2018) and *39*

Japan xi, 8, 28, 29, 71, 98, 146, 184, 186
  car production within 53
  China's rise compared to 16
  convergence and 53
  Co-prosper Zone 154
  exports and 72
  First World and 6
  GDP share of largest economies
    and 29, *30*
  global income distribution and
    1–2, 42
  Les Trente Glorieuses and 8
  managerial societies and 108, 109–10
  NATO and 27
  political West and 15, 20, 89
  relative income peak 22, *22*
  World War I and 95
Jiang Zemin 137, *138*, 167, 171, 240n

Kenya 97
KGB 174, 175
Kissinger, Henry 160, 223n; *On China* 72
Klein, Matthew: *Trade Wars Are Class Wars* 65–6
Kosygin, Aleksey 121
Kozyrev, Andrei 173
Kuomintang 172

labour 62, 68, 83, 85, 139, 140, 149, 220n, 229n, 230n
  austerity policies and 151
  division of 48, 50, 56, 184
  homoploutia 104, 112, *113*, 114, 115–16, 118, 119, 123
  managerialism and 111, 112
  neoliberalism and 156

free trade – *cont'd*
  New Deal order and 150
  organized 11
  tax and 92, 219n
Latin America 2, 7, 11, 17, 19, 27, 42, 94,
  97, 112, 118, 147, 217n, 223n, 227n
  GDP per capita range within
    20, 23
  Structural Adjustment Lending
    (SAL) and 148
  See also individual nation name
Legutko, Ryszard 121
Lenin, Vladimir 106, 173, 179, 227n
  division of the world (1920) as
    result of World War I according
    to 95–6, 95
  Hobson-Lenin-Luxemburg
    hypothesis 49, 50, 61–7, 78, 220n,
    221n
  New Economic Policy (NEP) and
    165–7, 238n
Les Trente Glorieuses ('the glorious
  thirty years') 8, 18, 19, 23
Li Yang 125, 132, 233n
liberalism 91–2, 145–6, 156–7, 170, 174
  liberal democracy 88, 89, 91–3, 98,
    98, 100, 100, 101, 103, 144, 186
  liberal societies 89–92, 226n
  national market liberalism *see*
    national market liberalism
  neoliberalism *see* neoliberalism
'libertas in imperio' ('freedom under
  constraint') 188
liberty or agency, domestic 46–7
Lin Biao 97
Lipton, David ix
longue durée thinking 80
Luxemburg, Rosa 49, 50, 61–7, 78,
  220n, 221n
Lyons, N. S. 122, 123

M-C-M scheme 117
Maddison Project 34, 123–4, 225n, 232n
malcontents xiii, xiv, 73, 92
managerialism/managerial class
  104–11, 116, 119–23, 125, 139, 231n
Mao Zedong 14, 36, 70, 94, 94, 96–7, 99,
  103, 137, 139, 143, 168, 169, 175, 176
Maoism 14, 94–5, 94, 99, 103, 139, 143,
  168, 169, 175, 176
marketization 149, 150
Markovits, Daniel: *The Meritocracy
  Trap* 77, 116–18
Marshall Plan 186
Marxism 49, 54, 61, 62, 63, 68, 77, 95,
  106, 220n, 222n
Mattei, Enrico 121
Matveev, Ilya 64, 65
May, Theresa 155
Maynard Keynes, John/Keynesianism
  x, 63, 66, 108, 220n
McNamara, Robert 121
Meloni, Giorgia 155
mercantilism 53, 57, 58, 69, 154, 158,
  218n
meritocracy/meritocrats 104, 111,
  116–19, 230n
Mexico 9–10, 11, 85, 86, 93, 112, 113, 113,
  155, 242n
Mian, Atif 63, 64
middle classes
  Asian vii, xiii, 30–38, 31, 33, 37, 73
  global/global median class 30–42,
    31, 33, 37, 39, 41, 45, 84
  US/Western vii, xiii, 38–42, 39, 41,
    72, 73–7, 78, 117–18, 141, 153
Middle East 92, 161
Mises, Ludwig von 157
Mitterrand, François 13
modernization theory 70, 170
Modi, Narendra 83

Index

monopolies 62, 109, 217n, 219n, 229n
   monopolistic capitalism 50, 67–9
   Smith and 56, 57, 58
Mont Pèlerin Society 147
Montesquieu, Charles-Louis de
   Secondat, baron de la Brède et de
   47–8, 53–6, 58, 62, 218n, 218n
   doux commerce 48, 54–6, 69–70, 72, 77, 218n
   Esprit des Lois (*The Spirit of Laws*)
   53, 55, 217n
multipolarity 52, 94, 144, 145, 177–92
   China, impossibility of absorbing into
   the US-led global system 183–8
   great men and deterministic forces
   188–92
   Russia–Ukraine war as catalyst of
   new global system 177–83
   struggle for multipolar world 94,
   94, 100–103, 100, 177
   transition to multipolar
   homogeneous system 182–3
Munich Security Conference (2007)
   101
Musk, Elon 161, 162

Narayan, Ambar 136, 235n
nationalization x, 13, 18, 105, 108
national market liberalism/national
   liberalism xiv, 141–92, 193, 195,
   235–43n
   'businessman' view of economics
   and 154, 156
   China, impossibility of absorbing
   into the US-led global system
   183–8
   democratic politics, Donald Trump
   and nature of 158–61
   fascism and 158
   friend-shoring and 154

global neoliberalism and national
   market liberalism table 157
goal of challengers to global
   unipolar neoliberalism 144–6
great men and deterministic forces
   188–92
'invisible hand' of market and 154
multipolarity and 177–92
neoliberalism decline and 148–52
neoliberalism spread and 147–8
neoliberalism transformed into 145–6
neoliberal order, main features/
   components of 146–7
New Economic Policy (NEP) and
   165–7, 238n
nihilists, Xi Jinping and rule of
   170–77
sanction regimes and 153–4, 156
statism 162–77
term 156–8
Trump and 141, 143, 144, 152–3,
   155–61, 237–8n
United States, rise and fall of
   neoliberal order in 146–52
national socialism 145, 158, 172
nation-state, role of xii, 197
NATO 13–14, 27, 43, 178, 179, 181, 184, 186
   NATO-Russia Council 178
naval routes 51
Navigation Act (1660), England 57
Nayar, Krishnan: *Liberal Capitalist
   Democracy* 150–51
neoclassical economics 50, 63
neoliberalism ix–xii, 188
   challengers to, goal of 144–5
   China's rise and xii–xiii
   counter-revolutionary reaction
   against 2, 3, 73–4, 141–92, 157
   decline/end of xii–xv, 10, 148–52
   elites and *see* elites

neoliberalism – *cont'd*
  Global Financial Crisis (2008) and xiii, 10
  government spending and 110
  main features of neoliberal order 147
  multipolar world and 144–5
  national market liberalism and xiv, 146–53, 156–8, 157
  nationalism, greed and property define era of 193
  origins ix, xi–xii, 10–11, 152–3
  peak of xii
  populist reaction to xiv, 141–2, 152
  social outcomes, nefarious 141
  Trans-Pacific Trade Treaty and 74
  Trump, Xi Jinping and Putin as products of neoliberal era 143
  United States, rise and fall of neoliberal order in 146–7
Nepal 23
nepotism 137, 161
New Deal, US xi, 107, 108, 110, 147, 150
New Economic Policy (NEP), Soviet Union 165–7, 238n
New International Economic Order (NIEO) 5, 10–11, 13, 17–18, 90, 97, 103, 211n
Nigeria 80, 102, 154–5
nihilism, ideological 170, 173–7
non-aligned movement 5, 7, 8–9, 13, 14, 94, 95, 97, 102, 103, 211n
non-disclosure agreements 160, 194
non-governmental organizations (NGOs) xii, 93, 159, 182, 183
Nord Stream pipeline 51
Novokmet, Filip 125, 233n

Offer, Avner: *The First World War: An Agrarian Interpretation* 51
offshoring xiii, 51

oil shocks (1970s) ix, 7–10, 211n
oligarchs 3, 47, 142, 143–4, 171, 176
Orain, Arnaud 69
Orbán, Viktor 101
Organization for Economic Cooperation and Development (OECD) 8, 13, 32, 36–8, 37, 44, 112
'other' 197–8
outlaw states 89, 92

parental income 115
people's capitalism 114
Peter the Great, Tsar of Russia 180
Pettis, Michael: *Trade Wars Are Class Wars* 65
Peyrefitte, Alain: *Quand la Chine s'éveillera . . . le monde tremblera* ('When China wakes up the world will shake') 7
physiocrats 47, 56
Piketty, Thomas: *Capital in the Twenty-First Century* 112, 150, 151, 237n
point U, Utopian 84–5
Poland ix, 11, 55, 108, 109, 179, 233n
  Solidarity movement ix, 233n
Polanyi, Karl: *The Great Transformation* 54, 62, 63, 77, 149
political economy 47
political West 20
  Asian countries share in global GDP (1952–2022) and 21
  average growth rate of GDP per capita and 20
  BRICS nations and 102
  China's absorption into, impossibility of 183–8
  End of History view of the world and 98
  Gaza, war in and 43

Index

GDP and population, percentage shares of world and 15
globally affluent and 42
international community and 102
international organizations and 155
relative peak income and 22, 22
rules-based global liberal order and 146
Russia–Ukraine war and 43
term 15
unipolar or multipolar world and 100, 100
United States at head of 183
unweighted inequality of GDPs per capita and 24
Pomeranz, Kenneth: *The Great Divergence* 165, 224–5n
population numbers
    Africa 19, 44
    BRICS nations 102
    capitalist core 6
    China 6, 7, 15, 17, 18, 30, 32, 33, 34, 35, 36, 37, 38, 39, 128, 185
    economic importance and 21
    First World 6, 6, 14
    Global South 15, 16
    Great Britain 21
    India 21, 29–30
    inequality and 23, 24–5, 25, 26
    OECD 36, 37, 38
    political West 15
    Russia 15, 15
    Second World 6, 6
    Third World 6, 6, 16
    US 27, 34, 35, 40
Portuguese Revolution (1974) 18
positional goods (Veblen goods) 87
princelings 137
proconsular power 184

production of goods 28, 47, 50, 53, 55, 83, 193, 197
property, private 48, 71, 97, 106, 108–10, 112, 114, 115, 118–21, 123, 193–7, 223n, 229n, 230n
purchasing power 31, 36–7
    purchasing power parity (sPPP) 20, 211, 213n, 214n
Putin, Vladimir 2–3, 23, 101, 141, 142, 143, 144, 171, 175, 181, 188

Qatar 10, 23
Quesnay, François 47–8, 56

Rassemblement National 156
Rawls, John 52, 88–93, 100, 145, 226n, 227n
    A Theory of Justice 88, 89, 90, 91, 92, 93, 227n
    Rawlsian accommodation 89, 145
    The Law of Peoples 88, 89, 92, 99, 225–6n
Reagan, Ronald ix, xi, 111, 147, 152–3, 223n, 229n, 235–6n
realignment, economic 3, 5–30, 46–103
    Asia, rise of 5–26; *see also* Asia
    conflict and 46–103; *see also* convergence, conflict and
    US decline 26–30; *see also* United States
redistribution of wealth 64–5, 76
relative peak income 21–2, 22
Ricardo, David 50
Romania ix, 11
Roosevelt, F. D. 108, 109, 147
Rostow, W. W.: *The Stages of Economic Growth: The Non-Communist Manifesto* 97
Russia
    absorption problem after end of Cold War 185

Russia – *cont'd*
  allies 27
  corruption in 142
  coup (1991) 163
  division of world in 1920 as result of World War I and 95
  elites in 141, 142
  End of History classification and 101
  GDP per capita 15–16, *15*, 20
  ideological nihilism and 174, 175
  inequality and *see* inequality
  Kozyrev and 173
  military potential 17
  national security complex 2–3, 141, 142, 144, 174–5
  nationalism 143, 158
  Nord Stream pipeline and 51
  oligarchs, reaction against 142
  Putin Munich Security Conference speech (2007) 101
  sanctions regimes and 153
  sovereign democracy 101
  Ukraine war 43, 93, 142, 172, 175, 177–81
  unipolar or multipolar world and 100
  'world majority' term and 101–2
  See also Soviet Union

Sachs, Jeffrey ix, 228n
Sakharov, Andrei 120
sanction regimes xiv, 43, 153–4, 156, 180, 226n
Sanders, Bernie 152
savings 64, 78, 97, 115, 116, 118, 226n
Schumpeter, Joseph 49–50, 54, 62, 66–9, 119, 222n, 236n
  Capitalism, Socialism and Democracy 50, 67, 109, 229n
  'The Sociology of Imperialisms' 66–8, 222n

Scottish Enlightenment 53
Second World 6, 9, 11, 14, 15, 94, 96, 97, 227n
sectoral planning 108
Shah of Iran, Mohammad Reza Pahlavi 10
Sharma, Ruchir 167–8
Singapore 22, 23
Singh, Manmohan xi, 148
Slobodian, Quinn: *Globalists: The End of Empire and the Birth of Neoliberalism* 157
Smith, Adam 48–9, 53, 54, 85, 154
  equality of power and 56–61
  The Theory of Moral Sentiments 60
  The Wealth of Nations 48–9, 50, 57, 58
social circle 137
social Darwinism 150
socialism ix, 9, 13, 18, 120, 212n, 236n, 238n
  China and 98, 99, 100, 163, 165, 166, 167, 168, 172, 176
  Cold War view of the world and 94, 95, 96, 97
  conflict with resolved to advantage of capitalism 110
  GDP percentage shares and x, 6, *6*, 19
  managerialism and 106–7, 109
  national socialism 145–6, 158, 172
  socialist internationalism 107
  Soviet Union and 150, 158, 171, 173
soft power 19
Solidarity movement, Poland ix, 233n
South Korea 6, 15, 20, 22, 27, 70, 71, 72, 89, 97, 98, 186
sovereign democracy 101
Spengler, Oswald: *The Decline of the West* 26
stagflation 7

Index

Stalin, Joseph 143, 158, 173, 174, 180, 212*n*
State Department, US xii
state-owned enterprises (SOEs) x, 65, 104, 125, 132, 148, 176
statism x, 162–77
stock market 113, 162–3
Straub, Ludwig 63–4
Soviet Union (USSR) ix, 27, 28, 49, 159
   China and 7, 19, 70, 72, 74, 172–4
   Cold War and 29, 94–6, 94, 177, 183
   coup, anti-Gorbachev (1991) 163
   dissolution (1992) xii, 10, 29, 71, 93, 172–4, 178, 179
   doux commerce and 69–70
   First Five-Year Plan (1928) 165
   global GDP and 29
   Gorbachevization 170
   Hungarian Revolution (1956) and 170
   largest economies in world GDP (1964–2022) (in PPP terms) and 30
   MAD (mutually assured destruction) and 60
   managerial society and 106, 108, 109, 110, 120, 121
   New Deal order and 150
   New Economic Policy (NEP) 165–7, 238*n*
   socialist countries aligned with 6, 11, 14, 18
   Third World/G77/non-aligned world and 9–10, 95
Sufi, Amir 63–4
Suharto 10
Sun Yatsen 186
supply chains 51
Surkov, Vladislav 101

tactical flexibility 168, 239*n*
Taiwan 7, 42, 70, 97, 172, 186, 223*n*, 228*n*
Tanzania 97
tariffs xiv, 9, 47, 51, 154, 155, 156, 157, 216*n*
taxes 47, 215*n*, 237*n*, 240–41*n*
   capital and xi, 92, 156
   cheating on 160
   Chinese income distribution and 136
   election promises to reduce 76–7
   global income distribution and 30
   government power and 147
   labour and 92, 156
   Piketty's advocacy of higher 151
technological progress vii, 9, 28, 29, 36, 48, 49, 52, 59, 71, 79–80, 109, 195
Tellis, Ashley J. 185
Thatcher, Margaret ix, xi, 111, 152–3, 235*n*
Third International 106
Third World
   challenges core capitalist countries in international economic arena (1974) 10
   China and 7, 96–7, 228*n*
   Cold War view of the world and 94
   divided among itself 10
   GDP 6–7, 6
   Global South and 16
   Havana conference (1979) 9
   liberation movements 19
   'migrating' nations to First World 13–14
   New International Economic Order (NIEO) and 5, 10–11, 13, 17–18, 90, 97, 103, 211*n*
   non-aligned movement origins 8–9
   political independence of 18
   religion, turn towards in 14

Index

Third World – *cont'd*
  ruling classes' dependence on US benevolence 10
  socialist bloc and 9–10, 13
  Soviet economic influence on 9–10
  term 3–4, 103, 211n
Tiananmen Square crackdown (1989) xi
Tolstoy, Leo: *War and Peace* 190–91
trade blocs 154–6
trade unions 11, 150, 221n
Trans-Pacific Trade Treaty 74
transactionalism 160
Trump, Donald xv, 2, 3, 188, 217n
  America First 159–60
  democratic politics and 158–61, 237–8n
  foreign policy 158–9, 237–8n
  Hillary Clinton and 138–9, 138
  losers of globalization support for 73–4, 77, 141
  migration and 85, 155–6
  national market liberalism and 141, 143, 144, 152–3, 155–6, 157

Ukraine 43, 93, 100, 142, 172, 175, 177–9, 181
United Nations (UN) 7, 182, 212n
  Charter 89–90, 181
  General Assembly 9, 227n
  People's Republic of China reintegrated into (1974) 94, 94n, 227n
  Trump speech at (2019) 159
United States of America (USA)
  American exceptionalism / America First 159
  China, relations with 29, 43, 69–79, 76, 78, 87, 153
  Cold War, perception of within 178
  Current Population Survey 104
  decline of 26–30, 28, 30
  democratic politics in, nature of 158–9
  doux commerce and 69–70
  educational mobility in 136–7, 137
  elites xiv–xv, 73–4, 78, 86, 104, 105–23, 113, 115, 136–40, 137, 138, 233n
  foreign policies 158–60
  GDP 26–9, 28, 30, 35, 37, 43, 137, 186, 215n
  Glass-Steagall Act repealed xii
  global output share 20
  government debt 64
  growth gap between China, populous Asian countries, OECD and (1960–2022) 36–7, 37
  High Globalization period (1988–2008) and 75–6, 76
  homoploutia 104, 111–16, 113
  imperialist competition and 69
  incarceration rates 149–50
  income distributions (1988) and (2018), positions of country deciles in global 39, 39
  income distributions (2018) 32–5, 33
  income gains by decile / growth incidence curves (1964–79) and (1979–2019) 12, 12, 12n, 13
  income inequality 64, 82, 112
  income positions of person with US median income and person at urban China's 9th decile, global (1988–2018) 87, 87
  inter-generational mobility 112
  largest economies in world, GDP share of and (1964–2022) 30
  largest economy in world (in purchasing power parity terms, or PPP), China overtakes as (2015) 20

Index

managerialism and 109, 122
median income 33
middle classes vii, xiii, 75–8, 76
migration and 86
neoliberal order, rise and fall of in 146–52
New Deal xi, 108, 109
opioid crisis 77
organized labour 11
pivot to Asia 73
political elite interrelationships in 136–9, 138
population numbers 27, 34, 35, 40
populism in 2–3, 142, 143, 152, 156
presidential election (1940) 108
presidential election (2016) 72–3, 77
relative income peak 22, 22
sanction regimes and 153–4, 156
tariffs and 155
Trump and *see* Trump, Donald
unequal growth in 75–6, 76

Valdai Discussion Club 181
Versailles Peace Conference (1919) 178, 185
Vidal, Gore 159
Vietnam 2, 10, 36, 97
  Đổi Mới economic reforms 82–3
  GDP 20, 21
  global income distribution and 2
  Rawls and 93
  relative peak income and 22
  war (1955–75) 83, 97
Volcker Effect 11
Vox 156
Vries, Peer 164–5

wages x, 8, 65, 66, 83, 84, 112, 113, 116, 118, 224–5n, 236n
Walter Lippmann Colloquium 147

Warren, Elizabeth 152
wars of aggression. *See* conflict *and individual conflict name*
Washington Consensus xii, 147, 154, 222n
Washington Post 162
Weide, Roy van der 136
welfare state xi, 10, 110, 157, 235
well-ordered societies 89–92, 226n
West Germany ix, 8, 227n
Wiles, Peter 9–10
'woke' ideology 122–3
World Bank 5, 9, 90, 121, 154–5, 182
  Structural Adjustment Lending (SAL) 148
world majority 100, 102, 228n
World System Theorists 8
World Trade Organization (WTO) xii, 35, 148, 154, 223–4n
World War I (1914–18) 26, 49, 51, 54, 61, 63, 66, 78, 95, 108, 178, 183, 221n
World War II (1939–45) 19, 22, 63, 108, 109–10, 121, 183, 185, 189

X 162
Xi Jinping xv, 3, 163, 188, 241–2n
  Anecdotes and Sayings of Xi Jinping 176
  cult of personality 169, 176
  elite corruption and 131–2, 135, 142
  national market liberalism and 141, 142, 143, 144
  New Economic Policy and 165, 167
  nihilists, against rule of 170–77
  political elite interrelationships and 137, 138
  'readjustment' or 'rectification', policy of 167–9

Xi Jinping – *cont'd*
  'Regarding the Construction
    of Socialism with Chinese
    Characteristics' 172–6
  Soviet Union break-up and 172–4
  zero-Covid restrictions,
    discontinuation of 167–8
Xu Caihou 132

Yaoqi Lin 132, 234n
Yeltsin, Boris 101, 142, 143, 163, 173, 174–5, 179
Yugoslavia ix, 11, 14, 70, 71, 93

Zhou Yongkang 132
Zhu Rongji 166
Zyuganov, Gennady 171